GEORGE BERKELEY
A REAPPRAISAL

George Berkeley
A Reappraisal

BY
A. D. RITCHIE

EDITED, WITH A PREFACE, BY
G. E. DAVIE, D.Litt.

MANCHESTER UNIVERSITY PRESS
BARNES & NOBLE, INC., NEW YORK

© 1967, MANCHESTER UNIVERSITY PRESS

Published by the University of Manchester at
THE UNIVERSITY PRESS
316–324 Oxford Road, Manchester 13

U.S.A.

BARNES & NOBLE INC.
Publishers, Booksellers, founded 1873
105 Fifth Avenue,
New York, N.Y. 10003

Printed in Great Britain by Butler & Tanner Ltd, Frome and London

CONTENTS

ABBREVIATED REFERENCES

An Essay towards a New Theory of Vision, 1709, two editions.   *NTV*
The Principles of Human Knowledge, 1710.   *Princ.*
Three Dialogues between Hylas and Philonous, 1713.   *Dia.*
De Motu, 1721.   *DM*
Alciphron or the Minute Philosopher, with the *NTV*, 1732,
   two editions.   *Alc.*
The Theory of Vision Vindicated, 1733.   *TVV*
The Analyst, 1734.   *An.*
Siris, 1744.   *Siris*

This list does not include short occasional writings, for which see Ch. VII below, nor the famous manuscript notes (short title, *PC*).

All references are to the edition of 1948–57, 9 vols., (Nelson), edited by T. E. Jessop and A. A. Luce (short title, *Works*): usually to paragraph or page number where convenient and for *PC* to number of entry according to Luce's order.

References to Luce's *Biography* are under *Life*.

In the chapters that follow I assume the reader to be familiar with *NTV* and *Princ.* or have the text before him and I quote sparingly. From less familiar works I give more and longer quotations.

PREFACE

SOME time ago, Professor A. D. Ritchie put into my hands the manuscript of the present book, in the knowledge that I had read it with admiration. It wanted, he said, the finishing touches, but his health was unequal to the task. Calling it 'his posthumous book', he asked me to undertake the responsibility of trying to arrange its publication.

Always a lively writer, Professor Ritchie is well up to form here. Because his style is aphoristic and pithy rather than argumentative such loose ends as there are do not hinder the communication. Because he has thought deeply about the ramifications of his subject, the incidental digressions do not detract from the main theme but counterpoint it.

What gives this book its very considerable distinction is, above all, that Professor Ritchie has something fresh and illuminating to say. If, he teaches, we are to appreciate the interest and importance of Berkeley, both for his own time and for ours, it is above all necessary to repudiate the kind of fashionable separatism which regards the psychology of the *Theory of Vision* and the metaphysics of the *Principles* as being only externally and accidentally related both to one another and to the economic and ethical writings. Instead of studying one part of Berkeley's thought with a reckless disregard of the rest, we must, according to Professor Ritchie, get our priorities right, and try to discover a central nucleus around which the other parts will organize themselves with an orderly subordination.

The value and originality of Professor Ritchie's Berkeley as a contribution to scholarship depend on the surprisingly simple solution he finds for this complex problem of priorities. Subordinate the *Theory of Vision* and the economic writings to the immaterialism of the *Principles*, as so many interpretations do, and you at once turn Berkeley into a purveyor of paradoxes. On the other hand, give pride of place to the *Theory of Vision*, and you find yourself at once possessed of the key to the hard-headed realism which inspires both the *Principles of Human Knowledge* and the economics of the *Querist*, not to mention the theology of *Alciphron*.

If one is to appreciate the realism of Berkeley, one must, Professor Ritchie insists, grasp first and foremost that the *Theory of Vision* is not meant to open up to metaphysical tourists a fantastic, isolated world of visual sense-data. In differentiating the visual world from the tactual, Bishop Berkeley had it in mind to execute the classic manœuvre of 'distinguishing to unite'. In this way, the original core of Berkeley's philosophy consists in realizing that experience, properly understood, consists not in the sensations of one single sense, such as vision, but in the comparison—i.e. the distinguishing and the correlating—of the sensations of one sense with those of another. What Berkeley's discussion of vision shows, and is meant to show, is that visual reports about the world, if considered by themselves and in abstraction from tactual reports, turn out to be a vehicle of unintelligibility, or at least of dimly indeterminate information. In short, from Professor Ritchie's point of view, the Berkeleian test, alike of empirical truth and meaning in regard to matter, consists in the coherence of sight and of touch.

Inevitably, the question will arise as to whether this interpretation of Berkeley, based as it is on the *New Theory of Vision*, does not unduly neglect the immaterialism of the *Principles of Human Knowledge*. However, I do not think that Professor Ritchie would be very troubled by this criticism. On the contrary, the very thing he wanted to do was to turn aside from those parts of Berkeley— sufficiently discussed by Mr Warnock (among others) in the wake of logical positivism—where Berkeley's target is materialism in the sense of the existence of unperceived and unperceivable bodies. Instead, Professor Ritchie is trying to switch attention to the unhackneyed and, as he felt, fruitful topic of the relevance of certain neglected parts of Berkeley for the argument about the sort of behaviouristic materialism which accepts only the publicly observable, and refuses the notion of private experience. For Ritchie, indeed, the Berkeleian doctrine which, of all others, has most importance for our time is the contrast—central to the *New Theory of Vision*—between the element in the fact of vision which has no tactual counterpart—viz. my awareness of the variety of colours—and the other element in the fact of vision, distinct but inseparable from the first, which is incapable of being seen by me, but which I am aware of tactually—viz. my eye's relation to the bodies seen in colours. According to Ritchie, the troublesome distinction between 'private' and 'public' will not begin to be understood until philosophers begin to analyse, in the light of Berkeley, experiences like being aware of seeing coloured things with one's eyes, or of feeling hard or soft things with one's hands.

The value of Professor Ritchie's approach is perhaps best revealed in the way in which it brings out Berkeley's realism, and practical-mindedness, showing how they are founded on his general philosophy. In the first place, it is no longer easy to brand as subjectivist the *esse-percipi*, when *percipi* is in its turn treated as equivalent to *videri et tangi*. The table I now see and feel acquires for me a species of actually experienced independence, in the sense that it is simultaneously seen as external to my impalpable organ of feeling and felt as external to my invisible organs of sight. Thus, the Berkeleian theory of externality, as analysed by Professor Ritchie, points towards the doctrine of the *'corps propre'* found in Sartre and Merleau-Ponty. But secondly and equally important, the exposition Ritchie gives of the Berkeleian experience as fundamentally a co-operation of sight and touch, not only in the manner just explained, confers a species of genuine independence on the things we see and touch, but at the same time brings out the fact that human cognition is rooted in the needs of practical life. According to the 'haptic-optic' basis of Berkeleianism, the kind of experience of bodies which founds natural science[1] is not so much a merely spectatorial observation but an observation which manipulatively experiments with its object and which by successful experiment learns to manipulate material objects at will. In this way the knowledge of matter which Berkeley brings on the scene is the kind of knowledge which is inseparable from power over matter, or, in other words, the Berkeleian empiricism culminates in a Baconian doctrine of a necessary connection between natural science and economic production. In short, Berkeley does not only prefigure bits of Sartre, for good value he also adds a limited measure of Marx.

But further, this reinterpretation of the *Principles* in the light of the *Theory of Vision* not only brings out the realist implications of the immaterialism; it also draws attention in an exciting way to the 'operationalist' intentions behind the negative critique of

---

[1] For a discussion of Berkeley's theory of science which clarifies and complements Ritchie, see G. W. Ardley, *Berkeley's Philosophy of Nature*, Auckland, 1962.

'abstract general ideas'. According to Ritchie, if one is to appreciate properly the distinctive originality of the introduction to the *Principles*, one must read it, not in isolation, but rather as a follow-up of what has been already achieved, in the *Theory of Vision*, in regard to the topic of abstraction. Looked at in this way, Berkeley's object is not the large and hackneyed one of propounding yet one more 'theory of universals'; rather, what he is doing is to contrast a legitimate model of abstraction[1] with an illegitimate one.

How do we think apart an inseparable aspect of some empirical object? What is it we do when, with reference to a geometrical diagram visible before us, we attend to the shape and neglect the colour? From Ritchie's point of view, the vital thing which Berkeley is trying to get over is that this concentration on the visible shape cannot be carried through in terms of visual experience alone, but depends on a conscious comparison with the diagram as seen with the same diagram as felt, in, for example, the tactual experience of drawing it. In attending to the shape and neglecting the colour we are concerned to note the respect in which the visible object before us has a certain peculiar (and very complicated) correspondence with the object as tangibly felt. Take away the comparison with touch, and visible shape becomes unseizeable. In this way Ritchie recovers the sense of Berkeley's doctrine of abstraction, revealing thereby also the very aspect of it which roused the interest of the youthful David Hume.

In the process of giving Berkeley a relevance to our own time, Professor Ritchie, it has to be noticed, is also transforming our conception of Berkeley's historical role. Ritchie's Berkeley is no longer a mere half-way house between Locke and Hume, a middle term between a half-hearted empiricism on the one hand, and a consistent thorough-going empiricism on the other. Instead, the Berkeley who now emerges is dualist rather than empiricist, having more in common with Maine de Biran and the tradition of French 'spiritual positivism' than with British common sense.

Empiricist in a precisely Baconian sense in regard to our knowledge of nature, the Berkeley that Ritchie presents is on the other hand a-priorist in a Cartesian or Platonic sense in regard to one's knowledge of oneself. In particular, the Cartesian theory of will, given so much prominence in Berkeley's own texts but so

---

[1] *Alciphron* vii is illuminating. See vol. III, *Works*, p. 293, lines 3–13, especially 8 and 9.

much neglected by his English-language expositors, at last gets its due from Professor Ritchie. Experience does not just consist in simultaneously seeing and tactually feeling things; it consists equally in that control of attention which is required to compare the intimations of sight with those of touch, noting their agreements and disagreements. In this way, Berkeley's rejection of Descartes' rationalistic interpretation of natural science goes hand in hand with the retention and development of the invaluable Cartesian insight that the science of nature rests upon the freedom of the human will.[1]

Berkeley's affinities with French dualism are made evident, in the Ritchie interpretation, not only in the emphasis given to the role of will and choice, but also and above all in the treatment of religion. In particular, Professor Ritchie shows how the doctrine of the haptic-optic primacy is fundamental to Berkeley's theology. This line of country is of particular interest to Professor Ritchie and, according to what he told me, the inspiration of his own Berkeleian studies ultimately stemmed from Father Sillem's[2] book on Berkeley's view of God. On Professor Ritchie's interpretation, our knowledge of nature is from Berkeley's standpoint rendered possible only by the fortunate accident that the data of sight and the data of touch, though externally and even accidentally related, nevertheless happen to be so arranged in regard to one another as to supplement one another's cognitive deficiencies. Thus, visual

---

[1] To develop Ritchie's position, it would be helpful to compare what Berkeley has to say about will in the *Principles* and the *Philosophical Commentaries* with Jean Laporte's magisterial articles 'La Liberté chez Descartes', and 'La Liberté chez Malebranche' in *Études d'Histoire de la Philosophie Française au XVII Siècle*, 1951.

In stressing the role of will in Berkeley's theory of perception (*percipere = velle*, i.e. *agere*), Ritchie is able to give a new and valuable turn to his haptic-optic interpretation. On this view, Berkeley's perceptual voluntarism would seem to get its most authentic statement in the *Dialogues*. First, Dialogue I, pp. 226-9 (Everyman), plainly implies that getting information from vision not only involves the passive experience of colours, but the non-visual and active experience of using the eyes; it is this latter side of the process (e.g. directing the eyes) into which will enters. But, secondly, visual knowledge requires not only the activity of using the eyes; it also involves the manipulative activity of placing the object under inspection now against one background, now against another, so as to 'detain' and 'awake' 'the attention'.— Dialogue II, p. 259.

[2] E. A. Sillem, *George Berkeley and the Proofs for the Existence of God*, 1957.

data, isolated from the tactual, give us only vague and indefinite information about the world, quite insufficient for the needs of science or intellectual life. Looked at in this way, the data of our experience have to be regarded as purposively adapted to the needs of human cognition, and as thus furnishing new and basic material for the teleological view of God's existence.

But if Berkeley's theology is rooted in his view of our experience involving a comparison of sense-fields, so also is his tendency towards an intellectualism of a Platonic sort which he, in Malebranchean fashion, combines with the Cartesian voluntarism. When, in *Siris* § 305, Berkeley tells us that 'sense, so far forth as sensitive, knoweth nothing' but only in combination with intellect, he refers us explicitly to the passage in the *Theaetetus*, which says that our knowledge of empirical things depends, strictly speaking, not on sense but on *the comparison of the senses* such as sight and hearing. So too, in the *Third Dialogue*, the argument for the existence of self as something non-empirical ('I am not my ideas') is made to rest on the very same Platonic principle that 'I, one and the same self, perceive both sounds and colours.'[1]

One of the most illuminating side-effects of Ritchie's emphasis on the Platonic intellectualism of Berkeley is to put in proper perspective the doctrine of the *Passive Obedience* and the other political writings. A devotee of the classical doctrine of the *via media*, Berkeley was concerned to repudiate a Hobbist absolutism without running to the opposite extreme of political permissiveness with Locke's disciples. The socially responsible Berkeley thus brought to light by Ritchie is the Berkeley of the remarkable and highly topical *Discourse addressed to Magistrates and Men in Authority*,[2] in which, as a reaction to the terrible simplifications of the free-thinkers, the question of a limitation on the liberty of discussion is frankly faced with a most impressive awareness of its complexity. Forbid unrestricted discussion, and you suppress evidence, endangering truth; insist, with the free-thinkers, on unrestricted public discussion, and you are liable to turn certain sorts of men into 'monsters' of moral scepticism.

These discussions of politics and theology are, of course, a kind of outworks to the system. From Ritchie's point of view, the central core of Berkeleianism lies in the contention that the prob-

---

[1] Everyman edition, pp. 269, 270.
[2] *Works*, vol. VI, pp. 201–22.

lems of externality-internality, of abstraction, and of selfhood, intellectual and volitional, can be effectively illumined only by fixing on the primitive human fact of the attentive comparison of the visual with the tactual. In this way what we get from Ritchie, in and through the interesting digressions and fragments of aphoristic wit, is the systematic build-up of a Berkeley who, far from being reductionist and atomist, represents experimental knowledge as essentially involving an effort of the spirit.

The Berkeleianism thus expounded is not a closed philosophy of the logical positivist sort which refuses meaning to whatever is overlooked in its first principles, but rather an open philosophy which can patiently bear with insoluble problems until such time as the progress of analysis will have disentangled from the ultimate haptic-optic complex the appropriate strand of evidence. Given this point of view, solipsistic accusations against Berkeleianism do not worry Ritchie overmuch. Following the line opened up by Maxime Chastaing in the remarkable articles[1] which show how on the question of other minds the work of Berkeley is carried on by Reid and his school, Ritchie also, in his own way, interests himself in the fruitful contrast between the internal or Cartesian knowledge of oneself and one's feelings and the external or behaviouristic knowledge of oneself which is got, and can only be got, from the reports of others. As elsewhere, the distinctive contribution of Ritchie consists in the suggestion that interpersonal experience ought to be explored on the model of intersensorial experience. For Ritchie, the contrast between the internal or, as he calls it, first-person view of myself and the external or third-party view of myself is already, in some sense, prefigured, in one's own experience, in the comparison between vision considered as colour experience and vision considered as the directing of the tangible eye on the tangible counterpart of the coloured thing. If this approach were properly worked out, the charge of solipsism could be countered in a genuinely Berkeleian spirit.

The enemy of 'abstractors', the foe of minute philosophy, Professor Ritchie's Berkeley is very different from the stereotype which prevails in the philosophy classrooms of the English-speaking world. As one might expect, the dualistic system Professor Ritchie finds in Berkeley has closer affinities with French

[1] *Revue Philosophique*, 1953, for the article on Berkeley, and 1954 for that on 'Reid, the Philosophy of Commonsense and the Problem of Other Minds'.

interpretations, such as the contribution of M. Leroy[1] in the centenary *Homage to George Berkeley* or the very stimulating article in *Recherches Philosophiques* tom. 6 from the pen of M. Chastaing.[2] Not that Professor Ritchie is wholly continental, however, since the basic place he gives to the *Theory of Vision* reminds one of Mr Turbayne's[3] interpretation of Berkeley. But perhaps the closest connections of Professor Ritchie on Berkeley are found in Berkeley's Scottish commentators, especially in the brilliant articles by J. F. Ferrier[4] which have been so mysteriously disregarded by latter day interpreters.

This latter reference to the Scottish background, if followed up with due care, can supply us with a formula for what is most central and distinctive in Ritchie's treatment of Berkeley, considered both as a contribution to scholarship and in its relevance to modern philosophical discussion. Deeply indebted as it is to the exact learning of the Luce–Jessop edition, Ritchie's work nevertheless marks a reaction in favour of the line of interpretation which runs from Reid and Adam Smith through Ferrier to Campbell Fraser. In the last analysis, the basic motif of Berkeley was not, from Ritchie's point of view so much the 'Immaterialism' as the 'Divine Visible Language'. Like other philosophers brought up on the Campbell Fraser tradition—Kemp Smith, for example, or John Anderson—Ritchie saw in Berkeley's *Theory of Vision* the key to all that was most fundamental in the 'sense-datum theories' which earlier this century were being so eagerly canvassed by certain British philosophers. Seen in this light, Ritchie's view of Berkeley reveals a surprising affinity with the approach of John Anderson's Australian disciple D. M. Armstrong, as in his book[5] about Berkeley's *Theory of Vision*. Both Armstrong and Ritchie, while no doubt considerably opposed in other respects, are nevertheless evidently in basic agreement that, in regard to one of the

---

[1] *Hermanthena*, LXXXII (1953) pp. 27–48, 'L'Influence de la Philosophie Berkeleyenne sur la Pensée Continentale'.

[2] Tom. 6, 1936–7. This remarkable survey of Berkeley's thought as a whole has been of great service in making comprehensible to me Ritchie's point of view.

[3] C. M. Turbayne, *The Myth of Metaphor*, 1962, not a study of Berkeley but valuable in bringing out the importance of his theory of vision.

[4] J. F. Ferrier, *Lectures and other Philosophical Remains* (1866), vol. II (or *Works*, vol. III), pp. 291–377 in both cases.

[5] D. M. Armstrong, *Berkeley's Theory of Vision*, Victoria, 1960.

most important movements in the twentieth-century discussion of perception, Berkeley's discussion of vision occupies a key position.

Professor Ritchie himself, as his illuminating discussion of Thomas Reid suggests, was well aware of the Scottish affinities of his work, and at the time his health was beginning to go he was looking carefully into the question of Ferrier's relation to Berkeley.[1] An heir of the Scottish intellectual tradition, Professor Ritchie sometimes liked to attribute his breadth of intellectual interests, scientific and literary as well as philosophical, to the kind of initial education he received at St Andrews University in studying for the traditional type of ordinary Scottish M.A.

But of course Ritchie's book on Berkeley has other sources of inspiration besides the Scottish background. The verve and wit reveal the Cambridge connections of his earlier years. The interest in science and technology—so important to his interpretation of Berkeley—remind us of the lively and fruitful years in Manchester where, as his colleague of the time, Professor Emmet, recalls, he found much in the way of intellectual stimulus and congenial contacts.

However, one does little to elucidate a book like the present one by treating it as the sum of separate intellectual influences. More than anything, Ritchie's interpretation of Berkeley depends on the idea of the whole as something which is not reducible to its parts. Unsympathetic by both tastes and training to any excessive narrowness of study, Professor Ritchie, in this book as in everything else he wrote, was campaigning with keen intelligence and biting wit against that kind of intellectual irresponsibility which in its zeal for the particular forgets the universal. His emphatic reassertion of Bishop Berkeley's intellectual breadth, his sustained attempt to see Berkeley whole, is thus far more than a

---

[1] The book, of course, was never properly completed. Thus, the important section on 'The Scandal of Immaterialism' was added as the result of a revisal. Not yet satisfied, Ritchie continued to work, and before his health broke down, had become interested in Ferrier's attempt to follow up Berkeley in regard to the question of the relations of sight and touch. From jottings that survive, it seems clear that Ritchie was going to add a note to Ch. 2 discussing Ferrier's position and quoting the footnote found on p. 336 of vol. II, *Lectures and Remains*, or vol. III, *Works*. Ritchie had before him a discussion of the significance of the Ferrier footnote by the present writer which is to be found in *The Philosophical Quarterly*, 1954, pp. 242 ff.

B

mere contribution to scholarship; it is a last great effort—the most
effective perhaps that Professor Ritchie ever made—of continuing
intellectual fight.

In conclusion, I should like to thank the Manchester University
Press and, in particular, Professor Dorothy Emmet. In the exact-
ing task of preparing Professor Ritchie's typescript for publication, her judgment and energy have been invaluable.

I have added notes in square brackets at places where the text
seemed to require elucidation. I am grateful to Mrs Ritchie for
her help in the reading of the proofs and in compiling the index.

GEORGE E. DAVIE

Department of Philosophy,
University of Edinburgh

I

INTRODUCTION

BERKELEY was lucky to live in a civilized and tolerant age, not in the twentieth century. Had a youth of less than 23 in these later times dared to write, and actually persuaded a publisher to print, a book that accused the leading experts on the science of optics of serious errors, while proposing to start a new kind of science, free from such errors, the whole gang of professionals would be calling for blood, saying (approximately), 'Grandpa knows best, children should be seen and not heard.' Had a clergyman dared to accuse those remote and godlike beings, the mathematicians, of arguing irrationally; saying, moreover, that the great new discovery of the age was a method merely of approximation, masquerading as exact, he would be told sharply not to interfere in things he could not possibly understand. Had an elderly Bishop lectured the medical profession about the treatment of epidemic diseases, merely because he had lived in a famine area, and done some amateur dosing of poor wretches who were dying anyway, and even more ignorant than he was, he would also be told, in stronger language, not to interfere in things he could not understand. Had the same Bishop accused responsible statesmen, as we call them, of gross ignorance and neglect of economic principles, he would, in many countries, in this century, be liquidated out of hand.

All these four offences were committed by Berkeley, and several others, but how differently was he treated! True, few troubled to read his books, but some did; nobody threatened him or was even rude except in the mild and civilized way of writing pamphlets in reply. In course of time some few people actually began to do some of the things he advised. The very next generation of writers on optics, and allied subjects, reformed their methods on Berkeley's lines and continue the practice to this day. Even godlike mathematicians began slowly to ponder the fundamentals of their science, not entirely on Berkeley's lines, but near enough to drop infinitesimals, in spite of the great authority of Leibniz. The medical profession was polite, on the whole, and quite interested; many recognized their ignorance of the fundamentals of their own science. The politicians were not interested, and just did nothing in the masterly eighteenth-century fashion, while students of the budding science of economics acknowledged Berkeley as one of the pioneers.

One book, *The Principles of Human Knowledge*, was jeered at in the coffee houses, and almost entirely ignored by the philosophers. But this case apart, the impact Berkeley made on his own time was quite considerable.

Berkeley's chief published works are listed above[1] in order of publication, with brief comments, preparatory to fuller treatment.

All these books deal with what is now called 'science', of one branch or another, from mathematics, experimental and theoretical physics to psychology and sociology. They all, however, introduce theology too; and for that reason, more than any other, caused some offence in their day and are liable to cause much more now; then because they might be heretical, now because all theology is despised.

NTV is not just the first, it is the main, central, constructive, and most strictly scientific work; also, in Berkeley's own view, the most strictly theological. It provides his basic controversial weapon for use against anti-Christians, of whom he saw many in his day. He relied on it directly for the argument of *Alciphron* and indirectly for the argument of the *Principles* where his *Immaterialism* forms the intermediate step. Berkeley does not refer to immaterialism in the later works, not because he abandoned it but because he had other controversial weapons. Berkeley was a genuine empiricist, a genuine enquirer, and genuinely believed in and used Ockham's Razor for getting rid of superfluous rubbish whenever it could be used, but he did not believe in using one weapon only.

NTV, though constructive, begins with an attack on characteristic lines, namely the misuse of unobservables in scientific discussion, the *Princ.* continue the attack and so does *DM*. *NTV* opens the attack on (i) *Theories of Unobservables*, and also very soon the attack on (ii) *Visualism*, less theory than a bad habit of supposing that only the visible is real, and other senses account for nothing. Then the introduction to *Princ.* brings in (iii) the

[1] See p. vii.

attack on *Abstract Ideas*, the misuse of visual imagination. These three are just bad habits, seldom noticed much less named, but all combine, inconsistently, in what has flourished as a full-bodied metaphysical theory, from Democritus to Hobbes, namely the Great Machine Theory of the Universe. Berkeley comes back to the attack in the last book he wrote, *Siris*, though more accommodatingly and without so much anti-metaphysical bias. His final word, if he has one, is in *TVV*, where he puts his whole position without the ambiguities of the early 'popular' statements (§§ 9–18 and 39 to end).

None of the books in the list were written as academic exercises; they all have a propaganda purpose, as we say now, which is most fully stated in the subtitle to *Dia.*: 'The design of which is plainly to demonstrate the reality and perfection of human knowledge, the incorporeal nature of the soul, and the immediate providence of a Deity; in opposition to Sceptics and Atheists. Also to open a method for rendering the Sciences more easy, useful, and compendious.' Several other subtitles could be added.

Berkeley is arguing *for* Christian faith and worship, to strengthen them and *about* the special sciences which he wishes to improve. His argument is to be seen in its simplest form in *Alc.* (*Works*, vol. III). It is as direct and empirical as he can make it, literally an appeal to common sense or experience. He could also support it by appeal to Old and New Testament authority, if called upon. He believed that anyone who refused to accept the argument was blinded by idolatry, by letting creatures stand in place of the Creator. The argument is in fact too direct and too empirical for many, perhaps most, Christians. Few religious persons, ancient or modern, care to be reminded of God and religion except in certain places, at certain times, in habitual and soporific phrases, or remotely metaphorical ones. Berkeley dares to tell them that the whole of sense experience of every kind provides a sign system, learnt from early infancy, which we ought always to recognize as telling us of God's perpetual care and support for our lives from birth to death. In short, we are asked to take Berkeley's favourite text literally or as nearly as we can: 'In God we live and move and have our being.' Note especially the verbs 'live' and 'move'; the worlds of biological science and mechanical science are 'in' God. It is not altogether surprising that there are idolaters who either blatantly or surreptitiously prefer their idols, of which they have plenty, and specially the Great Machine, which according to eighteenth-century myth is revealed by physical science as perpetually existing and needing no Creator, or according to nineteenth-century myth is self-created by Chance and Natural Selection. Ancient idols were carved out of stone or wood and were at least genuine stone and wood, both visible and tangible, modern idols are creatures of the human imagination, aided by abstract ideas; thus doubly powerful and doubly insinuating.

Two brief comments on Berkeley's relation to his predecessors are perhaps in place here. The words of the pagan Stoic poet quoted on p. 3 do not introduce anything that a Christian need hesitate to accept for fear of pantheism nor need they cause philosophical difficulties. The Platonic doctrine of the 'incorporeal soul', which comes from the *Phaedo*, should however rouse serious doubts in the mind of a Christian and makes a consistent account of body-mind relations difficult. The best that can be said for it is that it is not radically anti-Christian, nor does it make such an account quite impossible, as does the rival doctrine of the purely passive mind or 'Tabula rasa', which Hobbes alone plainly accepted, though both Locke and Hume played with it. There is no trace of it in Berkeley, though many academic expositions of Berkeley seem to presuppose it.

Berkeley must have been aware that Hobbes and Locke had theories about language. He himself did not, but was extremely careful in his use of that difficult instrument, and also could be daring, as in his *Querist*.[1]

[Here there is a break in the typescript, followed by a comment in which Ritchie calls attention to a central feature of his point of view.]

I expect to be accused of trying to turn Berkeley, anachronistically, into a twentieth-century *operationalist* (cf. P. W. Bridgman, *The Logic of Modern Physics*, 1932; also my *Studies in the History and Methods of the Sciences*, 1958) and here make a preliminary defence. Firstly, operationalism is much older than the twentieth century' when it first got its name. Its first known practitioner is Archimedes

---

[1] [*The Querist*, as Jessop points out, 'consists entirely of rhetorical questions' —vol. VI, *Works*, p. 90. See Berkeley's own comment: 'Whether he, who asks, asserts? And whether any man can fairly confute the querist?'—Loc. cit. pp. 90 and 161, query 316.]

(cf. his *Method* and *Sand-reckoner*). Secondly, Newton was an out-standing operationalist, but liable, as even the greatest artists, to occasional lapses. Wherever he lapsed his most outspoken critic has been, till quite recently, no other than Berkeley. This is not to say that Berkeley himself never lapsed, and where I think he has, I take the liberty to criticize him.

Among his works, those I would emphasize most strongly are *NTV* and *TVV*; in *Princ.* it is the Introduction, Replies to Objections, (§§ 34–84) and (§§ 85–134), where he anticipates *DM* and perhaps *An.*; then *DM* §§ 21–51, and lastly *Siris*, § 295, where he does sum up, if not quite finally nor constructively. Berkeley's immaterialism is dealt with separately in Ch. IV below. See also the section headings in the table of contents above.

II

THE NEW THEORY OF VISION

§ 1 Opposition to Berkeley

Berkeley was unaware of the kind and depth of opposition to the main theses of his Theory of Vision. He thought he only needed to correct a few incidental technical mistakes of a few scientific investigators, who would see the force of his arguments. Instead he was faced by ancient universal folklore, to which mankind are conditioned by the age of six, and which extremely few are prepared even to begin to doubt. Moreover many philosophers from Democritus to Descartes and Hobbes conspired to make the whole affair look scientifically respectable. The 'lore' is roughly:

i. A mind (or soul) is a Thing which inhabits a Place and belongs exclusively to an Owner. The Place is (vaguely) the Owner's Brain or (more vaguely but more adequately) his whole Body.

ii. It is assumed *a priori* that no Thing can be in two places at one time. Hence what has its place in your mind (or mine) has its place in your body (or mine) and what is outside your body (or mine) is outside your mind (or mine). As a convenient rough and ready simplification this may work pretty well in ordinary cases. It is doubtful if it could stand up to special examination of special cases of mental location, if mental events can be located anywhere.

iii. The learned world has added Transmission Theories of sensation, much discussed by ancient Greeks, all based upon hypothetical and unobserved processes. Even if some parts of some alleged processes can be empirically supported by means of second or third hand evidence, no complete account of any actual transmission has yet been produced in the twentieth century A.D., any more than in the fifth B.C.

iv. Berkeley ignores transmission theory, with good reason, to good effect.

v. He tried at first to save trouble and misunderstanding by using traditional terminology, as far as he could. This may have

6

been bad tactics, confused some readers, and occasionally perhaps himself. But had he invented new terminology, he would have had no readers before the twentieth century or even after.

§ 2 BERKELEY'S METHOD

Berkeley established two main theses in *NTV*, both novel, both decisive. The first was a matter of method, namely that what is observed should always be explained, if possible, in terms of the observable and not in terms of the unobservable. This rule of method is the means to his conclusion, the second thesis; namely that whatever we see and whatever we touch and handle is an object or thing, each different and distinct; not as red and green are different qualities which belong to one object or as rough and smooth are, but just that nothing visible is tangible, and nothing tangible, visible. We might have lived in a world where red things were generally rough and green things generally smooth, and popular opinion might have declared that red and rough, or green and smooth, were each one and the same. We do live in a world where a stretched rope both looks and feels straight and a slack rope both looks and feels curved, but *what* we see and *what* we feel are different and distinct, although always found related in this way under normal or usual conditions of perception. When not found together, as with the oar half in the water which looks crooked and feels straight, the conditions are judged to be abnormal, or out of the ordinary.

Berkeley's were the first definite steps away from ancient confusions, but first steps only. It is not certain that he was always quite free of the confusions himself; and afterwards Hume fell into them, to some extent even Reid, while in recent times Moore, Russell and numerous followers have wallowed. Ordinary language is all in favour of confusion for it takes as causes what may be only customary signs, as Berkeley complained.

The fundamental confusion is the belief that sight gives us direct intuition of REALITY, or if not that, direct intuition of a copy of REALITY, or if not that, then it is our own fault, for we ought to be having such intuitions by some means or other, since passively received intuitions are the proper road to REALITY; whereas adult human visual experience is not intuition of anything beside itself. Rather it is of the nature of prediction of further ensuing sense experience of various sorts, and necessary, useful prediction too, which only very occasionally leads us astray.

Berkeley's approach to his problems leads us definitely away from the usual assumption that experience is passive recipience and nothing else, to the conclusion that there is also something more, namely, learning by mutual encounter; and the more we actively explore the more and more effectively and instructively we encounter. A bodiless cyclops, such as many philosophers suppose themselves to be, never encounters, cannot explore and nothing for him can be either real or unreal, true or false. It is not likely that Berkeley himself fully realized what he was doing. There are passages in *Princ.*, which a bodiless cyclops might write if he were able, as he might most of Hume, J. S. Mill and Russell.

Berkeley was, however, the first to deny that Locke's Primary Qualities, geometrical forms, figures and relations, are common to both sight and touch; and to go on to indicate how they come to be correlated through experience, by active exploration in our early life. The term 'our' must now be taken to include not only men and the higher animals but even fishes, insects and molluscs; now, since the nineteenth century. Berkeley also hints (no more, unfortunately) that there are altogether three separate realms of experience that we correlate, namely, sound, sight and touch; and 'we' here means men pre-eminently, not dumb animals. His phrase 'natural visual language' is to be taken seriously.

Berkeley's first thesis is not quite so original as his second; Newton had said the first word in his experiments on the spectral colours. Let me emphasize 'experiments', for this is science, of the laboratory, of the holy temple of science, and Newton's procedure is strictly Berkeleian. From the days of the pre-Socratics on, people have been filled with curiosity about the mysterious transmission processes through which the eye responds to things happening far off and renders the possessor of the eye responsive also. They have filled the world with hypothetical entities to account for it, in defiance of Ockham and his Razor, and none of the entities have ever accounted for anything. Newton however was inventing no hypotheses, nor hypothetical entities of any kind, nor was he discussing theories of transmission of light or of anything else. For the purpose of these experiments he was interested only in what an observer (any observer) could examine for himself when he passed light through a prism under certain conditions, and correlated the colours he saw on a screen with other contemporary processes, belonging to things both seen and handled, and therefore measurable. These were the sunlight, the slit in the shutter, the prism, the position of the colours on the screen, and lastly the angles of refraction of the different colours. Notice that Newton worked entirely alone, yet anybody can follow his instructions and get the same result. Many have done it. The experiments can be demonstrated to a large audience and (granted only the sunlight) have never been known to fail.

Very few of Newton's contemporaries realized what he was doing, assuming that *he* must have been doing what interested *them*. Newton was naturally and properly annoyed at their mistake, which looked to him like a deliberate insult. It is perhaps useful to add that Newton had one predecessor in this Berkeleian kind of enterprise, who made an ambitious effort to correlate not only sight and touch, but sound also; namely Pythagoras. The absurd thing is that every one of us has carried out himself an extensive and on the whole systematic series of experiments on the correlations of sound, sight and touch; but we have all done it very young before we were able to reflect philosophically on what we were doing. Berkeley was not the pioneer experimenter but the pioneer philosopher. Molyneux's question and the answer to it in Chesselden's experiment are the most important steps historically and are fundamental for Berkeley.[1]

Transmission in general is popular because it can be endlessly discussed *a priori* and needs no actual observation, only imagination aided by abstract ideas. Another reason for the almost obsessive preoccupation with transmission theories of light is that people have supposed that such theories would explain the puzzle of how a man standing *here* can be aware of things over *there*, miles away, even millions of miles away, and so justify our own instinctive faith in things seen by our own eyes, though we seem to have every cause to doubt the report of others about what they see. The supposed situation is awkward. An observer at (A) claims to see an object at (B) where (A) and (B) are in different places as actually observed by an independent third party at (C). We suppose ourselves simultaneously to be at A and C. Under these conditions what is visible at A is never directly visible to C,

[1] What these are is explained below—especially pp. 13–18.

what is directly visible at C never directly visible at A. Even the object at B is not quite strictly the same object to both persons at both places, for no two can see it from the same place under the same conditions at the same time. In no case does anybody actually see the transmission processes outside his own body, which are in question; they are invisible hypotheticals. Those inside his body are doubly invisible and doubly hypothetical, because any serious interference with the inside of his body would bring his seeing to an end or grossly alter it. It is true that a great deal of indirect evidence can be brought to bear on the subject but all of it is obtained, in the last resort, not through third party transactions, but by the method of Berkeley (and Newton and Pythagoras) which ignores transmission processes and theories, and consists in what a person himself reports of his own visual (and other) experience. This may be called the *Direct Method*, as opposed to the *Indirect*, or (perhaps less accurately) the *Internal* view, as opposed to the *External* or *Third Party* view. The *Direct Method* provides no causal explanations, but something more valuable, namely criteria of valid or true judgments contrasted with invalid or false ones (cf. Ch. III, § 1).

At any rate Berkeley did ignore hypothetical transmission processes, but not (apart from lapses) bodily operations, to be discussed later. Transmission theories do nothing but throw doubt on the validity of sense experience by ignoring *isomorphism*[1] where it is presupposed and trying to find it where it cannot be found.

Newton's anticipation of his method on one special point probably influenced Berkeley's thinking very little. Some useful hints from Malebranche probably did (see Luce, *Works*, vol. I, pp. 117, 230n).

§ 3 Opening sections of *NTV*

Berkeley begins his discussion in the approved academic manner, by citing and criticizing the leading works on optics of his

---

[1] Some kind of 'isology' is assumed (? *a priori*), as for instance in the time and intensity relations of transmission. 'Isomorphism' has generally been sought in vision in spite of the warning provided by double vision (Ch. II, § 8) and the so-called 'inverted retinal image' (Ch. II, § 5). The isomorphism of haptic experience has been ignored.

day.[1] In dealing with the problems of how 'we perceive by sight the distance, magnitude, and situation of objects' (§ 1) he finds that the authors sometimes, though not consistently, use his own method, for they also use inobservables and transmission theory. He intends to show that the consistent use of his own method accounts for all that they can account for and also solves problems which they confess they cannot.

Had Berkeley been more cautious he might have omitted the ill-fated § 2 of *NTV* and gone straight to § 3 where he states, without ambiguous extras, the first point he sets out to establish and the universally accepted empirical basis for it.

I find it (also) acknowledged that the estimate we make of the distance of objects considerably remote is rather an act of judgment grounded on experience than of sense.[2] For example, when I perceive a great number of intermediate objects, such as houses, fields, rivers, and the like, which I have experienced to take up a considerable space, I thence form a judgment or conclusion that the object I see beyond them is at a great distance. Again, when an object appears faint and small, which at a near distance I have experienced to make a vigorous and large appearance, I instantly conclude it to be far off; and this, 'tis evident, is the result of experience; without which, from the faintness and littleness I should not have inferred anything concerning the distance of objects.

In other words, it is by combining visual and non-visual clues that we learn to *judge* of distance and when these judgments have become habitual we mistake them for direct sensory intuition. If we look across a stretch of calm water at floating objects, with no special form or colour by which we can recognize and name them at once, we cannot tell whether they are 20, 100, 500, 2,000 yards away. As soon as we have also a visual clue and can name them as 'ducks', 'swans', 'buoys', 'boats', we can make a pretty good guess. Surveyors, without bothering about recognition, but using scientific instruments, which add non-visual clues to visual ones

[1] Descartes (*Dioptrique*, 1637); Barrow (*Optical Lectures*, 1669); Molyneux (*Dioptrics*, 1692); Newton (*Opticks*, 1704); also *Phil. Trans.*, vol. 16, no. 187, 1687, pp. 314 and 323, where Molyneux and Wallis discuss the problem of the apparent magnitude of Sun and Moon.

[2] Some object to calling such an act of judgment 'inference'. 'Acquired skill' or 'conditioned reflex' will do, provided it is understood to be a skeletal or Sherringtonian reflex not an autonomic Pavlovian or Watsonian reflex which, though acquired, is unskilled.

can make very reliable and precise judgments. It is exactly such reliable and precise judgments that Berkeley's method is intended to supply.

In § 2 he accepts, from Molyneux, a statement he does not need, but which does not seem at the moment to do any harm, 'For distance, being a line projected end-wise to the eye, it projects only one point in the fund of the eye, which point remains invariably the same, whether the distance be longer or shorter.' Berkeley could not be expected to predict that careless readers would proclaim this as being the fundamental principle of the *New Theory* to be established. Nor that other readers, not careless perhaps, but rather bent on dragging in red herrings, would argue that this piece of geometrical theorizing from the anatomy of the eye was crude and inexact, and that it is an empirical fact, however it may be explained, that when we are using dark-adapted eyes and our powers of peripheral vision, as we cannot do in full daylight, then we do have a vague 'feeling' of 'depth' in the visual field as a whole.

It is open to Berkeley to reply, that even supposing this may be true, it is very little help in finding our way about in the dark. That contains the rudiment of the surveyor's scientific method of using non-visual clues, by holding a long stick in front of us. The non-visual clue is much more useful and reliable.

However, in the text as it stands, Berkeley before dealing with his main problem, discusses minor ones raised by the specialists on optics, which they solve only by introducing inobservables or fail to solve at all, but which he can solve on his principles without inobservables, and specially the famous Barrovian problem (§§ 29–40).

However, the problem of visual distance is not important by itself; indeed can hardly be discussed by itself, because visual 'distance, magnitude and situation' are closely interrelated and also related to tangible distance, magnitude and situation. These are the main topics of *NTV*, and we may as well pass directly to them and first to Molyneux's question, which is simple and crucial.

But one last preliminary remark. Berkeley, like everyone in his day and most people since, deals with sight exclusively in terms of daylight, central or *foveal* vision, under normal conditions of full attention and deliberate judgment. Peripheral, twilight vision, also the unattended, uncertain, sudden, dim or vague are ignored;

an ignoring which simplifies some things, complicates others, but is part of usual scientific procedure.

It is a fact of experience (fairly familiar to non-visualists I suppose) that after smelling a repulsive smell we keep on smelling it again, even where we are sure the original source of it must be absent. This may go on for half an hour or so. For even longer, normally innocent smells take on a similar repulsive tone. Other senses are not free from such curiosities or anomalies; but ordinary scientific procedure (I repeat) ignores or avoids all such complications.

§ 4 Molyneux's Question

A number of early entries in *PC* (nos. 27, 28, 32, 43, 49) show that in beginning to work out 'my doctrine' Berkeley realized the importance of this question for the theory of sense-perception and for his polemic against corporeal substance.

Locke had said (*Essay*, 1st edn., Bk II, Ch. 5), '. . . the ideas we get by more than one sense are of Space, or extension, figure, rest, motion; for these make perceivable impressions both on the *eyes* and *touch*.' Here we have the ordinary plain man interpreting his visual imagination or habit, without troubling to distinguish sign from significate, or realize that signs may be counterfeit. Indeed, signs are hard to distinguish as such when their relations appear to be reciprocal and invariable, or where exceptions can be ignored. Those whose thinking remains uncontaminated by eighteenth- and nineteenth-century philosophy, psychology or physiology would all, I suspect, agree with Locke. His statement here also fits perfectly with the famous distinction between Primary and Secondary Qualities of objects (i.e. Straight/Curved, Long/ Short, Equal/Unequal, At Rest/In Motion: contrasted with Hard, Cold, Yellow, which have no precise opposites).[1]

Before the 2nd edition of the *Essay* was published, Molyneux had asked his question, given a tentative negative answer, and Locke began to change his mind, It does him great credit that at his age he did so (Bk II, Ch. 9, § 8).

---

[1] Strictly and phenomenally, the Primary visual qualities are light, shades and colours. Sizes, shapes and motions are Secondary or even Tertiary, if bodily movements are reckoned as a phenomenal type distinct from feelings of contact (cf. *NTV*, § 129, and Reid, *Inquiry into the Human Mind*).

Molyneux's question may be put: 'Suppose a man completely blind from birth obtained the use of his sight, could he immediately, by sight alone, without touching or handling, be able to distinguish and identify objects already familiar to him by touching and handling, without sight; e.g., a cube and a sphere?' Were Locke's original statement correct, the answer would be 'Yes'. His eyes would now be seeing directly and immediately what his hand had previously felt; the same identical 'impression'. Had experiment corroborated the answer, 'Yes', then the doctrine of corporeal substance would have been nearly or quite impregnable. How could it happen that way unless visual and tactual 'impressions' both came from one and the same invisible, intangible independent somewhat, to do the 'impressing', as the majority of mankind, indefeasibly pseudo-Platonic, have always believed? Imagination can always let us suppose the self-contradictory, if we, conveniently, stop short of the contradiction (cf. *Princ.*, § 23, also below, Ch. V).

On the other hand if the answer is 'No', then some totally new doctrine is needed; if not exactly Berkeley's own, as he left it, certainly not that of Locke, Hobbes, Descartes, Democritus, nor even Aristotle. Part of his doctrine stands, namely that the eyes see a visible object, the hands handle a tangible object, and the relations between them have to be learnt by experience; we do not know them *a priori*, any more than we know *a priori*, which kinds of plants bear scented leaves and which scentless.[1]

Molyneux's question can be put to direct experimental test, provided that the technical difficulties are overcome, On this subject the First Aphorism of Hippocrates says the first as well as the last word: 'Life is short, the Art (of medicine or any kind of observation) long, occasion sudden, experience fallible, and judgment difficult.' This has to be said at the present day because so much philosophical discussion consists of noises or marks on paper made by devotees of common sense who have never observed, much less experimented, and take their own habits as infallible guides.

One of the early successful operations for congenital cataract of both eyes was performed in 1728, on a boy of 13, by Chesselden

---

[1] Is it necessary to point out that we must *actually smell* them once, but having lost all sense of smell, could still recognize the scented ones by sight alone?

who had prepared for the experiment beforehand to answer Molyneux's question (*Works*, vol. I, p. 276n.). In those days it was commoner for surgeons to be well read in philosophy, and it was even possible for philosophers (e.g. Locke) to perform surgical operations. Chesselden had read Locke, probably Berkeley, and made sure, before the operation, that his patient could identify, by handling them, a sphere and a cube prepared for the purpose. After the operation, as soon as he decently could, Chesselden confronted the lad with the same two objects and, before letting him handle them, asked him if he could distinguish by sight alone which was which. He could not; but later on after both handling and looking he learned to distinguish them by sight as an ordinary normal person has learnt to do in childhood. Indeed, had he failed to learn, everybody would have said his sight was abnormal and Chesselden would have had to try again with another patient.

As it was, he had the answer Berkeley's theory required, which was to all intents final. There have, however, been many other operations for cataracts supposed to be congenital and some observers have been less able or less lucky than Chesselden and have given or reported indefinite answers. The complicating factors in the situation are as follows:

i. It is seldom that a cataract is definitely ascertained to be present at birth. Defects in vision, even gross ones, are not usually noticed until a child begins to crawl and bump into things which a normal child would avoid. By then (say 9–12 months) it is too late to decide how much or how little it has learnt to correlate tangibles with visibles, a process which may be expected to begin during the first two months after birth. Once some correlation of the senses is established and elementary clues to the character and identity of familiar objects have been acquired, the clues may persist through a long period of partial or complete blindness.

ii. Even with modern techniques it is not easy to discover how much or how little use is made of vision in the first weeks of life; the necessary investigation is seldom attempted; in the past could not even be attempted. Conspicuous double cataracts may still allow for some discrimination of objects, specially if one or other is not in the centre of the lens.

iii. How much a child correlates or fails to correlate depends on its intelligence and interest as well as on the physical normality of his visual and motor apparatus. This applies equally after the

c

operation as before. (It is well to note that subjects of recent operations have generally been much younger than Chesselden's patient and thus mentally less equipped to answer questions on solid geometry, for that is what the test comes to.) A clever and interested subject picks up clues quickly and gives definite and articulate judgments. A stupid and apathetic one picks up clues slowly and answers questions vaguely and negatively ('Don't know', 'Can't see'), and possibly quite incorrectly. Newly restored sight is often painful or terrifying. Some subjects say that bright light seems to hit them in the eyes; most complain that everything at first is blurred and confusing.[1]

Berkeley's answer to Molyneux's question, when he published it in 1710, was an empirically well-based hypothesis and no alternative has ever had any empirical basis at all. He may be said to have predicted the result of Chesselden's experiment, a prediction which, without the hypothesis, could not have been thought of. The prediction was confirmed, and no subsequent observations, when carefully scrutinized, have thrown any doubt on its truth: in fact they have amply confirmed the conclusion that a previously blind subject can *learn* to identify new visible bodies with old familiar tangible ones, but *has to learn*. There is no immediate intuition at all, no identical 'impression' of sight and touch. Amid the confusing complications of all sorts of reports on all sorts of subjects there is no suspicion of it. This needs to be said only as a warning to those philosophers already mentioned who take a pride in being technically illiterate, and yet call themselves empiricists. In the long run empirical questions are technical questions and without proper techniques cannot be correctly answered. Discerning by sight the distances, magnitudes, shapes and situation of objects is a technique which has to be learned or else things are discerned badly or not at all. That is Berkeley's teaching, and the lesson to be learnt from the history of restoring sight to those who have been more or less blind from a very early age. There is other evidence for Berkeley from other sources, from his century to ours.

Berkeley's philosophizing turns upon assuming (reasonably, as I maintain) that each distinguishable item of experience is appre-

---

[1] Compare the not uncommon experience on a dark night when one is proceeding quite comfortably with completely dark-adapted eyes and a bright light is suddenly switched on.

hended separately, at such a time and place under such circumstances, yet it can be brought into relation with another item or set of items, as sign to significate, or *vice versa*; that this can be done correctly or incorrectly according as the relation turns out to be constant or inconstant, subject to systematic rules or not subject. Berkeley further assumes that our empirical knowledge of the physical world or world of tangible objects or bodies (including our own) and of all spatial and temporal order *begins in this way* and no other. So far he is on firm ground. When he goes on to say that knowledge must terminate exactly as it begins, he is on more doubtful ground, where we need not follow him just now. Instead, we must deal with a point that probably never occurred to Berkeley and may have been obscured to him by his early views about *sensory minima*, views he may have abandoned later.

It is the relations just mentioned, that point out for us stability and order in spatial and temporal relations, namely physical cosmos as distinguished from physical chaos; these relations are not most clearly nor simply seen at the lowest level of abstraction from concrete or particular experience nor in terms of *minima* of extension, nor in terms of simple sense qualities, but at a higher level of abstraction, exactly where Chesselden put it, for he was as successful a natural philosopher as he was a surgeon. Moreover, when Descartes, Spinoza and Leibniz said that thought clarifies sense they were not totally wrong, though seriously wrong in supposing it could or should clarify away sense altogether.

If we may suppose that Chesselden's patient knew some Euclidean geometry and the vocabulary of the learned world of his day, he could have said: 'I can see that *this* is a sphere, for the relations among my *relevant* visual ideas are all of a continuous uniformly curved surface, strictly one surface. *That* is a cube, because I see that it has several distinguishable surfaces, six of them, also six solid angles each between any three of the surfaces and eight edges between two surfaces. Further, the surfaces are all square and all equal when measured, and all the angles right angles. All the visual relations *under standard conditions of observation*, correspond with or correctly signify the relations among tangibles already familiar to me.' This minimum specification of what is meant by sphere and cube respectively is lengthy, and the process of observation for it lengthier still, but the roots of the distinctions and judgments made are simple enough and can be summarized as:

one figure is altogether continuous and symmetrical, the other composed of several distinct but similar parts and with its own kind of symmetry.

Moreover, it would take a long time to specify what is meant by 'standard conditions of observation' and also by 'relevant', but without an understanding of these and adherence to the proper rules, observation would go astray. Chesselden, we may assume, gave his patient a wooden sphere and cube, of convenient size and painted some uniform colour, let us say yellow. Had he been maliciously inclined he might have provided a polished glass sphere and cube, and left the wretched lad in complete confusion for days or weeks, until he sorted out and ignored all the confusing and distracting images in the visible objects.

The answer to Molyneux's question establishes the tangible and visible as separate realms of experience. It indicates too that the former is prior, that sight has the normal function of providing signs with which to predict touch, though it can be the other way round; but this priority needs further arguments to establish it. Most people even today are quite oblivious of them and even if not Lockean, are convinced visualists. Of these other arguments those on the Inverted Retinal Image, first and admirably put by Berkeley, come next, and those on Double Vision, first used by Reid, later; though we have not quite finished yet with the sphere and cube.

EIGHTEENTH-CENTURY REFERENCES

R. Smith, *A Compleat System of Opticks*, 1738.
Voltaire, *Édition de la Philosophie de Newton*.
W. Porterfield, *A Treatise on the Eye*, 1759.
Thos. Reid, *Inquiry into the Human Mind*, 1764. See also W. Hamilton's notes in his edition of Reid. Notes in A. C. Fraser's edition of Berkeley, 1901.

MODERN REFERENCES

D. O. Hebb, *The organization of behavior*, New York, 1949, who quotes:
M. von Senden, *Raum- und Gestaltauffassung bei operierten Blindgeborenen vor und nach der Operation*, Leipzig, 1932.
A. H. Riesen, also 1947, *Development of Visual Perception in Man and Chimpanzee*. See Hebb, p. 50.
J. E. Hochberg, *Psych. Review*, vol. 64, 1957.

§ 5 Inverted Retinal Image

The first thing to notice about the inverted retinal image is that it is entirely imaginary; a ghost and not a very reputable one (see below Ch. V, § 1, on Abstract Ideas). It springs from a kind of imagining that has a limited technical use, but used outside those limits causes confusion and becomes a nuisance. Let us consider the beginning of its career.[1]

Seventeenth-century students of physical and physiological optics using the ray theory of light (they had no other and no other was needed for contemporaty purposes), worked out the way in which the reflecting and refracting surfaces of the mammalian eye can bring the rays of light to a focus on the interior surface of the retina: this is a matter of anatomy and geometry. They concluded, *a priori* but reasonably, that distinct monocular vision can be obtained when the rays are so focused and not otherwise. So far transmission theory and third party method are working satisfactorily within their proper limits; but the working is all on paper by means of diagrams; it is not observation and never can be. Diagrams showed that when a supposed observer A is looking at an object B (for sake of later argument let us suppose that B is another man standing upright on the ground) the image of B in A's retina would be upside down, in the sense that the (imaginary) feet of B would be nearer the top of A's (actual) head and the (imaginary) head of B nearer to A's (actual) feet. This worried them and instead of putting their worries in their pockets along with their diagrams (observe the mixed metaphor), they went on worrying instead of getting on with their proper business; and some of their descendants have worried ever since over what is merely a mare's nest of red herrings.

The first step that Berkeley takes is to get rid of mixed metaphors, superfluous imaginary entities, and to ignore transmission problems, following the advice of William of Ockham. He insists

[1] [This whole section may be usefully compared with M. Merleau-Ponty, *The Phenomenology of Perception*, Second Part, Chapter 2 A, 'The High and the Low'. The problem raised for him by Wertheimer is analogous to that raised for Ritchie by Köhler. So too, up to a point, Ritchie's principle of solution has affinities with that of the French book, in so far as he works with the notion of 'a bodiless cyclops'. The difference is that unlike Ritchie, Merleau-Ponty does not go on to discuss the relevance to the problem of the fact of the correlation of sight and of touch.]

that when A looks at B, A never, never *sees* his own retinal image, or his own eye, or any part of his own body except perhaps the end of his nose or the ends of his toes, and these are irrelevant to his main intention, which is to see B. Nor does the C of the diagram observe any of these diagrammatic hypotheticals either.[1]

In the seventeenth century nobody could, quite simply and literally, see retinal images of any sort, and Berkeley is using a harmless and unmixed metaphor by calling retinal images, along with light rays and their angles, 'tangible' objects, not 'visible' objects. The nineteenth-century ophthalmoscope has complicated matters, but not substantially altered them. With an ophthalmoscope C can look into A's eye and see various things, including, with one kind of adjustment, reflected images from A's lens and cornea. All this is produced by light which C's instrument shines into A's eye and poor A is seeing nothing but a glare of light. The one important result that may follow these observations is that they may shake the faith of C in his diagram and make him understand that he is not omnivident any more than omniscient, and that diagrams may be just mixed metaphors. C in short is just like A and B, and can only see one thing at a time and by dint of not looking at many other things. This is true of things inside people's bodies as well as things outside.

Berkeley, as I have said more than once but say again, wisely ignored transmission theory about hypothetical entities and concentrated on what can be directly observed by any observer for himself, including anatomical data, e.g. that I see with eyes not ears and with two of them. The principal conclusion that follows from using his method is that the relations Up/Down and Higher/Lower do not belong to visual experience but to haptic experience, to the process of maintaining bodily position and moving about in a gravitational field. *Down* or *Lower* refers to the place on which the observer's feet rest. *Up* or *Higher* refers to places nearer his head, when he is standing or sitting up. Features of the visual field, whatever they might be initially or *in vacuo*, once they become familiar in conjunction with haptic experience are fitted into

[1] In *NTV*, 111 and 119, Berkeley uses Hobbist language as do writers on optics, and may appear to confuse 'outside my body' with 'outside my mind', and 'inside my body' with 'inside my mind'. In *TVV* he explains how he should be interpreted.

that field. The haptic field is assumed to be stable; when it is not there is trouble (see below on sea-sickness).

Berkeley points out that a proper consideration of the relations of this imaginary image to actual experience shows that no part of it is inverted at all. If A is looking at B, who is standing up, and C makes a careful sketch of the situation carefully imagined, leaving out metaphors, then he will discover that in the image on A's retina the feet of B appear next to the earth and the head furthest from the earth, as in real life: in short nothing is inverted in the image itself. The inversion takes place in C's imagination when it is allowed to have its fling.

Berkeley and his contemporaries were less well informed about the haptic side of the story than we are now. They had a rough idea of what are now called *kinaesthetic* processes; i.e. that we have some direct *feeling* of what our limbs and other muscular organs are doing when we move them. He specially mentions eye movements and focusing effort (*NTV*, 16–20). But he knew nothing of the labyrinthine organs in the skull, which signal the position of the head in the gravitational field (*Statocyst*) and head movements in the three spatial dimensions (*Semicircular Canals*). These nineteenth-century discoveries greatly strengthen his argument about the primacy of the non-visual over the visual. I hesitate to call the processes of these organs baldly 'haptic', or to say baldly that we have 'feelings' of their working. But they work in most intimately with haptic or kinaesthetic processes of the ordinary sort, which would be clumsy and inadequate without them and we certainly have 'feelings' in plenty when they go wrong (see, again, sea-sickness).

As to Berkeley's whole argument about the retinal image,[1] it has been brilliantly confirmed and reinforced directly by the experiments of Professor I. Köhler[2] of Innsbruck as well as from other sources, some more familiar and less technical. In *PC*, no.

---

[1] References for Inverted Image, etc., are to be found in:
J. E. Hochberg, 'Effects of the Gestalt Revolution', *Psychological Review*, vol. 64, 1957, pp. 73–84; but see also the pioneer attempt of G. M. Stratton, *Psychological Review*, 1897, vol. 3, p. 611, vol. 4, pp. 341 and 463.

His experimental periods were too short for complete habituation; the instrument was on one eye only and probably he saw too little of his own bodily movements and posture. He could make no film and his words fell on deaf ears.

[2] I. Köhler, *Über Aufbau und Wandlungen der Wahrnehmungswelt*, Oesterr. Akad. Wiss., *Philos.-Histor*. K.I.; *Sitz.-Ber.*, 1951, 227, 1–118, especially p. 74.

278, Berkeley anticipated the result of Köhler's experiment as performed by an infant learning to see. That Köhler could succeed with an adult is far more surprising.

In a vertical mirror we see right and left sides reversed, so that we find it difficult, without practice, to shave (for example) with the help of a mirror because all movements have to be *made* in the opposite direction to that *seen* in the mirror. With practice it becomes easy and the 'discrepancy' is hardly noticed. Anybody who spent his whole time looking at himself and everything else in a mirror would cease after a time to notice it at all (cf. *The Lady of Shalott*). This is what Köhler demonstrated by means of a horizontal mirror with respect to up and down.[1]

Köhler arranged an optical device containing a horizontal mirror that could be strapped to a man's head. There was a shield below, so that nothing could be seen ahead or near the ground except by way of the mirror and upside down in it (or if you prefer, 'with the retinal image re-inverted' or, if you really will insist on it, 'with the retinal image the right way up'). At first the subject had to make great efforts and many mistakes in order to handle things properly, walk about avoiding obstacles or go up or down stairs. With persistent practice (and no sitting about doing nothing) familiar objects gradually got refamiliarized in their new position. The subject wore the apparatus continuously during waking hours in daylight, and after a fortnight the new habit was sufficiently established for him to 'see' ordinary familiar things and indeed the whole visual field 'the right way

---

[1] Those who do manipulations under a compound microscope have a like problem with the visual field that is upside down and reversed from right to left. What is at first a very difficult conscious effort of adjustment becomes easier and less conscious with practice, but never quite unconscious and automatic because it is only practised for short intervals, never continuously. (Also I. Köhler, *Psychology*, 1956, vol. 3, p. 381. 'Effects of wearing distorting lenses'—or above at p. 21 n.) No account in words is as convincing as the film Köhler has made.

When first trying to ride a bicycle we 'instinctively' do the wrong thing, that is to say when we wobble to the right we wrench the handle-bar to the left and fall off. Gradually we learn to turn the front wheel a little more to the right, not the left, and push hard on the pedals to keep up speed, which is what really stops wobbles. Soon the correct procedure becomes 'second nature' and we never notice that we are doing it. The same is true of piloting an aeroplane, with respect to up and down, *mutatis mutandis*. (Cf. Polanyi, *Personal Knowledge*, 1958.)

up', with only occasional lapses in the presence of unfamiliar things, or when the necessary haptic clues were uncertain. Everything, however, was seen definitely either one way up or the other, not always quite consistently in all parts of the field.

The most interesting feature of the whole experiment was that when the subject, after his fortnight or so of habituation to seeing the visual field in the horizontal mirror, took the apparatus off and looked with his normal eyes he saw things upside down. In an hour or two this passed off; the habit of a few weeks does not for long stand up against the habit of a lifetime. To conclude, visual up or down is always habit, not direct visual intuition.

There is a much easier experiment of Professor Köhler's with an even more revealing result in one respect. He and his colleagues have worn continuously for periods of weeks, spectacles with prismatic lenses, prisms of small angles, which slightly displace objects in the visual field up or down, to right or left, or, if curved, distort them. They also produce coloured fringes round objects, as, optical theory insists, prisms must in polychromatic light. The displacement or distortion is scarcely noticed even at the beginning, because it calls for only very slight and occasional readjustments of movement: in fact, is almost irrelevant to ordinary activity. The coloured fringes are noticed for a few days and afterwards unnoticed; they are irrelevant to any adjustments in the haptic field and could not interfere with anything except precise optical measurements. Now, for the surprising final result. When after a long spell of habituation the prismatic glasses are taken off, the subject sees coloured fringes everywhere, for an hour or two, until the lifelong habit of ignoring the 'normal' coloured fringes of the 'normal' eye reasserts itself.

This observation establishes neatly and precisely that learned habits not only link together and reinforce, they also obliterate and/or suppress; this applies equally to actions we do or do not do, and to what we see or do not see, in the most direct and most nearly intuitive sense of 'seeing'. Habit makes us blind to what we are not interested in seeing, just as it rouses our sensitivity to what we are interested in seeing.[1]

---

[1] This helps to explain the extreme difficulty there is about sensory thresholds. There is, of course, a process of summation of *'petites perceptions'* as Leibniz said; there is also a process of inhibition that his generation could not even guess at.

§6 OTHER CASES OF VISUAL-HAPTIC RELATIONS

The previous discussion concerns relations that are explicitly between the visual field and the haptic. It will not do to forget the cases where the relation is implicit, which are often supposed to be purely visual; especially those of figures drawn on flat paper which are seen in perspective and, indeed, cannot be seen otherwise. I maintain that *figure* is never purely visual, even if seen as flat, and *a fortiori* not purely visual when seen in perspective, that is to say *not* flat. In an odd paradoxical way Locke was right in holding that perception of *figure* belongs to both sight and touch, but only when the argument against him has first been accepted.

Consider the simplest case. Draw two squares, thus:

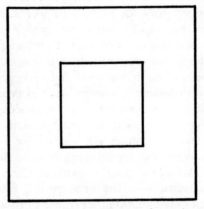

They are seen as flat on a flat surface and not in any other way. Now draw in the diagonals, thus:

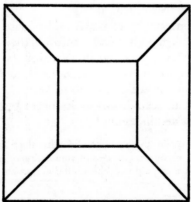

Then they cannot be seen as flat, but only 'in perspective', either the small one protrudes in front of the large one or sinks back behind it. The amusing and important thing is that the observer can 'flap' the small square in and out at will. It is perfectly clear that the field presented to sight is unchanging and motionless yet it can be visibly made to 'flap' one way or the other. Could a bodiless cyclops do this? If not, then the visual field is subordinate to the haptic.

Drawings are normally seen within a rectangular framework, of horizontal and vertical straight lines, and within the framework such lines are not interpreted except as flat. On the other hand diagonal straight lines are inevitably interpreted in depth, and the length of these lines or the number of figures or objects along them are clues to indicate distance in the line of sight. Hence objects otherwise visually equal in magnitude appear larger the more distant they are according to these criteria. This is essentially Wallis's explanation of the puzzle about the horizontal moon, which appears larger than the moon when seen near the zenith. Berkeley is needlessly harsh to Wallis over this; almost certainly it is part of the explanation and in no way conflicts with the other visual clues of distance, faintness and haziness which Berkeley emphasizes. In any case the puzzle is not important and cannot be dealt with in precise terms.[1]

To return to our main subject, the relation between the haptic and visual fields and the subordinate function of the visual; there is an example that calls for no laboratory techniques nor experiences difficult to come by, but is something frequently experienced, though not quite universally. Even the most ferocious upholder of the 'ordinary' as opposed to the 'technical' will find it hard to dismiss.

Nearly all adult human behaviour, static or locomotor, has become adjusted to be carried out on a stable platform in the normally stable gravitational field of the earth. In a ship at sea in rough weather there is only an unstable platform and moving gravitational field, and at first the result is extremely unpleasant. But most of us become adapted, or unlearn or forget, in a few

---

[1] It points to a conflict between a judgment based on measurement and one purely visual, as do the Muller–Lyer figures. In neither case do any operational consequences follow, except for those who deliberately ignore measurement.

days and 'get our sea legs'. This is a good descriptive phrase but does not go far enough: it should be 'sea legs-trunk-arms-neck-head-and-eyes'. If, while on board, we kept our eyes fixed on the horizon, which remains stable, we should be much worse off than we usually are and we should never become adapted at all. We become adapted by walking on, clinging to and looking at the moving decks and other parts of the ship itself, which has to be our new framework, leaving the horizon alone to fend for itself. The process of readjustment, or relearning after unlearning, is like that which Köhler's subject with the horizontal mirror underwent.

The end result is also like this. As soon as we step ashore on to the stable earth it is seen to heave gently up and down beneath our feet, as also all things attached to it. For the first few minutes we walk (in the view of others) as if drunk. The effect wears off in an hour or two, but it is unmistakable while it lasts, and more vivid the smaller the ship and the rougher the sea during the process of readaptation.

For the information of anybody who has not experienced the phenomenon it is perhaps necessary to insist that the heaving world is *seen* as directly and continuously as anything can be. One can sit quietly in a room and look carefully round for minutes on end and watch the floor and all the furniture heaving together. No one can unsee it at once, but by lapse of time we unlearn and then relearn the old adjustment to the old conditions.

Yet the highbrow physicist and lowbrow defender of common sense would both agree that nothing at all is heaving.

§7 Measurement not Visual

By far the most valuable corollary of Berkeley's doctrine that the visible and the tangible are two distinct fields of experience is that for classical physics there is no such thing as purely visual measurement; hence visual judgments do not by themselves have that kind of precision and certainty which measurement confers. This shows why the problem of the apparent magnitude of the horizontal moon is indeterminate, awkward and trivial. Strictly and visually the full moon has no magnitude, nor the sun, nor anything else, for by sight alone we cannot measure. We do have a 'feeling' that it seems bigger near the horizon and smaller overhead. The difficulty is not entirely that we never see it in the two positions simultaneously; for we can in fact see the half moon high in the sky and the setting sun near the horizon at the same time, and they sustain this 'feeling' well enough, as can a setting half moon, with the sun high in the sky, seen through cloud. There is no doubt about the phenomenon, as seen. The doubt is about its measurement.

There is a preliminary minor point to be mentioned. It is arguable, indeed highly probable, that we have no judgments of magnitude of seen figures that are not based on the process of *scanning*, that is of eye movement, as well as a single direct simultaneous visual impression of figure, supposing that there is such a kind of impression. Now for the important point, which is simple enough. When we do measure the magnitude of the moon's disc (or the sun's) we do so by means of instruments, that is to say haptically, with visual aid; first by what we do to and with the instrument, secondly by what we see happening. The puzzle about the horizontal moon would never have been a puzzle for the ordinary man, had not astronomers been professionally puzzled. From the time of Hipparchus on they still had this primitive feeling that the horizontal moon looked or seemed bigger while their astrolabes told them it measured just the same. The nineteenth century with photographic methods amply confirmed the old astrolabes, and yet the old feeling remained also.

In the first instance measurement means the application (actual putting together) of a standard or test object to another object, the one to be measured, according to a prescribed and specified procedure and then noting agreement or disagreement with respect to one specific relation between the objects (or among them, if more than two are involved). The process is repeated with various readjustments until the nearest possible agreement is obtained. The elementary examples are, measurement of lengths with a graduated straight edge, or a graduated stretched line, or the use of dividers; or else weighing with a balance. All other measurements are elaborations or sophistications of such elementary procedures.

Ordinary methods of measurement of length consist in comparing lengths by hand and eye simultaneously. A bodiless cyclops cannot do it. A blind man, however, can do it by hand only, though with instruments made for him, rather than made by him, and rather slowly and clumsily. The man with sight can start from scratch, making his instruments as he goes along. It is doubtful whether a completely blind man ever would start by himself. He certainly could not go very far nor attain great precision. He could not produce and use an astronomical telescope, not even an astrolabe. This, however, is speculation.

What is not speculation is that the combined use of hand and eye provides for measurement of lengths and for derived geometrical measurements (e.g. angular), a self-checking, even self-standardizing method. If our selected standard unit of *mass* (selected arbitrarily and by convention, for there is no other way) happens to change between two successive measurements of mass then it is just too bad; but we can do nothing about it except hope for better luck next time with some other standard, which we hope is more stable. But as long as hand and eye agree in geometrical measurements we know that our selected unit is stable in one way, relatively if not absolutely. What we are doing provides an independent check on what we are seeing; and what we are seeing on what we are doing, so we are less completely at the mercy of our selected standard unit, which still is and always must be arbitrary and conventional.

All this would be unnecessary if it were not that so many philosophers have never measured anything or if they have, one would not know it. To mention no lesser names, let Lord Russell and the late Professor Moore suffice for examples. It is the non-metrical aspects of mathematics which interest the first. The second always put his faith in ordinary common sense and ordinary language, and assumed all technical matters to be without interest or importance for philosophy.

To come back to Berkeley; in the early entries in *PC* there are indications that he *might* have claimed that measured lengths are sums of *minima tangibilia*. He once actually uses the terms 'punctum visibile & tangibile' (no. 70), but he nowhere says specifically that lengths are sums of tangible points or even *minima*, not even in *PC*, much less in his published works early or late, though it might have seemed a useful weapon with which to attack Leibniz. The statements at the end of *NTV* are almost entirely negative. Berkeley shows (§§ 150, 151) the hollowness of the arguments that 'incline one to think geometry conversant about visible extension' and refers back to his contention of §§ 59-61, that visible extensions have no settled determinate greatness and that men measure altogether, by the application of tangible extension to tangible extension. Visible figures (§ 152) 'are of the same use in geometry that words are'. Lastly (§ 158), 'What we strictly see are not solids, nor yet plains variously coloured: they are *only diversity of colours*' (my italics). In other words, Euclidean geometry is a metrical science of tangibles which are, incidentally and helpfully, also visible; a bodiless cyclops cannot use it. He then adds a caution in his last paragraph (§ 159). We have no difficulty in distinguishing between the sound and the sense of words in a language we are just beginning to learn, but in our own mother tongue we have the greatest difficulty; and if we knew of no other we might find it quite impossible.

This may perhaps suffice as a survey of the main topics of *NTV* and *TVV*, works which should, provided only they are read, speak for themselves.

§ 8 REID ON DOUBLE VISION

Reid's experiment on double vision[1] (*Inquiry into the Human Mind*, 1764, VI, ii.) needs to be quoted, as it is the first original and relevant contribution after Berkeley. It brings up a fundamental point. Also the experiment is simple, done in a few seconds, and anybody can try it for himself without special apparatus. Reid's explanation, though not definitely anti-Berkeleian is not Berkeleian nor entirely satisfactory.

The experiment, which has two parts, is this: First, fix the gaze, with both eyes, on some object ten feet or more distant, then hold up one finger directly in front of the eyes, while still *looking* at the distant object. Notice that there are now two fingers visible, rather faint and hazy but quite evidently *not one*, while the gaze is directed beyond them. The experiment cannot be done successfully by those whose vision is monocular (with one dominant or

[1] [What is the point of discussing Reid in a book on Berkeley? Anxious to show that the key to whatever is most fruitful in Berkeley lies in the *Theory of Vision*, Ritchie appeals to those philosophers who have found their inspiration in following out the Berkeleian views on the correlation of sight and of touch. Hence Ritchie's discussion of Reid, hence his interest in Ferrier.

In the case of Reid, Ritchie might indeed have gone further than he does in calling attention to Berkeleian affinities of the discussion of vision in the *Inquiry into the Human Mind*. In this connection, Reid's sections on squinting are of the greatest interest (*Inquiry into the Human Mind*, Sections 14, 15, 16).]

leading eye, the other functionally subordinate or mostly or entirely out of use). Nor can it be done by those who are very myopic and do not use correcting glasses. It should succeed with all who are normally binocular and can accommodate for near and distant vision. The only difficulty about it is instructive; to *fix the gaze* on one object and *direct attention* to another involves some degree of *strain*, a definite effort not easy to maintain for long. It is only under conditions of strain, that anybody ever sees anything double, which, as we say, ought to be single, e.g., the forefinger of his own right hand (cf. D. C. Blumenfeld, *Phil. Quart.*, vol. 9, 1959, p. 264). The strain, which is something *felt*, and the faintness and haziness, which are *seen*, provide sufficient grounds for dismissing duplicity of appearance as insignificant. While the clearness, distinctness and absence of strain when the seen finger is single, and the correspondence between binocular and monocular visions and of both with haptic experience, are guarantees of truth or reality. It is not surprising, nor puzzling, that the deceptive appearance is habitually suppressed or inhibited and passes unnoticed as do the coloured fringes round objects, except under special circumstances such as those of Reid's experiment. But we have only reached the first half of it.

The second part is more difficult and not everybody can get it to work. After the first part, still keeping the finger at arm's length or some shorter convenient distance for near vision, transfer the gaze (direct the eyes) from the distant object to the finger, but note the appearance of the distant object when it is done. The finger is distinct and one, the distant object faint, hazy and double. This, as I have said, is not easy to do; and, myself, I can do it only momentarily and after several trials. The second part also involves strain and of a more awkward kind. It is easier, perhaps more 'natural', to *attend* to something near while *looking at* something distant, than to perform the reverse feat.

On this point there is a useful note in Hamilton's *Reid* (p. 169n.) where Reid is discussing the phenomena of vision in subjects with an uncorrected squint. Hamilton quotes the physiologists Purkinji and Volkmann as saying that short-sighted persons under certain conditions habitually see distant objects double. Uncorrected myopia was very common in those days. Such myopics would be habitually in the position of one attempting the second part of Reid's experiment, but never of attempting the first part.

Their eyes would be accommodated and focused for a small range of near vision and never for distant vision. Their attempts at distant vision would always be strained and the objects indistinct.

The simple Berkeleian account of these observations would be that strictly each eye perceives its own object, right and left, as is discovered by opening and closing them alternately. If the two objects are near enough small differences can be discerned between them. Under the guidance of haptic experience we have learned to fuse the two visual fields. Under special conditions (e.g. Reid's experiment) we can partially and momentarily resolve or 'unfuse'.

Reid's experiment is valuable and the information to be got from it I consider decisive; his explanation of the information less so. He explains double and single vision and the phenomena of squinting (his experiment involves a temporary artificial squint) in terms of the theory of corresponding retinal points (perhaps his own invention). He suggests that in normal binocular vision when single objects appear single the retinal images, right and left, of these objects fall on geometrically similar parts of the retina. When the images fall on different parts then the objects appear double. There is some obvious confirmation of this suggestion. Intoxicated persons are subject to *nystagmus* (wandering eyes) as can easily be seen by sober onlookers; and the intoxicated report seeing things double. But this observation establishes nothing about corresponding points, which are more hypothetical and less observable than the retinal images, on which they depend for the bare possibility of existence. Sherrington's work on binocular flicker[1] bears strongly against their anatomical or physiological respectability. The familiar experience of onlookers at tennis that the gaze can flick rapidly across between right and left without the ball, players or court ever appearing double to those free from nystagmus bears rather strongly against them. If they exist at all they must belong to the central regions of the retinae not the peripheral. There is no evidence, so far as I know, of anything but single appearance of single objects with dark-adapted peripheral vision; but of course this may be monocular, not binocular. Here is an interesting subject for a Ph.D. thesis for which the enquirer

[1] *The Integrative Action of the Nervous System*, 1906, Ch. 10.

D

will have to devise his own methods instead of repeating old observations with more complicated and more expensive apparatus devised by somebody else.

In short, retinal corresponding points will not work at all unless Berkeleian principles are accepted first, and then do no real work; they make nothing more precise, determinate or intelligible. Moreover they belong to the transmission theory of sense at its weakest; at a point where it has to abandon *isomorphism* in order to explain how something that began (in the evolutionary sense) as two processes has become one process and when, under special conditions it reverts to two, can be a source of falsehood or illusion.

It is necessary to indicate the source of weakness in Reid's explanation; but the value of the facts to which he points is not diminished by that weakness.

Summary of conclusions (not necessarily Berkeley's own) from §§ 1–7.

  i. There are distinct realms of the several different senses.

 ii. Between, as well as within, these realms, we learn to discover stable sign relations; the most useful of which are between the haptic and visual realms.

iii. The natural sciences have developed out of those specially stable groups of perceptual relations we call *objects*, *things* or *bodies*, and the specially reliable relations we find by experiment and measurement; two forms of active interference.

iv. Because of this, haptic experience, without which there is no active interference, has become the predominant realm of experience; it is also directly the most useful or dangerous, though remembered only by passive imagining.

 v. Corroboration (or the reverse) between two different realms is more precise and reliable than within one realm, because the sensed qualities are entirely different and we are not confused by vague likeness or unlikeness. What was active interference, reappears in memory as passive imagining.

§ 9 TEST OF TRUTH AND FALSEHOOD

Berkeley did not discuss the test (or criterion) of truth and falsehood in *NTV*, nor elsewhere; he had no need to for his purposes. Yet the test is there, presupposed by his method and can be derived from it by cautious generalization; the more easily because it is used by him in a specially simple and direct way. Berkeley first arrived at the test because in *NTV* he escaped from both visualist and 'third party' illusions and dealt with correlations among experiences within one field as well as those between different fields. Visualism is so deeply imbedded in what is commonly called common sense, and in the minds of most philosophers ancient and modern, that Berkeley himself relapsed into it occasionally (see Ch. IV, pp. 62–65 and V, 84 ff.).

As I understand it, there is and can be only one test or criterion for judging between true and false in sense experience and the sciences of observation; one *genus* but many *species* according to the different types of situation to which the test is applied. In the process of use, matter and form cannot be separated, even when distinguishable; the situation and its details enter into the precise way of using the test.

To deal with judgments of this kind it is best to begin by using the most general of available terms; *True* (*Right*) and *False* (*Wrong*), rather than any more special terms. For example, the contrasted terms *Real* and *Apparent* suggest certain metaphysical theories; the term *Illusory* suggests them more strongly; the term *Erroneous* suggests rashness, stupidity and bad logic (cf. Descartes on Error). Bad faith or fraud is another type opposite to Truth (Right). These terms do not all apply to all cases; there are non-metaphysical problems about which we may be right or wrong; sober, sane and honest people make mistakes; clever people using good logic can arrive at false conclusions if they observe badly. Berkeley's argument and the type of case to which it belongs is less specialized than these examples. He does not consider the highest levels of abstraction, nor introduce the kind of obscurity that such arguments do. Nor on the other hand does he introduce the obscurities belonging to difficult observation or where there is no conscious, precise or deliberate judgment. Rather he deals with the level of elementary scientific observation and judgment, and specifically that of experiment and measurement.[1]

---

[1] The poets have always known that there is also a kind of truth and falsity very remote from the technical, scientific or Berkeleian. For example, in *Midsummer Night's Dream*, who is the true lover of Hermia or Helena, and who the false, or are both false, or is the melancholy truth as Lysander says? (Act I, Sc. 1, 132). This problem is often treated frivolously, and the similar

The Berkeleian perceptual test of truth and falsity applies where two or more parts of chosen perceptual situations are found either to confirm or corroborate, or coordinate or cohere with each other, or to be mutually inclusive; or else, in contrast, to do the reverse. In the contrasting case the parts remain single, unconfirmed, uncorroborated, incoordinate, incoherent, exclusive, and because of this unreliable, uncertain or deceptive. A certain difficulty crops up at the beginning. True and False are not simple Positive and Negative; such numerical analogies can be very misleading; specially so when a double negative is assumed to equal a positive. This is one of the deceitful conventions of logicians, denied by most plain honest men in many languages.[1]

Granted that we are free of this first illusion, we need to be free of the next, that experience consists, first, of single separate items, which then have to be glued together with logical glue. On the contrary, first, *we* select, single out and differentiate the items *we* choose, then, secondly, *we* observe them as fitting together or not. When there is failure to fit, *we* reject the more single, solitary, weaker, or less determinate.[2]

The pure Humean impression, which even Hume could see beyond,[3] which he could have called 'Categories', or pure *sense datum*, by itself and in itself, is a fabulous monster, but if anything which looks like it crops up in experience it is treated as negligible, neither true nor false, unless it is found masquerading as something else; then it is rejected as false. Experience can sink down to something like strings of Humean impressions, as in dreaming. At its highest and furthest from dreaming, it is the experience of skilled craftsmanship or precise observation, which is also a skilled craft.

Hallucinations, even, are not so low as dreams, for they can sometimes be shown to be false, and could in principle be fitted into or coordinated with valid experience, though in fact they fail

---

one in *Cosi fan tutte* even more frivolously; though it is very serious as all true poets know, but not the false ones.

Perhaps it is relevant that all large scale music is based on Choral Song and Dance and its aesthetic value depends upon the cooperation of many persons in sound, sight, and bodily movement.

[1] R. G. Collingwood, *Essay on Philosophical Method*, 1933, Chs. II and III.

[2] W. A. Sinclair, *The Conditions of Knowing*, 1951, pp. 35 ff., and Appendix A.

[3] 'Of Relations', *Treatise*, Bk I, Pt I, I, § 5.

and are therefore condemned as false, not just insignificant. For example, A says, pointing, 'There are pink rats.' B, who hears him and sees him point, fails to corroborate him by seeing, touching, hearing or smelling anything ratty or pink in the region pointed to at the time of pointing. B also observes certain abnormalities of behaviour on the part of A, which lead him (B) to conclude that A is suffering from delusions or hallucinations. B however cannot *demonstrate to* A the falsity of A's pink rats unless A himself is willing and able to cooperate, and to investigate for himself whether or not he (A) finds something tangible, audible or smell-able and not just visible in an odd kind of way other than the way in which the walls and floors of the room are visible to him, A, and also to others, such as B.

A, even if intoxicated, can collaborate to some extent and so help to demonstrate the defect or abnormality of his experience, but his collaboration will be inferior to that of a sober and other-wise normal man. The sole, but important difficulty caused by hallucinations and the like, is the unusual personal situation in which they arise; namely, the effect of drugs, fear, fatigue, and other pathological states. Practically all the collaborating has to come from sober B, and very little from drunken A. It is very different when a normal A mistakes a tree for a man in a bad light, easily discovers his mistake for himself, and has no difficulty in arriving at agreement with B, who says that at first it did look rather like a man, but now on a nearer, clearer view it looks extremely like a tree.

So far discussion has been in terms of what may be called the standard Berkeleian case, which involves coordination between two sensory fields, the most impressive and perhaps the most important aspect. There is, however, coordination within one field which has its own necessary part to play, one often forgotten. Agreement between two eyes or two ears are simple examples, so simple and so common that nobody notices them except when, very occasionally, agreement fails, and that is taken as a diagnostic sign that something is out of order. Coordination within the haptic field is equally unnoticed but displayed continually in a most intricate way and necessary for normal life. It is displayed when anyone uses the combined movements of any two or more organs; as for example the two hands in using tools or the four limbs in climbing. It is unlikely that anybody ever considered this kind of coordination before Berkeley did, and it was Molyneux's question that put it into his mind. (I refuse to use the pedantic inaccuracy of 'put it into his head'.)

Let me repeat; without attempt and failure to corroborate there is no falsehood and without success, no truth; the contrast between the two constitutes the test.

By emphasizing haptic experience in *NTV*, Berkeley does not claim that it reveals *causes* as necessary relations, any more than that it reveals *essences*. The special kind of *reality* he claims in *NTV* is that it is most directly useful as a means of life and therefore more important. Nor, lastly, does he claim that it is infallible in principle; but only that normally it is better and more continuously corroborated than visual experience. This is because the normal use of visual experience is for prediction by the use of imagination and not directly for corroboration. Occasional failure is the price to be paid for the advantage of prediction, and most failures can be corrected before they have done much harm, many by sight before they have occurred. Most failures are the result of our mistaking unfamiliar conjunctions of experience for familiar ones, when we are aware of part only of the total relevant situation. Mistakes and their partial correction or complete correction are the beginning of new knowledge, or can be if properly (scientifically) used. The central and most important conclusion of Berkeley was that the relations among experiences should be treated, *prima facie*, not as causal, necessary nor essential, but as symbolic, therefore not final nor free from all risk. In this he anticipated Hume but, like Descartes and Locke, held that by the goodness of God which fits His creatures to His creation, the risks are not too great; but, I would add, great enough to sharpen human wits. (This is the 'survival value' argument in its theistic form, not in its nineteenth-century atheistic form.)

Let me now consider the classical example of a perceptual situation which may, when unfamiliar, cause false judgment: the oar which *looks* bent when half in water, though it is *really* straight. Here, if you please, 'oar', not 'stick'. A 'stick', while still *real*, might be of any size, shape or material; it could be flexible, and could get bent by the process of partial immersion in some kind of liquid. But when it is a question of 'oars', they have definite specifications. However we may choose to vary the specifications as to material and form, we must include in our statement that an oar is an instrument for the purpose of propelling a boat, in one or another of several different ways. For that purpose it must be *straight* (apart from the end of the blade, which may be either straight or bent) and also *properly balanced*. Straightness is not basically a matter of how a thing *looks* to the eye but of how it *feels* when handled in the ways that oars are handled in use. It must also be rigid and strong. Apart from superficial matters of paint or varnish, specifications will not lay down how oars should *look*.

Here we seem to be starting from the higher ground of conceptual thought, as indicated by the term 'specification', and it may be so: nevertheless we are brought back at once to the perceptual level and to Berkeley's treatment. *Straight* is a geometric relation between spatial *ideas* (in Berkeley's sense) of haptic experience, with which visual *ideas* are correlated. If we notice at any time that visible relations appear to be connected with tangible relations in an unusual way we dismiss the visible as *mere appearance* or false prediction, for the visible is usually taken as predicting the tangible, and seldom *vice versa*.

Now if an oar is held up in the air it *looks* (as well as *feels*) straight. Only under the special conditions of partial immersion does it *look* (but does not *feel*) bent. By leaving out the bracketed words, we can make the statement imply that *looking* itself could suggest something wrong about the *look* of an oar half immersed. Against that I would maintain that for human animals there is no mere or pure looking and that even if there were (as perhaps in dreams) there would be no right or wrong (no truth or falsehood) about it. No rules would govern variegated play of lights and colours: anything might be succeeded by anything (cf. the case of Chesselden's subject had he been presented with a cube and sphere of polished glass; § 4 above).

False judgment comes in when an observer of relations of things or objects combining visible with tangible properties infers that what feels straight must invariably look straight under all conditions. When however the observer pauses, refrains from such a judgment and considers instead what are the conditions that produce a combination of visible crookedness and tangible straightness, he will then be opening up a new branch of science; the investigation of the Laws of Refraction.

Notice, in concluding this stage of the argument, that we say that a thing *is* straight because wherever we 'try it out' it feels so, though occasionally it may look bent, but never the other way round. For we 'try things out' by handling, never by merely seeing.

Next I ask leave to reintroduce two contrasting cases and attempt to answer a question which I asked in my book *Scientific Method* in 1923 (pp. 28–9) and failed to answer. Nobody took the question seriously, though I meant it seriously, and still think it needs an answer. The cases are:

i. Everything we see under the standard form of compound microscope is different from anything we see with the naked eye or handle with our hands in the ordinary way. Everything under the microscope is differently orientated (upside down and left to right), of different size, often of different shape and colour as compared with 'real' objects: yet nobody ever calls them 'unreal', false, wrong, erroneous or illusory, but surprisingly, and most metaphysically as being 'really' the same as 'real' objects. Why? The foregoing gives the answer: because correlation and corroboration is always obtained under ordinary working conditions among the relations of naked eye and microscopic objects, *mutatis mutandis*. That is to say there are constant and precise rules of mutation from the one type of object to the other.

There are many and complicated rules, but each special one is simple. That is because in the history of microscopy there have been small steps in magnification and no sudden jump from none to the highest possible magnification. Each step has been made deliberately and systematically, by modification of instruments and methods of use. Always, the necessary general standing conditions for seeing any valid and interpretable microscopic object, e.g. a single red blood corpuscle, streptococcus, or, if you wish, virus, is the correct use of a suitable type of microscope.[1]

ii. Now for the contrasting case. The necessary general standing condition for seeing pink rats is the consumption of large quantities of alcohol over a long period. Why then the doubt about the truth of the appearances? The answer is given in the rules of mutation. Those for seeing a single red blood corpuscle under the

---

[1] *Electron-microscope* is a misnomer: there is no 'scope' about it, only 'micro-'. The '-scopic' part of the business consists of persons looking at photographs in another room. The rules of mutation are more complicated.

microscope are precise, detailed, specific, entirely reliable; those for seeing pink rats are not. Nobody can specify precisely when, where, under what conditions, and by what persons they will be seen, or will not be seen. Every pink rat remains a simple Humean impression. It is not that nobody has yet bothered to investigate the subject, but that nobody is so stupid as to try. A further question needs to be considered. Admitted that there could be no truth or falsehood in terms of Humean impressions or of relations among them (supposing that there could be general relations among them), then truth or falsehood belongs to *apperception*, in the sense of Leibniz or Kant: that is to say conceptualized perceptions. Does it follow that truth and falsity are always conceptual, not perceptual at all? I think not.

Consider our three examples: oars, red blood corpuscles, pink rats. In discussing such cases we use these and similar general class names for speed and convenience: but I suggest that we could do without them when the objects themselves (if genuine) are before us and can be pointed at, so that we can say 'This . . .', 'That . . .', and 'The other . . .'. Even then, we do need some general names, e.g. *straight, bent, surface, upper medium, lower medium, seen, felt when handled.* We can do without *oar, air, water,* as we can do without *paint, varnish, wood, boat.* We need geometrical relations, certain categoreal or sub-categoreal terms, and verbs that refer to sense experience generically or specifically. But I think we could manage with a reduced strictly Berkeleian vocabulary in the presence of the things discussed: we could not eliminate concepts altogether but we should definitely be dealing with truth and falsehood in perceptual terms. It might be tiring but would be possible. At any rate I do not take this objection seriously, and am more inclined to put the question the other way round, as Berkeley does himself. Can there be truth or falsity that is purely conceptual?

As has been said above (p. 34) the true and the false are not just plain positives and negatives: if they were, then there could be degrees of truth, in the sense that we might have propositions of ten degrees of truth on the one hand and of ten degrees of falsehood on the other, and their sums would be zero. That does not happen, even though there are propositions or apparent propositions whose truth or falsehood is zero, e.g. that equilateral triangles are virtuous. If there is anything positive or negative

about truth or falsehood the positivity seems to belong to falsehood rather than truth, and truth to be the absence of falsehood,
not the other way round. Certainly it is generally an easier and
more direct process to establish falsehood, completely, definitely,
both in matters of experience (fact) and of theory: specially so in
theory. Certain fallacies have been refuted once and for all. That
does not prevent some Sophists from trotting them out in every
generation again and again, but it means that the refutations are
the same old refutations, again and again. On the other hand,
while certain truths need to be proclaimed again generation after
generation, they are not so completely the same, they are in
slightly different terms for slightly different conditions. There is
a kind of growth in new experience under new conditions. It is
not *philosophia* that is *perennia* but *sophistica*. (To say this is not
pessimism nor misology, but the recognition of original intellectual sin.)

On the less abstract, but factual, perceptual or Berkeleian level,
it can be shown once and for all, that it is false to say that the
tangible oar is bent at the surface of the water because the visible
oar is bent. The refutation suffices for any one who troubles to
consider the facts, and he will be the more convinced when he
considers also the laws of refraction of light. But as to the whole
theory of light and of the structure of surfaces, the whole truth
has not been revealed to any.

As has been hinted in a footnote (p. 33) the story of this kind
of truth and falsehood is not the whole story, but is the part with
which Berkeley in *NTV* was specially concerned. He is also concerned with it in *DM*, but before that we need to know his
criticism of *abstract ideas* and specially of corporeal substances
which is one of the worst of them.

In *NTV* and *TVV* Berkeley said something quite new, but
his statement is specialized, technical and fits into an already
recognized framework of thought, which framework should be
noted.

Aristotle's idea of *dialectic* as the second best method of improv-
ing knowledge (where demonstrative science by deduction from
first principles is not available) is the notable example. *Dialectic*
proceeds by a systematic scrutiny of various hypotheses that have
been suggested. Any one of them that is found internally incoherent or inconsistent is rejected, as also any which contradicts

accepted empirical facts. The process of scrutiny is continued until a hypothesis (or possibly several) is found which passes all tests.

Francis Bacon has nothing to say against this; rather he transfers the procedure more firmly to the sphere of experience by making hypothesis the guide to systematic observation, and emphasizing that observation is a cooperative human undertaking and an experiment, a deliberate interference with things for the testing of hypotheses.

Berkeley now provides examples of certain kinds of experiment and hypothesis hitherto ignored, as, for example, the answer to Molyneux's question; also the analysis of the physical process of linear measurement. He assumes the general framework, and makes no general statement beyond his immediate purpose.

III

REFLECTIONS ON THE THEORY
OF VISION

§ 1 The Direct Method

In the works that followed *NTV* Berkeley emphasized his destructive aim, the idols he wanted to destroy. These were, in his view, both religious and scientific, and both related, springing from the misuse of visual imagination. He attacked, for example, the doctrine of corporeal substance, which he held to be responsible for the Machine Theory of the Universe, and Locke's theory of 'abstract ideas'. Among these attacks Berkeley says less than he should about what he defends, his own positive doctrine, which can well bear to be expanded. Berkeley believed that all our knowledge of the world in which (by the Grace of God) we live is based on observation, so that all theorizing from past observation should be referable to future observation. Thus inobservables should be eliminated from accounts of the natural world or at least reduced to a minimum (his later more tolerant view). What is wrong with Locke's 'abstract ideas' is that everything which is properly, carefully and clearly observed has its own specific character and no other; and that is why it is worth observing. The generic image that Locke described and many philosophers beside him have believed in, can have each, any or all specific characters, so has in effect none, and nobody can do anything with it except make mistakes. Berkeley was wise to reject inobservables and see through the farce of generic images; he was not quite so wise to say so little about the conditions of observation which make our ideas exactly what they are and nothing else, and make them concrete, not abstract, but he did open up the way to new developments where Locke and Hume failed.

Berkeley's *Direct Method*,[1] or less accurately, *Internal View*, is the

---

[1] [In this section and its successor, Ritchie is occupied in trying to formulate the distinction, so central to his discussion of Berkeley, between the Internal or Direct view, and the Third Party or External or Indirect view. The subject is resumed in Ch. IV, especially pp. 64–65, where Ritchie adds

correct way of beginning any empirical investigation, either psychological, or belonging to the Natural Sciences. It can lead to a conclusion which is definite and shared by any or all observers. The common alternative, the *Indirect* or *Third Party Method* is arbitrary, *a priori* in the bad sense, and leads only to rival conflicting hypotheses. In practice the users of it smuggle in a bit of *Direct Method* secretly and inconsistently. Beginning with the *Direct Method* the practitioner is free to incorporate, at the right place, openly and consistently whatever he needs of the *Indirect Method*.

Unless Berkeley's *Direct Method* is understood and used we shall never be rid of three common confusions:

i. Confusing objects of sense with objects of imagination (see *TVV*, § 10). This confusion can be avoided in spite of the serious difficulty of avoiding confusion of objects of sense with objects of recollection as Hume tells us (vainly) we ought to do by his distinction between impressions and ideas.

ii. Confusing objects of one sense with objects of another as Locke did and very likely Hume also (*TVV*, §§ 46–7).

iii. Failing to notice that sensation, perception, memory and imagination are self-including activities, often discussed, and perhaps of necessity in self-referring terms. I use 'self' here with two different meanings for there is no convenient alternative. The activity is of our-self; the term refers to it-self.

These confusions could be found all cooperating on a celebrated occasion when G. E. Moore tried to persuade an audience of the truth and value of his kind of common sense, and apparently succeeded. Moore held up one hand and said that he could not doubt that it was a hand and one. Then he also held up the other and said he could not doubt that now there were two and both hands. He might have been more usefully employed had he

---

important clarifications. The line he develops may, as Ritchie was himself aware, be pushed further with the help of J. F. Ferrier's two articles on Berkeley in *Lectures and Remains*, vol. II (sometimes vol. III, depending on the edition), especially pp. 366 ff. and pp. 388 ff. Expressed in contemporary terms, the point in question is that developed in M. Merleau-Ponty, *The Phenomenology of Perception* (1962), Pt I, § 2 (especially contrast of pp. 106 ff. of French edition) or in J-P Sartre, *Being and Nothingness* (1957), Pt 3, Ch. 2 Introduction (pp. 303–5 of the English edition).]

performed before them Reid's experiment[1] and instructed the audience to try it for themselves. Then he could have added: 'Now try to sort out your confusions about "one" and "two".' Unfortunately he was content for them and himself to remain as confused as before.

§ 2 THE DIRECT METHOD *versus* THE THIRD PARTY VIEW

Let us suppose we are in a well-conducted psychological laboratory; that is to say one where human behaviour is studied as such by direct examination, not inferred *a priori* from rats running through mazes, or dogs salivating, or even neurotics exhibiting fantasies. Suppose further that we are in a room where work is in progress on the phenomena of visual after-images. It is likely that we shall find there a number of persons or *subjects* whose *experience* of or *reaction to* certain visible *situations* and other *environmental processes* are being tested. Call these persons A, B, C, etc.[2] What is seen by them will immediately be seen by us (X, Y, Z) who come in to look on; and we can take a share in the tests too. The crucial part of the test consists in what A, B, and C each report on what each *sees*, separately and independently of the rest. The reports may be just 'Yes' or 'No', or a complicated written statement. The whole *situation* however is being controlled by another person R, the recorder, who collects and collates the reports. Suppose that R is for the moment mainly concerned with what he is *doing* for control purposes; switching lights on to a large screen that A, B, and C are looking at, switching them off again and instructing the *subjects* about what he is doing and they are to do. R may also be acting as subject and reporting what he himself sees on the screen. Indeed we might come into the room and find R all by himself acting as both *subject* and *recorder*. In any case before he starts *recording* he should have made some direct acquaintance with visual after-images.

In many types of study of human sense experience the *recorder* expects all subjects to behave in the same or very nearly the same way, but in the case I have supposed he will expect a small but

---

[1] [Ritchie, presumably, has in mind the experiment described on p. 29–30 above.]

[2] Note: Messrs A, B, C, etc., here are not the same as those of Ch. II.

significant minority to behave differently. That will not worry him, quite the contrary. It means that he will sort out the *subjects* into a majority with full *normal* colour vision and a minority with deficient colour vision of various and interesting kinds. Whether he himself has normal or deficient colour vision makes no difference to his work as *recorder*, provided he knows how to classify himself.

I have chosen the special example of visual after-images, because it shows well how sense experience can be at the same time private or subjective (if you like to put it so) and public or objective (if you like). We have to start from and by means of our own private individual experience, but we can publicize it to others and they equally can publicize theirs to us. This can be done even with after-images, which are neither things nor objects nor yet *corporeal substances*, yet not to be dismissed with insulting names as illusions, hallucinations, products of indigestion, alcohol, or a frenzied imagination, as they probably were before Berkeley's day, if anybody ever stopped to notice after-images. It is doubtful whether he himself ever did, but by using his method they can be dealt with almost as easily as the familiar objects of everyday life. This is because Berkeley first drew attention away from imaginary hypothetical singular entities to certain general relations upon which our publicly available information depends. Berkeley did this in spite of his insistence (in his early days) on sensory *minima* and his alleged nominalism (really an attack on mock universals).

Consider now an instance of Berkeley's *Direct Method*. Mr A, who may be Berkeley, you or me, and is given the *Mr* for reasons that will appear later, explains how the things he himself observes are interrelated so as to supply him with a set of empirically discovered rules which he names or describes in his own general terms; e.g. *hard, soft, cold, warm, straight, curved, long, short, equal, unequal.* (Note the intrusion at the end of the list of typical Platonic forms.) None of these terms need be taken visually, though we can speak of a 'hard light' or a 'cold light'. They are chosen because they belong basically to the processes, active as well as passive, of touching, handling, moving about, to the tangible or haptic realm of experience. Had the terms been invented *de novo* by Mr A, he could communicate their meaning to Mr B by putting suitable objects into Mr B's hands and naming them at the appropriate moment, provided only they both can hear as well as handle. If they both can see also, so much the quicker and easier; but sight is not necessary. Finally, in case there is any doubt, Mr B can hand them back to Mr A again saying the appropriate words: *straight, equal* and so on. The process is mutual and reciprocal; though one person is reckoned active, the other as passive. Their experiences are closely similar; it may do no harm to call them *identical*, at least in certain cases.

Over the last and most abstract of the terms mentioned (*equal, unequal*) there is no great difficulty as to identity of experience or objective meaning of terms. Apart from rash or careless judgment, Mr A and Mr B can easily agree whether two tangible objects are equal or unequal, and are not likely to make different judgments at different times provided they stick to familiar and rigid bodies, wood and metal, not butter or clay. But all that is meant by 'equality' is 'possessing no discernible or significant inequality'. Because it is negative, equality might stand as absolute. Inequality is directly observed, positive and relative. We can ask about it, 'In what way?', 'By how much?' Also, it is judged by external standards. Unless Mr A and Mr B agree to select (arbitrarily in the first instance) standards of comparison they will not agree with one another at one time or with themselves at different times. So also with *long* and *short*, which really must be written *longer* and *shorter*, to show that both are relative terms. The terms refer to a specific inequality, one kind only, thus reducing the arbitrariness of choice of standards, pointing to one kind of standard, one kind of process (bodily action) of measurement and finally placing the science of Euclidean geometry at the disposal of two observers.

Cold and *warm* are more difficult because not themselves geometrical, and it is even more urgent to use the relative terms, *colder* and *warmer*, because of the trouble Locke got into (*Essay*, II, Ch. 8, § 21).[1] He is referring to the experiment: Put your right hand into a bowl of hot water and your left into a bowl of cold water, then after a time place both hands in a bowl of lukewarm water (equal quantities of the waters in the first two bowls). This one sample of water then feels cold to the right hand and warm to the left. There is no contradiction, no paradox, no illusion, no serious difficulty of any sort in terms of the comparatives, *colder* and *warmer*. Thermometry provides a method of measurement and a

[1] Locke, *Essay Concerning Human Understanding* (Pringle-Pattison, Oxford University Press, 1924).

science, not so easy nor so well worked out as geometry but available here and sufficing for ordinary practical purposes, for controlling temperatures.

The brief sketch above should be enough to enable the reader to work all these examples out in as much detail as he wishes, to add to them the more awkward pair, *softer* and *harder*, and any other analogous pair of correlatives. By starting from a Berkeleian basis any two or more human persons, though each starts independently and each experiences some things differently, can conclude by understanding each of the others. All equally and mutually share a common world, the world of the physical sciences. A Berkeleian could be a solipsist if he wished, but has no need to wish or to indulge in such perversity, a perversity which denies the existence of human language and could be maintained by a bodiless cyclops only.

On the other hand any one who tries to start from and maintain a completely behaviourist (or, if you like, materialist) External, Indirect or Third Party view runs into trouble for he cannot arrive at mutual understanding with any other person and has to finish as a solipsist with no language or with a self-contradictory private language. That is why I speak of the *Direct Method* or the *Internal* or the Berkeleian view, but of an *External* or (possibly) anti-Berkeleian View. The first can and does develop into a universal or objective view, the other cannot. Let me explain further, if it is not clear already.

Mr A is now supposed to have changed his mind and to be a consistent metaphysical Behaviourist or Externalist. He starts examining the *reactions* of object B, not Mr B; for him there is no such person, only something that is allowed to be alive and to *react* in a way that lifeless things do not. For convenience let us suppose that the other objects towards which B *reacts* are the test objects of Molyneux's question, a cube and a sphere (*NTV*, § 132). Mr A looks at B while B is handling these two things, and interprets what is happening in terms of his own Internal View (he has no other) while rigidly excluding B from it and excluding any view of B's own. Mr A remembers how he has handled cubes, spheres and other similar objects while looking on at the process. By these means he can distinguish B from cube and sphere as reacting or behaving after the Mr A fashion up to a point, while the cube and sphere do not *react* or *behave* in any such fashion. For

E

instance when B puts the cube down on a table he lays it on one of its sides and not on an edge or a point, while he puts the sphere down just whichever way he happens to be holding it; also he may place the sphere on the top of the cube but not the cube on the top of the sphere.

Mr A cannot, of course, speak to poor B about it, but let us suppose for the moment that we can communicate with Mr A and he with us telepathically or by some other esoteric means. We say to him: 'You can watch B handling those things and infer that it is handling behaviour from what *you see*: but does B *see* anything? Mr A can only reply: 'Not so far as I can make out. When B shuts its eyes it makes no significant difference in its behaviour and when it is not handling the cube or sphere it is not behaving towards them at all, even if its eyes are turned that way.' Mr A's assumptions exclude his admitting that B *sees* anything because he himself does not actually *see* the *seeing*. But, because he both *sees* and *feels* his own bodily movements and can see B's also, he inconsistently admits B to a partial equality with himself as *behaving towards* the sphere and cube in an intelligible way instead of saying that B differs from sphere and cube no more than they differ from one another. If Mr A is to be consistent he must either become a solipsist, or else a Berkeleian by talking to B, and then discovering that B sees just as well as he does himself, and that seeing is part of his behaviour. In short, B is allowed to become Mr B.

If A (we can now drop the formality of *Mr*) tries to persist in strict externalism he has to assume that his own experience and judgment are the only ones and are infallible. He cannot make the necessary first step in distinguishing truth from error by appealing to the experience and judgment of another person. If he sees B repeatedly putting the cube down on one corner, picking it up when it falls over and again putting it down on one corner, he cannot say: 'B is making a mistake'; nor, if by some trick B succeeds in standing it up on one corner can he say: 'B is cleverer than I thought.' If A himself fails to do what he wants with these objects he cannot say: 'I am doing it wrong': he can only say: 'These are queer objects, always changing and slippery.' Therefore, when after trials, he does what he wants with them, he cannot say: 'Now I have learnt how to do it': only 'Now they have changed again.'

Externalism or Behaviourism can lead to fallacies and confusions, when it is made the starting point and pursued so as to exclude the *Direct Method* or *Internal View* in the places proper to it. Most psychological observation and experiment has to be of what people *do*, that is what is visible externally. By combining that with what they *say* about what they *do* and with what the observer (or recorder) *does* and *says* also, fallacies and confusions can be avoided. This is not to claim that everybody always tells the truth; quite the contrary. Telling lies is one of the privileges of high grade intelligence, as is play-acting and pretending.

On the other side, the pursuit of the *Internal View* has led to fallacies and confusions too; to the vicious kind of subjectivism and introspection. Here it is the peculiar and easily misinterpreted privacy of visual experience that leads to difficulties and particularly to the ambiguities of the terms outside and inside; as I indicated, I hope sufficiently, when first using the terms *Internal* and *External* in a special sense.

In conclusion, both Internal and External Views are needed, in that order of priority; and they need to be combined in the right way. This last is not always easy. In ordinary life and practice it is done automatically, unconsciously, but not always correctly in unusual situations. When we say that two people hear the same sound, or touch and see the same object, the word *same* often gets us into trouble. It needs qualifying with *ceteris paribus* and *mutatis mutandis*, and we are not always clear what has to be changed and what has to be taken as equal. I believe that Berkeley took the necessary first steps towards dealing with these problems, but not the last, and apart from Malebranche nobody had ever begun to see what the problem was. They had asked the wrong questions and therefore obtained the wrong answers or none.

The next step is to follow up the *Direct Method*. Unfortunately it has to be done in two different ways, each of which needs a separate section though in practice they should be combined. First of all a preliminary difficulty has to be considered.

§ 3 THE HUMEAN VIEW OF IMPRESSIONS[1]

For the most part Berkeley showed the way out of difficulties and avoided the Humean blind alley in which most British philosophers have groped about, but he did raise one apparently insoluble problem. Berkeley's theory, at least as he first expressed it, seems to require single, indivisible atoms of experience passively received by minds, which are themselves pure activities, indivisible, eternal, spiritual substances. Admittedly an indivisible, eternal substance, if it is spiritual, is not absurd *prima facie*, as is such a material substance; and it obviously can and must be active. But Berkeley had to combine this Platonist theory of spirits with what most people consider to be extreme Nominalism (*Princ.*, Introduction), and extreme empiricism, whereas it usually goes with rationalism and the dismissal of sense experience as inevitably obscure and confused, if not totally illusory. The Gordian Knot could not be untied because Gordius took care to leave no visible ends; but can be cut, and cut it shall be.

Berkeley was defending, as was a later eighteenth-century philosopher, the doctrines of God, Freedom and Immortality against atheist, determinist and nihilist (I can find no other suitable name) metaphysics and took what appeared to be, in the early eighteenth century, a short cut against spiritual nihilism and against Locke's notorious Ch. 27 of Bk II of his *Essay*; though it can now be seen that Locke is no nihilist. On the other hand Berkeley should have seen that this kind of Platonism, with its compulsory and merely numerical endurance of soul-substance is a deification of the human intelligence and incompatible with the Christian doctrine of Eternal life as a freely bestowed divine gift. He should also have been aware of the extreme awkwardness of Aristotelian or preNewtonian mechanical theories of 'activity' and 'passivity'. He was clearly aware that Intelligence and Will must not be separated (here he did rather better than Kant), and took care to link them. But when they are linked, then activity and passivity follow the Newtonian model in psychology as well as mechanics, and here Locke's theory might have helped him. At any rate Berkeley's statements in *Princ.*, § 27 and later are rash, and possibly we can

---

[1] For comparison do not consult Hume's *Treatise*, Bk I, where he is concerned with 'ideas', but Bk II where he is concerned with 'impressions', i.e. passions: especially the early and last §§ of Pt I.

find in *Siris* a partial correction, bringing another aspect of Platonism to counter the indivisible soul-substance theory.

If we can set aside the spirit theory and consider only the *idea* theory, then we can see that part (not the whole) of the function of ideas is to stand as signs for others, that one stands for many, that it may be separate and stand for what is different, complex, structured and undergoes change. For performing this function some *ideas* must be, in some way, single, simple, uniform and passively received all by themselves; on the other hand others cannot be like this. At least some sign systems must contain simple, single signs as beginnings. Association is an elementary cognitive process, though it would not be cognitive at all if it operated by itself. That is why Associationism is a false theory whether in the hands of Hobbes its originator (at least for modern thought) or his numerous unwitting followers. That is why Locke put his finger definitely on its main defect (*Essay*, II, Ch. 33); association, by itself, is irrational, illogical, and by itself not fully cognitive.

Let us consider examples of sense processes which operate as simple signs by association, deliberately leaving visual experience to the very end; for whatever may be the case with insects, human visual processes hardly ever work this way, but other senses do. We never speak of *a sight* except metaphorically or sarcastically. The sole exception to the rule would be in a thick fog when we experience quite literally *a sight*; one, single, uniform, circumambient colour, pale grey, dark grey or dirty yellow. We do not speak in these terms because no speech is necessary, we and others all have the very same experience and it tells none of us anything about anything. We do however speak of *a smell*, *a taste* and even *a sound* and properly, because we have one experience which operates by association as a sign standing for something else quite different.

The best kind of example is *a smell*; our whole olfactory field is filled for a time by one quality, which may, according to our past experience of such a quality of smell, act as a warning sign of something wrong or something unpleasant, to come, or else something pleasant to come. In either case for some active response. For the most part a smell just comes to us passively, and if it is a bad smell obtrudes itself in a compulsory way. We can however deliberately seek out and to some extent select a smell. Another character of smells to be mentioned is that for the most part they are there one at a time, and if any displacing takes place it is usually involuntary, the worst displacing the better. You cannot arrange smells in a systematic order in time as you can sounds; much less in space.

Tastes are in many ways similar, but are more definitely sought out or selected by taking something into the mouth, to swallow it if it 'tastes' (is a sign of something) edible, or spit it out if not. Taste qualities are more specific, classifiable, and nameable than smell qualities, e.g. the names sweet, sour, salt, bitter. They vary less according to strength or concentration, and are also less mutually antagonistic, more compoundable, e.g. we can taste sour and sweet, salt and sweet together.

For smells we have no names except names of chemical species characteristically possessing or producing a distinguishable smell which remains distinguishable, sometimes even in the presence of rival or different odiferous substances. That is why, for the chemist, smells are very useful, delicate, even precise diagnostic signs, in spite of their limitations, perhaps because of them. One more peculiarity should be mentioned. Most smells are pleasant or at least not unpleasant when faint, or very faint though just distinguishable. Very few smells are pleasant when very strong. Good cooks know this, but do not divulge certain secret parts of their knowledge. At any rate smells are diagnostic signs for those who have the experience and skill to use them.

One last point needs a few words, the unclassifiable[1] nature of smells. What may be called 'ammoniacal' smells include the smell of the pure chemical substance out of the bottle, the smell of a flock of sheep on a hot day, the smell of smouldering carpet. If anybody who had never smelt the pure substance or anything like it were first introduced to ammonia by carefully waving the stopper of the bottle not too near his nose until he declared he smelt something, and then had the open bottle thrust right under his nose, he would almost certainly suppose that he had smelt two entirely different substances, the second pungent and painful experience would seem to have no resemblance to the first pleasant and slightly exhilarating one. Only after experiencing a series of graduated doses would the common 'ammoniacal' quality be realized; and probably only after that would it be recognized in hot sheep and smouldering carpet.

[1] Meaning that classifications are vague, arbitrary and difficult to use; there are no correlatives like hard/soft, only nice/nasty.

It will generally be said that burnt carpet smells of impure ammonia and is a mixed smell, but it is hardly possible to say what it is mixed with: similarly with sheep, though the mixture there may well be something different. The smell of burnt carpet is generally held to be unpleasant, but is that only because of its sign function, its associations, its warning that something is wrong and needs to be put right, or is the unpleasantness inherent in that specific sense-quality? To my nostalgic memory the identical smell of singed horse-hoof, smelt long ago in a village smithy, was a pleasant one, but again very possibly by association. For us humans the smell of sheep is mostly unpleasant but mildly so, the different smell of rats much more unpleasant; but for terriers that smell is nectar and ambrosia, and their response ecstatic. Is it all association?

These are interesting but unprofitable speculations; what seems more certain is that smells and tastes in their rather different ways each fill their whole field at any one time with *a* quality; pure or impure, classifiable or not, but usually a sign of or for something else.

This is about as much as need be said about smells and tastes, except for the last and important point that their associations are random, unsystematic, without reason or logic, solely according to habit, and entirely according to Hume. That is why they are mentioned first, and why there is something odd about their apparent aesthetic qualities. I say 'apparent' because 'aesthetic' may be the wrong word.

We could go on next to consider sounds as signs, because they seem to be similar, but it may be better to go straight to the opposite extreme where reason and logic do come in, and no sign is simple or a unit.

The field of haptic experience is that of *apperception* in Leibniz's sense, and never of bare *perception* (impressions) in Hume's sense. Every new portion of experience comes into and has to fit into a field already complex, patterned, articulated, referring back to the past and forward to the future as well as spatially extended; a field of relations that are not random, but systematic and metrical, where reason and logic belong.

Because our human bodies are all much the same size and have to balance themselves and move about in a uniform gravitational field they provide us with a ready-made set of metric standards and geometrical relations corresponding to one another and all falling into a system, which combines the advantages of the *a priori* with those of the empirical and has nothing apocryphal about it.

The story that some Saxon king defined the standard English foot (or yard) as the length of his foot (or arm) may be apocryphal, but makes very good sense.

Many years ago, in *Our Knowledge of the External World*, 1914, Lord Russell suggested that 'objects' or 'things' could be explained as logical constructions out of 'sense data', but ran into difficulties when he tried to work out the theory and never went further with it. The difficulties were the result of his assuming that the sense data had to be visual. Professor H. H. Price, who made far more ingenious and systematic efforts, also ran into difficulties because, though allowing for haptic experience, he took it (in his book *Perception*) as secondary and in some sense parallel or similar to visual experience instead of totally different. Professors of 'common sense' have all scoffed at the whole notion of 'construction' and of 'logic' having anything to do with sense data. But take Russell's suggestion first of all entirely in terms of haptic experience and then the suggestion is what 'common sense' has always said about 'objects' being constructed out of 'objects'. If the objects in question are models of the Five Regular Solids, how are they constructed? By the operations of human hands and other tools, according to the laws of Euclidean geometry, which are logical laws of the metrical relations of spatially extended bodies, including the human hands (if you like you can add human brains and anything else human you care to mention). It is perfectly true that a workman using sight as well as haptic experience will do the work with a speed and precision impossible for a blind man, and he can also make his own tools, but in principle, given his tools, a blind man could do it in course of time.

Now we must turn back to the field of sound, of auditory experience; and let me add at the beginning that there is a correlation between auditory and haptic experience, in some ways like that between visual and haptic, namely through the human voice and its two functions of speech and music, which we both make and hear. We can, however, be aware of *a sound* which fills the field (more or less) and may be single, associative and simple (more or less), and be an associative sign, referring to something that is not a sound. Such experiences are rare in modern urban life which fills the auditory field with artifacts, significant ones of speech and music, insignificant ones of noise, that have to be ignored or avoided; but we must first consider the basic type to which they belong; uncontaminated natural sounds, excluding even animal sounds or signals, namely those of wind and water. The first thing to notice is that they have aesthetic quality, purely aesthetic, not mixed with human wants, wishes or even fears. The sounds of running water have musical quality which human composers most often envy and which cover a wide range from the tiny bell-like tinkle of invisible streams buried deep in heather, to the roar of a cataract. By association, however, the sound of running water has become an invitation to drink, as the roar of the cataract is a warning to keep away. The sound of the wind in trees also has musical quality, but no definite human associations apart from violent wind, and then only the vaguest kind of warning. In connection with natural sounds it may be relevant to mention natural silence, when wind and water are silent and even birds and insects. Town dwellers find it terrifying. Why?

This again is idle speculation. The only reason for mentioning natural sounds is to contrast them with those human artifacts, which are not just noise. The relation of human music to natural sounds is easy to understand, but the difference is great; it has a complex articulated structure, which possesses a kind of logic of its own. This can be said without going all the way with Pythagoras and claiming logic to be just numerical. Lastly music is almost entirely useless. Speech also has a complex articulated structure, but quite possibly no logic of its own. To compensate for that defect, it is useful.

No more need be said here about sound. Temperature sense, wrongly included with touch, better taken as similar to smell and taste, need not be discussed at all. So we now come to sight, the stumbling block of the philosophers, the source of all fantasy (not the derivation and the more fancy spellings of the word).

The field of pure visual experience if we care to attend to it in its pure form, is that of lights, shades and colours.[1] They are

---

[1] Colours are not so simple as most people think they look. The U.S. National Bureau of Standards has published a colour dictionary giving 7,500 colour names with definitions from the fields of zoology, botany, geology, philately, horticulture and haute couture.

noticeable in human experience for their pure aesthetic quality and not for anything else. As associative signs their value is slight for human experience, though not apparently for insect or bird experience. But pure visual experience however cannot be had except by an effort of abstraction, an effort seldom made at all by those who are not artists, and not always effectively by them. So much for pure visual experience apart from the usual impure vision contaminated by haptic experience, intrinsically and extrinsically.

Hume's description of Impressions, Ideas and Relations between them is a truthful account of certain parts of experience, but as Locke could have told him, of parts below the human level of the rational, systematic and logical. Thus it needs to be supplemented by what we can learn from Leibniz and Kant. This is the subject of the next section.

§ 4 APPERCEPTION

The Leibnizian doctrine of Apperception has been found difficult. This has been firstly, because it would compel us to admit something very disagreeable about the most conspicuously conscious and voluntary aspect of life, namely taking careful note of our surroundings while reacting effectively towards them in a continuously varying fashion (as, e.g., in playing tennis or cricket); namely, that it depends upon and cannot escape from a background that is neither conscious nor voluntary. More shortly, our *grandes perceptions* depend upon *petites perceptions* of which we are not aware. If we grant this we might as well accept a few of the rationalists' *innate ideas* at the cheaper wholesale rate instead of taking them continuously and expensively retail. Secondly, a further consequence, when we link together a simple item of experience as a diagnostic or prognostic sign of other items, this is no new departure nor a beginning of a learning process, but rather an end part of a long process. Thirdly, it would compel us to accept, with Kant, that 'percepts without concepts are blind', an even more repugnant proposition than the other half of his dictum.

Leibniz and Kant both made themselves unpopular by making our minds appear more complicated and less familiar than we think they ought to be. Moreover they were misleading, since they stressed the easier temporal aspect of apperception, and kept quiet about its spatial aspect. Visual imagination can be precise, systematic, rational, when it is controlled; but cannot control itself and when left to itself smuggles in things that make it deceptive, irrational and *a priori* in the wrong way. The true function of visual experience is to forewarn us of the immediately impending future; the true function of visual imagination is to suggest alternative future possibilities near and distant. Neither of them should be left to itself to pretend to make decisions about truth and falsehood. Further, if visual perception operated by itself, as it never does in man, it would not be spatial in any precise or detailed way, but only vaguely, in the way that the pain of lumbago is more extensive than that of earache, while a headache is usually intermediate. Precision and control both begin with correlation of the fields of haptic and visual experience; as when we move our eyes, heads and bodies in the process of observ*ing*, and in many of our most important observations, as in doing skilled work, what is observ*ed* is the combined motions of our own and other bodies. Finally we have to call in a third sensory field for combined acoustic-optic-haptic experience.

After this preliminary, it will be asked: 'Can Berkeley's theory possibly include apperception?' Those who interpret Berkeley in the light of Hume will say it cannot be done; but they need to be reminded that Berkeley had never read a word of Hume at the time he was writing, probably not even later, and would certainly have objected to Hume's hard and fast distinction between *impressions* and *ideas*, and his oversimplified view of *relations*. For all that there are difficulties about reconciling him with Leibniz and Kant; they appear to be five.

i. *Minima visibilia* (or generally *sensibilia*) are very hard to fit into any kind of apperceiving; but Berkeley does not need them. They are prominent in the notes in *PC*, less so in *NTV*, barely appear in *Princ.*, and after that disappear.

The notion of *minima* is *a priori* rather than empirical, and better fitted for metaphysical argument against Leibniz's infinitesimals by use of an antinomy.

However, anyone who tries can observe the *minimum visible*, singular and not plural.[1] It is seen as it was before the primal act of Creation, 'without form and void'. It has no determinate colour,

[1] Cf. A. D. R. on 'Achilles and Tortoise' in *Mind*, 1942.

form or magnitude; it is merely not invisible. No actual visual field can be described as a complex or mosaic of such quasi-nonentities. If any other sense could display a *minimum*, it would be likely to be similar. A mere *minimum* is no genuine obstacle to anything and no use for anything.[1]

ii. The rejection of innate ideas, after Locke, is more serious. If we possessed Berkeley's comments on Leibniz's *petites perceptions* it would be easier to judge how serious, but we must do our best without them. Leibniz expressed himself numerically, with his eye on the problem of infinitesimals and with no thought of anything Berkeleian; but we should be cautious about his numerical terms. When a number (if the word cannot be avoided) of unconscious processes operate in conjunction ('sum up' is the wrong word) to reach up to a *threshold* and produce a conscious process, that process is something that was not there before; it is emergent; the merely potential has become actual. Could Berkeley have seen anything to object to here? Locke had been protesting against the metaphysical sleight of hand which tells us that we are 'really' in some esoteric fashion aware of things which are quite unknown to us, and Berkeley could well accept his protest. The dictum 'Esse est percipi vel precipere' (the whole is needed, not the first half only) does not exclude from existence everything that is not now actual; the whole *sensible* world is left for us as it has been and is.

iii. Berkeley's rejection of the *abstract ideas* of Locke should not be taken as rejection of universals in usual nominalist fashion. It is rejection of universals as generic images. Berkeley's own *notions* and *relations* are universals (cf. Ch. IV).

iv. The complete passivity of *ideas* of sense would be a serious difficulty if we had to assume that Berkeley was completely committed to it. A visualist probably is, but in *NTV* at least he is not a visualist. If there were no relations between *ideas* except only sign relations, then complete passivity would be possible. But in such a world could there be relations of incompatibility (logical contradiction or contrariety)? For it would contain no causal relations at all in the sense in which Berkeley acknowledges *causes*?[2]

---

[1] It is hard to believe in *minima* of smell, taste or sound—not even *pizzicato*.

[2] [For further light on Ritchie's view here, see p. 84 below, especially the sentence: 'Anybody who takes a lively and ill-trained dog for a walk knows perfectly whether he is pulling the dog or the dog is pulling him.' So far as Berkeley himself is concerned, § 113 of the *Principles of Human Knowledge*

Such *causes* are determining acts of will, decisions for either A or B, one and not both. In a visual world or a passive world everything is compatible with everything else. Did Berkeley need to assert the pure passivity of ideas except to defend the pure activity of spirits?

v. The basic difficulty is the Platonic (Plato of the *Phaedo*) doctrine of soul-substance. This appears most specifically in *Princ.*, and I suggest that at that stage Berkeley had not thought very seriously about it. It was for some reason very popular in the seventeenth century; both Descartes and Leibniz held it, and when Locke appeared to attack it bishops rushed to defend it as if it were part of Holy Writ. It is hard to reconcile it with the more Aristotelian metaphysics found in *Siris*.

The soul-substance theory is *a priori* metaphysics of the weakest kind, as Kant argued. Empirical study of the *notions* we have of our own mental activity, of our relations with other persons and of our relations with God do not lead inevitably to it; indeed lead away from it, in the direction of Locke and Kant.

Let us suppose that Berkeley could have abandoned it without loss, he could have accepted apperception with great gain. Finally, there is no *ad-* to the *perception* without haptic experience and no fully human experience which is not combined acoustic-optic-haptic, therefore conceptualized. Conceptualization can provide freedom from any particular perceptual situation without loss of control by rational constraint; the animal intelligence does not know freedom, nor control either.

This attempt to expand Berkeley's theory of sense perception is

---

would seem to accord very well with Ritchie's interpretation. When we walk along the street, says Berkeley, we see our body and the pavement stones changing their position relatively to one another, but we are not on that account entitled to say that the stones move. Why? Because experience makes us aware that our body's change of place is the result of our own efforts of will—it is 'that to which the action is applied'. As Ritchie makes clear, the activity involved in causality, consisting as it does in the act of will, cannot be a visual datum. He discusses Visualism further in the Appendix to his *Studies in the Methods and History of the Sciences*, pp. 209–19. It may be mentioned that the same sort of ideas about Visualism which Ritchie finds in Berkeley are also present in Maine de Biran and Whitehead. Compare Jean Laporte, 'L'*Idée de la Necessité*', P.U.F. 1941. 'Whitehead, like Biran, thinks that Hume has falsified and mutilated experience; he has reasoned like a man reduced to the sense of sight'.]

intended to set the stage for his theory of scientific conceptions.

Those who doubt the validity of Berkeley's theory of perception or its general philosophical importance should read first *TVV*, §§ 9–18, and 36 to end, then the nineteenth-century controversy in which J. S. Mill ably supported him against Samuel Bailey and T. K. Abbot.[1]

[1] [Samuel Bailey, *A Review of Berkeley's Theory of Vision*, 1842; J. S. Mill's critical notice of Bailey, reprinted in *Dissertations*, vol. II; T. K. Abbot, *Sight and Touch*, 1864.

Ritchie ought in addition to have referred to the Ferrier articles (mentioned above as having interested him) 'Berkeley and Idealism' and 'Mr Bailey's reply to an article in Blackwood's Magazine', *Lectures and Remains*, vol. II (sometimes vol. III), pp. 289–377, since originally they were written in 1842 in reference to Bailey's book.

These articles, like everything else Ferrier wrote in his youth (in fact all the articles: this volume) have been unfortunately overshadowed by the less brilliant if more systematic work of his maturity. See Arthur Thomson's centenary study of Ferrier in *Philosophy*, January 1964.]

IV

'THE SCANDAL OF IMMATERIALISM[1]'

THE special hullabaloo caused by the appearance of Berkeley's
Principles, not by any other of his books, is generally accounted
for as a protest of common sense against the extravagances of
philosophers, but common sense is more extravagant in its claims
than *bona fide* philosophers have dared to be, and with far less
justification. There is no harm in common sense nor even serious
ambiguity in it, as long as it is recognized for what it is: a rough
and ready way of dealing with rough and ready problems of
ordinary practical life by ordinary rough and ready persons. The
once famous firm of Boulton and Watt, Engineers, Soho, near
Birmingham, dealt with all their very difficult practical problems
solely by means of common sense, for they had nothing else to
help them; though Watt's original invention was not the result of
common sense, but of academic researches ignored or pooh-
poohed by common sense. The modern engineer still has to use
common sense to guide him when he has nothing else; but he
would be an incompetent engineer if he did not use the other aids
he now has, for instance the data in *The Engineer's Pocket Book*,
none of which is available to mere common sense. Any philosopher who professes to speak in the name of common sense is
bound to be talking through his hat. The extravagant claims of
common sense break down wherever more than ordinary precision, more technical details, and more thorough enquiry are
called for than the rough and ready can supply. Sooner or later,
generally sooner, its errors are uncovered for those who do not
deliberately shut their eyes. Common sense says 'all', when it
should say 'some', or 'most', or 'necessary' when it should say
'probable', in defiance of the science of statistics. It says 'always'

---

[1] [Written later than the rest of the book, this chapter was never revised,
and, as it stands in the original typescript, its lucid and fruitful insights are
sometimes overlaid with points which have not been sufficiently developed
to communicate. These latter passages have been excised in the editing, and
at the same time a couple of footnotes have been introduced with a view to
elucidating what is central in Ritchie's position.]

or even 'eternally' when it should say 'for a very long time', in defiance of the sciences of geology or other special chronological sciences. It says 'everywhere' when it should say 'in many places', in defiance of special topological sciences including geography and astronomy; and so on and so on. The process of grudging retreat against science began when the round earth of the astronomers displaced the old flat one, a process that has taken centuries and is possibly not yet complete. Another stage came when the moving earth displaced the stationary earth. Fortunately these stages were all protected by the sacred science of mathematics, of which the rough and ready stand in awe, as they do not of other less remote sciences. When mathematics speaks, common sense goes away grumbling, but hardly ever dares to interrupt. No special clash was felt at the supreme moment in history when common sense should have raised its voice in protest or else 'hereafter for ever held his peace'. That was when Newton's *Principia* were published, but he was both lucky in his time and clever in his method, for he put up the best barrier of the most severe mathematics he could devise, saying to the reader 'if you are not content with my rough sketch of general method and my partial proofs, work them out in detail for yourself'. Common sense did not even know what to grumble at. Berkeley was not so lucky, he was dealing with familiar generalities which common-sense people thought they understood at a glance, without even reading his book or any book, while in fact these were the parts of common-sense faith they least understood, the scraps of metaphysics that had got worked into it; catchy, rough and ready formulae, ambiguous enough to be used for a variety of purposes. Also, Berkeley had no mathematical screen and attacked in the name of theology, never a popular subject with the rough and ready.

The outburst of rage against Berkeley came first in the London coffee houses, with jokes and jeers and display of Cockney wit. The solemn Scots took it solemnly and quite a few even read his books, both *NTV* and *Princ.*, and even discussed them in a philosophical spirit. It is doubtful whether David Hume read the first; he certainly read the second, and strongly approved of its daring and original Introduction, which struck no coffee house sparks from Cockney wits. He approved of most of the rest, not all; he even took the trouble to expand and improve some of Berkeley's special arguments against traditional views of Substance and Cause. But in the eighteenth century nobody heard of, much less read, his *Treatise* except a few fellow Scots and one Welshman. If Hume escaped obloquy from outraged common sense, it was because he was a lazy man, and openly confessed that he was tired of perplexing speculations and content with mere habits of thought, as all of us would like to be in our slack moments and not all of us are prepared honestly to confess. (See Ch. VI, § 1 below, discussion on *Alc.*)

Thomas Reid made many valuable comments in detail on Berkeley and Hume, but made the error, no philosopher should make, of calling common sense to his aid. Thus he left little to his Scottish successors except confusions. Though they went on discussing, the world has forgotten them more completely than it has forgotten Berkeley, scandal or no scandal, or Hume, lazy or not.

The legacy of the great twentieth-century champion of common sense, G. E. Moore, for all his skill and pertinacity in argument, has been much the same, negative, timid and not free of confusion. Lord Russell, though slightly older, must be reckoned as Moore's disciple on most subjects. Though bolder and more constructive, Russell was inhibited by Moore in his constructive efforts, but not in his extravagances.

Popular caricatures of Berkeley pretend that he took the human mind to be a solitary ghost, a bodiless cyclops, peeping at a cinema screen showing 'ideas', with which a ghost could not interfere. It might do well enough as a hostile account of Hobbes's picture of the world. Descartes or Locke might have some difficulty in refuting it. As an account of the common-sense view it would be completely adequate, but for the fact that common sense contradicts it every now and then, without noticing any inconsistency. But it also corresponds to the old Pythagorean myth about the superiority of the spectators at the Olympic Games over the vulgar contestants.

What Berkeley needs to say, if I understand his position, is that human minds (plural always) are active; they cognize, perceive and *will*. They are not excluded from any rigid, predetermined projector and screen, for there is no such thing to be excluded from. The possessors of these minds (there is a difficulty here that a brief account must skip over) are partaking in the activities of others, either by collaborating or opposing. The sciences known to men

F

are the result of prolonged and careful collaboration, hindered continually, if seldom seriously, by those who cannot or will not collaborate, among them, worshippers of common sense. There is a natural order which has to be discovered, not just imagined, but it includes even worshippers of common sense, and is flexible, not rigid, and not an order of independent absolutes. For there is one sole absolute, continually creating order at various levels. Berkeley, in *Siris*, holds that Platonists and Aristotelians have said this, even if in a peculiar way. In our generation, Macmurray and Polanyi are saying it in a new and peculiarly interesting way.[1]

Let me mention first a recent warning to drivers of cars which has been published in the newspapers, not a matter of scientific technicalities but one about which everybody should use his or her 'common sense'. In my words, not quoted from any text, 'Drivers are warned not to wear glasses with thick opaque rims while driving their cars, as such glasses produce a blind area towards the periphery of the field of vision.' The fact can be tested by any one for himself by standing in an empty street with a row of parked

---

[1] [Note carefully how Ritchie, in the next two paragraphs, deals with what is for him the chief paradox of Berkeleianism—the 'subjective idealism'. Roughly speaking, the principle Ritchie follows is the introduction of a plurality of active human perceivers of the chair or table who are also conscious of being perceived by one another. He thus invokes again his central contrast (pp. 42–49 and 72) between the internal view, and the third party or external view, but in returning to the topic, he adds two new and important clarifications. (i) The internal view, although privileged, is nevertheless inherently defective in the sense of not revealing the medium, e.g. we do not see the spectacles through which we see, we do not feel the glove through which we feel. (ii) The external view of myself which reveals the existence of the spectacles or the glove is not dependent only on a third party in the sense that someone else may call my attention to the fact that the spectacles are on my nose, or that my hand is gloved, but I can also, up to a point, get an external view of myself and my perceptual process in solitude—by touch, I can reveal to myself the existence over my eyes of the invisible spectacles; by sight, I can reveal to myself that the fingers with which I feel are gloved. Though Ritchie did not work out the implications for the problem of facts like these, it was, I think, a very considerable service to have called attention to them: the sense that they seem to present a perspective which does justice at one and the same time both to the insights of the logical positivists with their stress on the privacy of experience, and to the rival attempts of observationalists like Professor Ryle to uphold the publicity of experience and to deny 'privileged' access. It was this attempt of Ritchie to do justice both to the inner and to the outer which enabled him to understand what Ferrier had been driving at.]

vehicles on one side, and on the other side of the street, with such glasses on, turning the eyes carefully backwards and forwards along the line and noting whenever a gap appears in the line from time to time. Then let him do it again without glasses, or with rimless glasses, noting whether or not similar gaps appear. Reference to REALITY or any other fictitious absolute is quite useless for a test of this kind or any genuine test. Berkeley knew nothing of modern traffic problems but in principle he could have predicted this problem and its solution, given the data of the present day. He did predict the results of Chesselden's experiment and the findings of I. Köhler (cf. above, p. 21). Nobody else in his day could make any such prediction, and the boasted objectivity of their beliefs was the hindrance.

I may perhaps be overstating, for sake of emphasis, the case for Berkeley. The case against common sense cannot be overstated. Before Berkeley, if any one had asked the question 'With what can I check my observations to find out if they are true, or correct?' philosophers, such as Descartes, Hobbes, etc. would have said with one voice, echoed by common sense—REALITY. Berkeley's answer would have been: First, find out how far your own observations are consistent among yourselves, using every possible sensory means and every possible kind of change of conditions. Second, and more important still, compare them with the observations of others, under all possible changes of conditions of all concerned. There is no REALITY with which to compare observations; there is only the systematic order of all actual observations, carefully and honestly made. That is also the answer of twentieth-century science, which common sense has hardly begun to hear of; and all the thanks that Berkeley got in his own day was to be called names, especially 'subjective idealist'.

All sense experience requires a medium or media. The observer by himself cannot *observe* a medium that he is *using*, while *using* it, but another person very often can *note* that there is a medium and find out something about it. The single observer by making a series of observations and by *calculation* from them can infer that a medium is probably having a *distorting* effect and make *corrections* for it. Media cannot be directly observed but can be corrected for, and that is the only way in which observation can be made reliable and precise. Thus, long ago, surveyors using optical instruments for angular measurements of distant objects began to construct maps, and noticed that discrepancies in horizontal positions of objects were very seldom found, either between those calculated from simultaneous observations by different observers of the same object from different places, or from those of one observer at different times and places. But that observations of altitude and specially of more distant objects did give discrepant results until recalculated to allow for differences of refraction in the intervening medium, the air.

Another paradox is mentioned by Lady Percival (cf. *Works*, vol. VIII, Letter No. 12, pp. 37–8). This letter is Berkeley's reply to her question; how if only spirits and ideas existed, he would explain the history of Creation as recorded in the Mosaic books of the Old Testament. Put in this form, Berkeley could make his answer easily and simply. To answer a corresponding question put by a Hobbist or Cartesian would need the whole of the arguments of *NTV* and *Princ*. Berkeley's reply was:

I do not deny the existence of any of these sensible things which Moses says were created by God. They existed from all eternity in the Divine intellect, and then became perceptible (i.e. were created), in the same manner and order as is described in Genesis. For I take creation to belong to things only as they respect finite spirits, there being nothing new to God. Hence it follows that the act of creation consists in God's willing that those things be perceptible to other spirits, which before were known only to Himself. Now both reason and Scripture assure us there are other spirits (as angels of different orders, etc.) besides man, who 'tis possible might have perceived this visible world according as it was successively exhibited to their view before man's creation. Besides, for to agree with the Mosaic account of the creation it is sufficient if we suppose that a man, in case he was then created and existing at the time of the chaos, might have perceived all things formed out of it in the very order set down in Scripture, which is no ways repugnant to our principles.

On all questions of history and pre-history Berkeley is in a very strong position. Even Hobbists, Cartesians and other kinds of metaphysicians have to deal with history and *a fortiori* pre-history in terms of hypotheticals. The one definitely weak point of Berkeleian immaterialism is that it leans too heavily on hypotheticals unsupported by actuals. Moreover, a question put in terms of Christian and Hebrew theism has already granted more than half Berkeley's case. (Cf. below, Ch. VI; and see also the discussion in *Princ.*, §§ 82–4.)

Berkeley objected on moral and religious grounds to the Great Machine Theory of the Universe, which represents the full development of the general and possibly quite vague doctrine of corporeal substance (or substances, it can be taken either or both ways). It was not his sole objection nor his complete theory. The Great Machine is easy on the imagination and calls for no intellectual effort; it is very ancient and varies its form conveniently according to which kind of machine is fashionable. It came to the fore in the seventeenth century with the versions of Gassendi, Descartes and Hobbes, held in check only by the powerfully religious atmosphere of the age. (I am not imputing insincerity to anybody.) But at the end of the century, religious fervour decayed along with religious strife and the apparently complete synthesis achieved by Newton's Natural Philosophy seemed to justify the quip of Aristophanes many centuries earlier, 'Zeus has been kicked out and Whirligig is King', though it was Descartes, not Newton, who put his faith in whirligigs. At any rate, Berkeley grew up in an age where whirligigs competed for supremacy with gravitation and inertia; and everything else was reckoned to be out-moded superstition. For the first time since the age of the Emperor Constantine it was intellectually respectable, and in some countries politically safe, to scoff at religion in general and Christian faith in particular (cf. *Advertisement* to Joseph Butler's *Analogy of Religion*, 1736). As the eighteenth century went on, things got worse rather than better, as Berkeley partly foresaw and later also more definitely realized.

Berkeley could see and declare that materialism in philosophy *tends* to make people materialist in their behaviour, *some* of them, never quite *all*; just as today Pavlovian or Watsonian psychological theory *tends* to make them inhuman in their behaviour. Berkeley did not just turn *some* or *many* or even *most* into *all*. He had respect for both fact and logic. He sought to support his moral attack from the side of metaphysics, which attempts to be universal; and there his critique of scientific method came to his aid. Immaterialism in general and scientific reductionism in specific instances are not the same theory, but may be allied.

Berkeley's general position is conveniently put in a neat phrase used by J. S. Mill, whose own position was near to Berkeley's (but *via* Hume, Reid, Hartley, James Mill and Hamilton, while his religion was Wordsworthian). Mill held that the natural world is an order of 'permanent possibilities of sensation'. If that is so, the obvious questions to ask are: i. What kind of entities are *possibilities* that have not been actualized in any person's sensations, and almost certainly never will be whatever pains are taken by enthusiasts to experience to the utmost all *possible* experiences under all *possible* conditions? and ii. What can *possibly* make them permanent?

It seems unreasonable to look to the merely possible, and not actual, to make anything permanent; and of all things known to us sensations themselves are the least permanent, not accidentally but by their very nature. Moreover, such vast numbers and unimaginable varieties of hypotheticals have to be conjured out of nothing that Ockham's Razor cuts the wrong way for their theory.

We need three kinds of metaphysical criteria to establish hypotheses: i. Logical Consistency, ii. Aesthetic Value, iii. Utility or Technical Efficiency. These are often rivals, not mutually supporting criteria. Ockham is relevant to ii and iii, and may give us an ambiguous answer. Thus, there are serious difficulties about Berkeleian theory, but it does not follow that they are enough to damn it altogether.

We must remember, on the other side, he claims that the concept of a universe consisting entirely of 'bodies in motion' is downright self-contradictory because in such a universe there are no concepts, nor theories, nor are there any percepts in terms of which bodies and their motions, their qualities and relations, can be perceived, measured and described. It would be in the completest and strictest sense 'without form and void'. Body by itself does not know body, nor speak to it, nor about it.

V

PHYSICS WITHOUT ABSOLUTES OR FALSE ABSTRACTIONS

§ 1 ABSTRACT IDEAS[1]

In the Introduction to his *Princ*. Berkeley attacks errors that arise from habitual misuse of visual imagination, and, incidentally, also attacks a form of ancient psychology, which provides a perfect example of such misuse. This psychology may be taken to be ancient folklore, but it found its first expression among the 'learned' of the West with the Epicureans; was continued by Hobbes who put it simply and ingeniously; chunks of it survived in Locke; it still crops up in many places notably in those 'moderns' whose thinking stops short with Hartley and James Mill. The psychology of Hobbes embodies (literally, as befits a materialist) the picture-name theory of language. According to him sensation consists of the arrival from outside the body into the brain of a train of physical disturbances; these set up further disturbances inside the brain, a kind of persistent echoes, which go on long after the external disturbances have ceased. Hobbes calls the echoes *phantasms* and takes them to be faint pictures, images or representations of the original sources outside brain and body, or, as we commonly say, the 'real objects'. Such *phantasms* receive adjectival labels, such as *green*, *soft*, *cool*, with which are connected substantive labels, such as *grass*. The process of thinking consists of some kind of shuffling about of *phantasms* of the first sort along with *phantasms* of the second sort, for the labels are presumably *phantasms* too, or images, auditory, visual or

---

[1] [The section on abstract ideas, though it gives the impression of fragmentariness, nevertheless manages to put over a central insight of, I think, great interest. Ritchie's distinctive position is that the remarks on abstraction in the Introduction to the *Principles* are to be read as a follow-up of Berkeley's critique of 'Visualism'. Berkeley's point then would be that 'diagrams and models' in so far as they 'are or provide "ideas" in abstraction from operational contexts' can be misleading (p. 75). Berkeley's attack on 'abstracters' is thus, so to speak, anti-atomist in its aim; his 'minute philosophers' are those who concentrate on details or aspects to the exclusion of the whole.]

whatnot. This fantastic story cannot be dismissed offhand as totally false, yet it will not do. Whatever else thinking may or may not be, it is that which decides, judges, acts, and it is *about* or *of* or *aimed at* something other than itself. Hobbes's *phantasms* should be bits of matter or motions of bits of matter and can have no *about* or *of* in them, nor be *aimed at* anything. One point only remains clear; that this kind of theorizing about the brain is idle reverie or day-dreaming: what might be supposed to be seen to happen inside somebody else's brain, if we could creep inside it and look round at everything going on there without destroying it all. This kind of day-dreaming is an example of the *abstract ideas*, which Berkeley objects to because it leads to pseudo-science of the worst and most popular kind in his day and in ours. Note here that advances in brain physiology between Hobbes's day and ours have made no significant difference, though fashions in terminology have changed.

Locke's theory is better than Hobbes's in one respect. Locke's *ideas* are not just bits of matter, neither small, thin, ghostly, *phantasmic*, nor yet large, thick, solid and *real*; they are mental, without self-contradiction they can be *of*, *about* or *aimed at* something: they can *represent*, *picture* or *image* something other than themselves. In short, Locke had the beginning of a possible theory, as well as a bad day-dream; all the same, not a good theory in Berkeley's view, and with it a bad theory of language (expounded mainly in *Essay*, Bk III), which retains far too much of day-dreaming, of common mental processes that are not relevant to rational discourse, assuming that such a process does actually occur.

For the most part, words are related to other words and images to other images, and each kind should be related according to its own kind of rules; but both have to be related also to that at which discourse is aimed, apart from words or images; and that aim should also be governed by its own rules. There is not one set of rules but three at the very least, assuming only one set for words, one for images and one for aiming. If discourse is to be rational, logical or scientific, it aims finally at action and experience, and not at words or images. This is as far as day-dreaming goes, and without any definite rules at all, only indiscriminate undirected change-over between words of any sort and images of any sort.

Like Hobbes, Locke had no conception of *concepts* and their relation to *percepts*. Concepts are not images, nor phantasms, but *rules for synthesis*, in Kant's terminology, governing a process where percepts, along with signs of all sorts (including images and words), should each play its own kind of part, not another's. When we are thinking, discoursing or working scientifically or systematically all relevant symbolic processes should be controlled, and if we are working within the realm of physical science, controlled operationally. In any particular case we can specify how that operational control should work, even if it is difficult to specify in general. We are concerned with certain metrical properties of certain things to the exclusion of other properties and other things. We can specify what measurements are to be carried out and how. Then we can see whether or not the results turn out as specified, within certain limits of error.[1]

The anxious reader may now ask: 'What has Berkeley to do with all this Kantian and post-Kantian stuff?' My reply is that Berkeley was not so Humean as is frequently supposed, and more Newtonian, and both of them looked forward not backward; nor into the blind alley in which Hume's admirers lurk. They looked in the direction of Kant and Bridgman. Unfortunately Berkeley used a limited vocabulary in which the already exhausted word 'idea' was worked overtime. He also tried to make things easy for ungrateful readers of *NTV* by quasi-materialist expressions, and in *Princ.* for equally ungrateful readers by quasi-visualist expressions. On the whole, for all its omissions, *DM* is nearer to Kant with his concepts and percepts, and Bridgman with his *operations*; and that is because the book is specifically directly concerned with Newtonian physics and not vaguely with things in general.

For the basic difficulty we must go back to Hobbes and Locke. Hobbes knew exactly what he was getting at and equally obviously was wrong; while Locke was a puzzled man and never quite knew where he was going. He began rashly in Book II by making *idea* stand for everything whatsoever; 'equality' is an idea, and needs the singular because all equals are equally equal. But 'men' and 'horses' are also *ideas* and cannot get on without their plurals for all collectively are not definitely anything, as Berkeley

---

[1] Cf. P. W. Bridgman, *The Logic of Modern Physics*, 1927. I doubt whether any later developments call for serious modification of his view. Also, for an earlier view, N. R. Campbell, *Physics: the Elements*, 1920.

points out. In Book III *ideas* seem also to be names for *ideas*. It is as though Locke were in the Garden of Eden naming the beasts. Like Adam he sees something walk past and says, 'This shall be called Lion.'[1] Then Locke noticed, as Adam did also, that things worked the other way too. If the word 'Lion' came into his mind by any means, or none, when no real lion (as we say) was present, he might start imagining lions of divers sorts doing divers things in divers places and divers ways, and that nothing special would come of it all, but his fancies might go on indefinitely, unless Eve called out that supper was ready, when they would all fade out as easily and promiscuously as they began. There are many odd things about words which intrigued Locke, though not Berkeley, who wanted no nonsense, but scientific precision, system, caution and decisiveness; as probably Eve did too.

Consider now Berkeley's complaint about the *abstract idea* of 'triangle'.

§ 13. To give the reader a yet clearer view of the nature of abstract ideas, and the uses they are thought necessary to, I shall add one more passage out of the *Essay on Human Understanding*, which is as follows.

'*Abstract ideas* are not so obvious or easy to children or the yet un-exercised mind as particular ones. If they seem so to grown men, it is only because by constant and familiar use they are made so. For when we nicely reflect upon them, we shall find that general ideas are fictions and contrivances of the mind, that carry difficulty with them, and do not so easily offer themselves, as we are apt to imagine. For example, does it not require some pains and skill to form the general idea of a triangle (which is yet none of the most abstract comprehensive and difficult) for it must be neither oblique nor rectangle, neither equilateral, equicrural, nor scalenon, but *all and none* of these at once. In effect, it is something imperfect that cannot exist, an idea wherein some parts of several different and *inconsistent* ideas are put together. It is true the mind in this imperfect state has need of such ideas, and makes all the haste to them it can, for the conveniency of communica-tion and enlargement of knowledge, to both which it is naturally very much inclined. But yet one has reason to suspect such ideas are marks of our imperfection. At least this is enough to shew that the most abstract and general ideas are not those that the mind is first and most easily acquainted with, nor such as its earliest knowledge is conversant about.' B.4. C.7. Sect. 9. If any man has the faculty of framing in his

---

[1] We should try to remember that the lion might have said to the lioness 'This shall be called Adam'.

mind such an idea of a triangle as is here described, it is in vain to pretend to dispute him out of it, nor would I go about it. All I desire is, that the reader would fully and certainly inform himself whether he has such an idea or no. And this, methinks, can be no hard task for any one to perform. What more easy than for any one to look a little into his own thoughts, and there try whether he has, or can attain to have, an idea that shall correspond with the description that is here given of the general idea of a triangle, which is, *neither oblique, nor rectangle, equilateral, equicrural, nor scalenon, but all and none of these at once?*

§ 14. Much is here said of the difficulty that abstract ideas carry with them, and the pains and skill requisite to the forming of them. And it is on all hands agreed that there is need of great toil and labour of the mind, to emancipate our thoughts from particular objects, and raise them to those sublime speculations that are conversant about abstract ideas. From all which the natural consequence should seem to be, that so difficult a thing as the forming abstract ideas was not necessary for *communication*, which is so easy and familiar to all sorts of men. But we are told, if they seem obvious and easy to grown men, *It is only because by constant and familiar use they are made so*. Now I would fain know at what time it is, men are employed in surmounting that difficulty, and furnishing themselves with those necessary helps for discourse. It cannot be when they are grown up, for then it seems they are not conscious of any such pains-taking; it remains therefore to be the business of their childhood. And surely, the great and multiplied labour of framing abstract notions, will be found a hard task for that tender age. Is it not a hard thing to imagine, that a couple of children cannot prate together, of their sugar-plumbs and rattles and the rest of their little trinkets, till they have first talked together numberless inconsistencies, and so framed in their minds *abstract general ideas*, and annexed them to every common name they make use of?[1]

As Locke says, we can visualize triangles of all shapes, colours and so on, each one turning into another without order or connection except bare triangularity. They can be of all possible compatible and incompatible characters and relations. All taken together constitute a genus by wiping out everything specific. Locke describes a process that is only too fatally easy. I cannot believe that Berkeley found it difficult, but he certainly found it useless and senseless (in any sense of 'sense'). It is not by daydreaming that geometry becomes a science and establishes its conclusions. If however Hobbes's materialism were a possible kind of

[1] Introduction to the *Principles*, §§ 13; 14.

theory at all, day-dreaming, i.e. association, would be the only kind of thinking, and if machines think, as many now suppose, then this is the way they do it, and a stupid way too. Moreover, it can sometimes, with safeguards, be a route to 'the enlargement of knowledge, (§ 13, quoted above), by suggesting possibilities. Berkeley was too much concerned with all the very necessary safeguards, and reluctant to admit this.

I have spoken as though day-dreaming were always visual; it need not be. I have not insisted that it may use words, visually, auditorily or otherwise; but I do insist that visual day-dreaming is typical, and any words that come in are not playing a proper linguistic part, for that is communication. Because there is usually no communication in day-dreaming there is usually no logic or reason in it. Day-dreaming proves no theorems about triangles, solves no problems and butters no parsnips, even if it may occasionally be a first step to doing something new.

The geometrician has some choice of methods, but within strictly prescribed limits, excluding day-dreaming, needing the handling of things, looking at them and even listening to them. The old Euclidean method will suffice for illustration. Euclid wishes to prove a theorem about triangles; he therefore draws one specimen triangle, a tangible-visible thing, selected by him at random from the various possible species of triangle. (It is *one* specimen only and not itself *any* triangle, much less *all* triangles.) Euclid however mentally abstracts this triangle from its peculiar physical environment, and attends only to what is relevant to his purpose of proof. The abstraction is helped by giving it a name, ABC, to distinguish it from DEF; but if Euclid is actually speaking to an audience this is not necessary; he can point to it instead. What he has to make clear is that he is using it or operating with it or on it symbolically, for a purpose; namely to show that some general proposition is true of this *triangle*. He then goes on to conclude that because it holds of *this* one, it holds of *all* and *any*. If Euclid's audience are sceptical he may have to go on to draw a number of different kinds of triangle to make them admit that the differences are irrelevant, provided only that all figures are triangular and thus the proof becomes universal. This last part of the proof is the difficult one; because of their abstract function symbols are treacherous.

Triangles raise no grave difficulties, since they are never referred to except for technical purposes, namely for practising an art or craft the purpose of which is scientific, not industrial, commercial or magical; day-dreaming is at a discount.[1]

Berkeley introduces a more awkward example, 'man'. It is awkward because there is either no art or craft of humanity, or there are half a gross of them, including industry, commerce, even magic. Idle reverie, day-dreams, even sleeping dreams cannot be excluded offhand, as irrelevant to man.

In one small matter Berkeley seems to me at fault, though, since he was young and a bachelor at the time he wrote, he may be excused. I suggest that 'a couple of children' can perfectly well 'prate together, of their sugar-plumbs and rattles and the rest of their little trinkets' to the accompaniment of *abstract ideas* if they feel like it. On the other hand, if they are intelligent children they may stop to reflect that any *abstract ideas* they indulge in will not serve to settle the question whether Tweedledum or Tweedledee possesses the better rattle. Fighting a battle might settle it, though better methods are available. I suspect that Berkeley was not entirely a visualizer,[2] while Locke was.

So far I have taken *abstract ideas* in their extreme and obviously irrational form. But a great deal of apparently respectable symbolic apparatus used in scientific discourse can be irrationally and irrelevantly used. Diagrams and models are or provide 'ideas' in abstraction from operational contexts and can be made misleading when wrongly abstracted. How many lunatics have pored over diagrams of perpetual motion machines or non-working models of them with no results beyond day-dreams.[3]

Let us return to Locke for a moment. Undoubtedly *ideas* are associated in the mind, but all theories which base learning or any higher form of cognition solely on *association* are useless. Locke realized this (*Essay*, Bk II, Ch. 23) and sufficiently refuted Hobbes and all later *Associationists* to the present day. Why then was Locke deceived by *abstract ideas*? They depend on *association* by resemblance, which is no more and no less rational in itself than

---

[1] More difficult geometrical figures such as the Chiliagon and Myriagon discussed by Descartes offer no obstacle, as explained in a letter to Molyneux (*Works*, vol. VIII, p. 26).

[2] In the psychologist's sense of visualizer: one who has rich and habitually used visual imagery, not one who adopts visualism as a philosophical theory

[3] Cf. Ch. II, § 5 above on inverted retinal image.

association by contiguity, the favourite form of association of the professed *Associationist*. Locke's theory of language may have been at fault. If he forgot that language is communication between persons then he may have taken words to be arbitrary labels attached to mental images (*association* by contiguity) and thus had to assume that the rational aspect came in through image *association* by resemblance building up a generic idea or fused portrait, the *abstract idea*. In non-linguistic realms, music for example, pedants once laid down rules for musical composition. Music composed strictly according to such rules is harmless but dull. Compositions which violate the rules wholesale avoid dullness but are harmful to the ears. Classical composers used the rules when they were useful, and broke them when they were not; occasionally and judiciously. There are rules for the use of language and pedants would like to enforce such rules as they can think of. If they had their way, then it cannot be doubted they would impugn the use of puns under all circumstances. Yet even these vulgar jokes have their place in communication, if used with tact and discretion, as a good musical composer can use dissonances. The pedants also are suspicious of metaphors, not entirely without reason, as anybody who listens to the talk of pedants themselves will discover. Yet language entirely devoid of metaphor is practically impossible, and even mixed metaphors may play a humble part without causing grave inconvenience. Convenience is the test, and the unscrupulous breaker of rules may succeed better in communication than the timid conformist.

Within the limits of technical scientific discourse, where the intention of all interlocutors should be directed solely to attaining truth and avoiding error, and no tricks or ornaments are needed, attempts to be funny are tiresome, and attempts to deceive should be taboo, it might be supposed that rules could be easily and clearly laid down and that any breach of them would always lead to disaster. Yet even here general rules are not easy to formulate, rules are not always kept, disaster does not always follow the breaking of them.

Mathematicians are generally scrupulous enough in their use of mathematical notation (but cf. Berkeley's *Analyst*) though often loose and metaphorical in the names they give to such operations. The reason (or excuse) given for the difference is that rules are specific for each type of operation and of context and not freely interchangeable and that metaphorical nomenclature does not reflect back on the operations named.

Initially there is an arbitrary element in all rules for technical procedure. Some one person has to start by a *fiat* of his own will. (This is still true even if the *fiat* is issued in the name of a Committee.) Thus all physical units have been chosen arbitrarily; for instance it has been laid down that the unit of length shall be the length of *this* bar of metal or else the wave length of *that* band of light in the spectrum of *that element*. To the first *fiat* is added another, that the name of the unit shall be 'Abracadabra' and no man shall use it except as prescribed.

Now, it so happened that in the year 1855 Rankine introduced to physical science a new unit, which he called *Stress* and he defined it, as he was entitled to do. He did not behave quite as the pedants would have him do for the name was a metaphor. In earlier English usage and still in ordinary usage the word 'stress', like 'distress', means a psychological state, a feeling: it is only by a metaphor that it can be transferred to stretched wires which have no feelings that we can discover. Still, this is a small matter, for the name itself is short and easy and its definition, one would suppose, offered no difficulties. That was not so. In the following year Thomson (Lord Kelvin) used the term 'stress' in a different sense. He said quite calmly (*Phil. Trans.*, vol. 166, p. 485), 'It will be seen that I have deviated slightly from Mr Rankine's definition of the word "stress", as I have applied it *to the direct action experienced by a body from the matter around it*, and not, as proposed by him, *to the elastic reaction of the body equal and opposite to that action.*' The italics are mine, and intended to emphasize that when it came to metaphors the great Lord Kelvin was quite without shame, as also in the matter of changing the meaning of the term. But strictly he ought to have used another name, and we should all have measured our stresses either in *Rankines* or in *Kelvins*. In practice the engineers who have most dealings with stresses would seldom notice the difference. Kelvin's *stress* can be directly determined without difficulty. Rankine's definition sounds simpler but to determine it precisely you would need to know whether the body concerned was perfectly elastic (within significant limits of error) or not. The conclusion appears to be that even in technical matters linguistic rules are not sacred, but are for convenience, or, perhaps I should say, operational.

There is a more recent example, for which I have not looked up names and dates (another breach of the rules and possibly a more serious one). In the 1920's some international committee decreed that henceforth laboratory vessels for measuring fluid volumes should be graduated in *millilitres* and not, as previously, in *cubic centimetres*. (The reader can look up the difference for himself.) Laboratory workers were not so stupid or extravagant as to smash all the existing apparatus and wait till the new stuff came along. Most of them had no need to worry about errors less than $\frac{1}{2}$ per cent and used the old vessels graduated in *cc*, but wrote down obediently *ml*. The few who did need to worry, and whose apparatus was sufficiently accurately calibrated, made the necessary numerical correction at the cost of a little arithmetic, and again wrote down obediently, but more conscientiously, *ml*. This went on until the new apparatus appeared. Nobody seems to have been a penny (or cent or even centime) the worse.

When we leave the realms of strictly technical terminology of mathematics and of the experimental and observational sciences, which use mathematical methods of measurement and calculation, we find there are few explicit rules at all and that if there are, rules vary according to who it is who lays them down, about what, for whom, for what purpose, under what circumstances. Most frequently nobody has ever deliberately laid down any rule. Rather, all those concerned in any manner find themselves in an environment or context, linguistic and non-linguistic, not always stable, but more given to us than made by us. In that context there are some well-established linguistic usages, established perhaps by a process of natural selection, perhaps by artificial selection. With these nobody has much difficulty and nobody has any quarrel. But there are also ill-adapted usages which interfere with communication instead of furthering it. For example, take the writing of most journalists, many highbrow novelists, quite a few lowbrow ones, and all writers of advertisements. At any rate linguistic usages now are many and conflicting. There is more noise and less understanding. The basic empirical fact about signs of all sorts, linguistic or not, is that at the beginning any one thing may be a sign for any other one thing, under certain conditions, for certain persons, for certain purposes. Perhaps it is in accordance with this that we possess nervous systems in which every cell is connected directly or indirectly, by more than one route with every other which lies in a forward direction. These are the basic empirical facts, and there is one universal rule, namely that we must always be careful or signs will mislead us. Berkeley's attack on *abstract ideas* points out one way in which we can easily and quickly be misled, while scientifically controlled procedure is one way to avoid being misled, though it is not a quick or easy way.

Berkeley had already, without seeing how much he was doing demonstrated in *NTV* an elementary working model of experimental scientific method, a basic form before the invention of tools or apparatus other than the human limbs. With that and the warning against abstract ideas, the stage is set for his philosophy of science and that is the preliminary to his argument for faith in God.

§ 2 DE MOTU

Had the arguments of *De Motu* been published as Pt II of *Princ.*, shortly after *NTV* and Pt I, some few readers might possibly have understood them, who had been prepared by these two first books. (Cf. *Princ.*, § 97, 102–5, 110–16.) But the continental readers, who awarded the prize in 1720 to someone else, were quite certainly not so equipped. The most that they could well have extracted from the text was that the author went far further than Newton in condemning anything looking the least like an *occult cause*; that he refused to take seriously the original title, 'The Cause of Motion'; that he claimed the sole concern of physics or natural philosophy to be with perceptible bodies and their motions (plural, not singular); that he rejected offhand any general scheme or cosmology of physical or natural causation, as well as all traditional theories about space and time. They were not likely to be favourably impressed by such a reductionist programme. They would have asked: 'What scientific advantage is to be gained by accepting Berkeley? What scientific error can follow from adhering to a more orthodox programme?'

At that time scientific advantages could hardly be foreseen, and the contrasting scientific errors had to wait till after Ernst Mach published his *Die Mechanik in ihrer Entwicklung* in 1883, leading Einstein in due course to the *Special Theory of Relativity* (1905). Since then there has been less excuse for ignoring Berkeley. Mach, however, seems to have been a complete visualist and probably missed the main point of *NTV*, by taking observables to be pictures of mechanical relations instead of mechanical relations mechanically perceived or predicted through visual signs.

Too many philosophers who call themselves empiricists are a-priorists gone wrong. Berkeley was a genuine empiricist, inter-ested in experience of every sort, and not interested in meta-physical speculation for its own sake nor in anti-speculative criticism for its own sake—he did not value words as such, but persons, the things persons could use, and words only so far as useful. His philosophy is not to be seen as a whole till his method has been seen at work on special subjects and in the right order, first on the more elementary kinds of perceptual learning, then at the basic stages of the special sciences, and lastly, generalized. The general argument in *Princ.*, as again in *Siris*, is directed explicitly and mainly against the Great Machine Theory of the Universe. That theory is attractive just because it is vague, woolly, merely general; nobody has the least idea how to apply it to any particular case, which could be examined empirically, in detail. Thus it is assumed as true, in the absence of evidence. For all that, those who believe in it claim that its truth is guaranteed by science. It is the lowest kind of metaphysics.

Berkeley points out that in no particular scientific argument about any special natural operations do we need to suppose that there is occult machinery at work; we start from past observation of sensible operations of sensible bodies, past, present, or future. Occult substances and occult causes merely serve to distract the attention of the investigator from the work in hand, and encour-age bogus solutions to bogus problems. If this is true in each special case it is also true in general.

The world had already seen a notable scientific failure of occult substances and occult causes in Descartes's vortex theory of the Solar System, which Newton had refuted on empirical grounds, namely that observable vortices do not produce motions of bodies like the observed motions of the planets. On the other hand, Newton's theory, by sticking to the prescription, Sensible Motions of Sensible Bodies, could do all the work that Descartes's failed to do, and more too. When the time came for revision, after two centuries, Newton's theory was not revised by going back to Descartes but further forward beyond Newton.

De Motu is brief, incomplete and largely taken up with special instances of pre-Newtonian physicists wasting their energies on vain speculations about those *abstract ideas* Berkeley attacked in general terms in *Princ*. These speculations are now entirely forgotten and hardly as comprehensible as mediaeval speculations. It is best now to ignore them and stick to Newtonian methods, taking care only that we adhere to them and not to popular misunderstandings of Newton, however distinguished the misunderstanders. To be extended in space is not the essential or determining property of bodies, as Descartes supposed, but a variable property or relation varying with density and form. The Mass and Inertia of a body are not other properties, they are the body itself, that which makes it bodily not just geometrical, and therefore, in any given body, are invariable.

Gravitational mass is a force which we can directly observe. 'While we support heavy bodies we feel in ourselves effort, fatigue and discomfort. We perceive also (not by sight only) in heavy bodies falling, an accelerated motion towards the centre of the earth; and that is all the senses tell us' (§ 4). It is also all that physics requires. *Gravity, mass, force*, should be used concretely 'to connote the body in motion, the effort of resisting' and also the actual processes of measurement used by the physicist. 'But when they are used by philosophers to signify certain natures carved out and abstracted from all these things, natures which are not objects of sense, nor can be grasped by any force of intellect, nor pictured by the imagination, then indeed they breed errors and confusion' (§ 6).

Thus *mass* as a force is measured directly, as it can be felt, by supporting the body in question on (or suspending it from) a vertical spring balance. *Inertia* can be felt by the muscular effort needed to catch hold of a moving body and similarly can be measured directly (but inversely) by the speed of horizontal displacement of a body to which a given horizontal force is applied (as with a torsion balance) when suspended from a vertical wire and set swinging. Let us leave out here the use of the ordinary horizontal beam balance and the pendulum where both gravitational forces are involved. But they would do as illustrations for anybody who cared to consider both gravity and inertia together.

Berkeley says of attempts to assign causes or origins for motions:

§ 20. . . . . All these indeed either say nothing particular and determinate, or if there is anything in what they say, it will be as difficult to explain as that very thing it was brought forward to explain.

§ 21. To throw light on nature it is idle to adduce things which are neither evident to the senses, nor intelligible to reason. Let us see then what sense and experience tell us, and reason that rests upon them. There are two supreme classes of things, body and soul. By the help of sense we know the extended thing, solid, mobile, figured, and endowed with other qualities which meet the senses, but the sentient, percipient, thinking thing we know by a certain internal consciousness. Further we see that those things are plainly different from one another, and quite heterogeneous. I speak of things known; for of the unknown it is profitless to speak.

Berkeley then goes on to state, in terms as nearly Cartesian (not Newtonian) as possible, his major distinction between sensible bodies with their sensible motions, which are the sole subject matter of natural philosophy; and Minds, Souls or Spirits, who are the sole subject matter of First Philosophy, and are the sole active agents or efficient causes in the Universe. Bodies and their motions are only secondary causes. It is perhaps unfortunate that Berkeley here makes the distinction between bodies and minds as sharp as Descartes does, but not so simple, while his intentions are different. He emphasizes the famous saying of Anaxagoras, so strongly approved by Plato and Aristotle, namely, that *nous* is that which sets everything in order (not just that which thinks), the supreme cosmological principle. Berkeley also emphasizes that the two categories of bodies and minds are both of the known (even if imperfectly) and not of the occult or unknown. Occult bodies, motions or causes are not needed for natural philosophy. First Philosophy is not about a Higher Occult, but is Psychology (if you like) provided only that it is Theistic Psychology; inclusive not exclusive.

Certain questions are excluded from natural philosophy or any other special science, which does not enquire into *natures, essences, virtues*, nor yet *principles* or *original causes* of *motions*, nor any *absolutes*, not *absolute space* or *time*, nor *empty space* or *time*, but only into *sensible motions* and other *sensible properties* of *sensible things* (bodies or objects). Thus:

No motion can be recognized or measured, unless through sensible things. Since then absolute space in no way affects the senses, it must necessarily be quite useless for the distinguishing of motions. Besides, determination or direction is essential to motion; but that consists in relation. Therefore it is impossible that absolute motion should be conceived (*DM*, § 63).

From the foregoing it is clear that the following rules will be of great service in determining the true nature of motion: (1) to distinguish mathematical hypotheses from the natures of things; (2) to beware of abstractions; (3) to consider motion as something sensible, or at least imaginable; and to be content with relative measures (*DM*, § 66).

Berkeley does not add that 'relative measures' are of necessity approximations and that absolute exactness or precision is excluded along with other absolutes, but it is hard to believe that he did not think it, since for him all measurement is of sign relations between items of our experience, which hold for the most part, not universally nor precisely. He does go on to say:

§ 66. . . . If we do so, all the famous theorems of the mechanical philosophy by which the secrets of nature are unlocked, and by which the system of the world is reduced to human calculation, will remain untouched; and the study of motion will be freed from a thousand minutiae, subtleties, and abstract ideas. And let these words suffice about the nature of motion.

§ 67. It remains to discuss the cause of the communication of motions. Most people think that the force impressed on the movable body is the cause of motion in it. However that they do not assign a known cause of motion, and one distinct from the body and the motion is clear from the preceding argument. It is clear, moreover, that force is not a thing certain and determinate, from the fact that great men advance very different opinions, even contrary opinions, about it, and yet in their results attain the truth. For Newton says that impressed force consists in action alone, and is the action exerted on the body to change its state, and does not remain after the action. Torricelli contends that a certain heap or aggregate of forces impressed by percussion is received into the mobile body, and there remains and constitutes impetus. Borelli and others say much the same. But although Newton and Torricelli seem to be disagreeing with one another, they each advance consistent views, and the thing is sufficiently well explained by both. For all forces attributed to bodies are mathematical hypotheses just as are attractive forces in planets and sun. But mathematical entities have no stable essence in the nature of things; and they depend on the notion of the definer. Whence the same thing can be explained in different ways.

§ 71. In physics sense and experience which reach only to apparent effects hold sway; in mechanics the abstract notions of mathematicians are admitted. In first philosophy or metaphysics we are concerned with incorporeal things, with causes, truth, and the existence of things. The physicist studies the series or successions of sensible things, noting by what laws they are connected, and in what order, what precedes as cause, and what follows as effect. And on this method we say that the body in motion is the cause of motion in the other, and impresses motion on it, draws it also or impels it. In this sense second corporeal causes ought to be understood, no account being taken of the actual seat of the forces or of the active powers or of the real cause in which they are. Further, besides body, figure, and motion, even the primary axioms of mechanical science can be called causes or mechanical principles, being regarded as the causes of the consequences.

§ 72. Only by meditation and reasoning can truly active causes be rescued from the surrounding darkness and be to some extent known. To deal with them is the business of first philosophy or metaphysics. Allot to each science its own province; assign its bounds; accurately distinguish the principles and objects belonging to each. Thus it will be possible to treat them with greater ease and clarity.

There is no great difficulty about the passages so far quoted; and Berkeley is in general careful to say 'sensible' where many would say 'visible'. But a reader on the look-out for visualist errors may have his suspicions roused and when he reaches §§ 69 and 70 they will be more than suspicions. It will suffice to quote two sentences from § 70 where Berkeley first refers to Newton's Third Law of Motion. (Cf. Kant's 3rd Analogy.)

. . . For if the true nature of things, rather than abstract mathematics, be regarded, it will seem more correct to say that in attraction or percussion, the passion of bodies, rather than their action, is equal on both sides. For example, a stone tied by a rope to a horse is dragged towards the horse just as much as the horse towards the stone; for the body in motion impinging on a quiescent body suffers the same change as the resting body. . . .

This is visualism. Berkeley is merely looking at his horse and stone, as Hume merely looked at his billiard balls (*Enquiry concerning Human Understanding*, VIII, Pt I). Anybody who takes a lively and ill-trained dog for a walk on a lead knows perfectly whether he is pulling the dog or the dog pulling him, as might the dog if he cared to reflect on what was happening. The vector relations of haptic experience, or interactions of our bodies with other bodies are discovered directly, empirically; no mathematical hypotheses nor conventions are needed to discover which is active, which passive; the purely visual temporal priority of cause to effect is reinforced by non-visual experience; and Newton's 3rd Law looks after it all. Even prior to Newton, could the terms 'active' and 'passive' be used meaningfully except as contrasted correlatives, as e.g. 'matter' and 'form'?

A fanatical visualist might well take pre-Newtonian astronomy as his model of scientific knowledge. Here there are only initial optical measurements of angular positions and motions, then from these are developed geometrical constructions or theories, with the help of arbitrarily introduced, but formal, mathematical hypotheses. Within this world there are no causes, no effects, nothing active, nothing passive, no distinction of opposition enters except that of *plus* and *minus*, which is conventional, and could be taken either way as we choose to decide. The accepted convention is that the terms on the left side of an equation are reckoned positive and those on the right negative; but any Dictator who wanted to proclaim his superiority could command his subjects to take it the other way round. In pre-Newtonian astronomy theory is pure kinematics; 'heavenly bodies' display their heavenliness by being visible but, in principle, intangible. The same fanatical visualist could try to interpret the whole of physics in the same way; but for most of us it is too difficult. Berkeley did not appear to be visualist in *DM*, §§ 3 and 4, where he recognized that with the help of our own bodies we can feel and roughly measure forces affecting them; Berkeley cannot have been satisfied with his position as stated in *DM*.[1] Later he made an important advance in *Siris*, which remains to be discussed in Ch. VIII. Meantime, certain minor points should be mentioned in passing.

i. It would be more reasonable to claim primacy for the audible world than the visible, because audibility is the first requirement for human communication, and the audible is closer to the tangible, since intelligible sounds are made as well as heard, and the processes of making and hearing are reciprocal and public. It is more nearly accurate to say that many people can make the *same* sound and also hear the *same* sound, than that they can see

[1] Post-Newtonian astronomy is not compatible with astrology for in it all bodies are the same kind of body. Pre-Newtonian astronomy had no such defence against astrology.

the *same* sight; and they cannot *make* sights at all in the sense that they can *make* sounds by the process of *making* movements.

We can for special reasons passively receive lights, colours and smells; so far Berkeley is right but no further. A deaf man can make sounds, which he cannot hear, and for him they are pure haptic experience. His *ideas* of them are of activity more than passivity. Others can hear them (passively) and interpret them correctly (passively or actively?). Consider the case of Beethoven composing some of his best music which he could not hear himself and other people did not in fact hear till after his death.

You may say that I have dragged in a red herring about intelligibility, but I claim that it is strictly relevant. Compare the case of Chesselden's patient who had to *learn to see*. Though relevant to the whole question, it need not be taken further here.

ii. If Berkeley can be defended on the subject of passivity, it has to be on the basis of his distinction between primary causation, the decision to act or the fiat of the will, and secondary causation, the bodily process of grasping something or standing up and walking. (Remember Hobbes's question to Descartes: Why 'I think therefore I am'? Why not: 'I walk therefore I am'?)

iii. The phrase 'sensible bodies' or 'sensible motions' also needs amplifying by a statement about the conditions of sensibility, in order to exclude abnormal experience, hallucinations and nightmares, from the world of physical science. A full specification of what constitutes normal conditions would be a long complicated affair. For experimental science, however, there is no difficulty, because an experiment is by definition that which can be repeated at will on several occasions and by several observers. Very serious difficulties arise for historians and lawyers, who have to consider the kind of evidence that belongs to a unique occasion and a unique observer.[1]

iv. Scientific procedure starts from what has been observed in the past and recorded, and it concludes with further observations which can now be made. They may belong to the present, to what is being done here and now. Or they may belong to the future, and then caution is needed. We can usually predict what can or what cannot be observed by use of existing techniques, but future techniques are nearly unpredictable. If there are definite assignable

[1] No two *independent* witnesses can tell *exactly* the same story, unless it has been learnt off by heart.

limits to what men can do they are limitations of the human organism, rather than of the tools that organism can use. This question is important because enthusiastic theorists aided by abstract ideas speculate about future observations almost as though they had been made already and could be used as evidence. (Cf. space travel and thinking machines.)

v. Berkeley assumes that particular observations made individually by individual observers can establish a public permanent system of general relations among things. This introduces the classical problem of Inductive Generalization, which he did not discuss and which (unfortunately) Hume did discuss later. Though in one way Hume did it well by putting the problem in its most acute form, he also made it insoluble. He discussed it in terms of causation, quite properly, but as a visualist to whom causation is invisible. The visualist looks on passively at the game and does not participate in it; but causation is participation. Vision alone cannot discern Euclidean geometrical relations, much less dynamic relations, so that the whole of physical science is beyond the range of the visualist. Berkeley is not to be accused of Hume's errors, though he has his own difficulties to be discussed later.

vi. The world of Berkeley has been accused of being a world of loose transferable adjectives, with no substantive nouns except names of unitary self-subsistent souls. Leibniz has to meet the same accusation, and so in a way has Newtonian physics which thrust aside the qualitative aspect of nature as entirely lawless. The alchemists assumed that all qualities were loose and transferable. The statistical study of characters belonging to populations (e.g. human populations) can proceed on such a basis. Thus Berkeley is not alone in this predicament, so far as it is a predicament.[1]

§ 3 GENERAL CRITICISM OF BERKELEY

We must now consider the main criticisms that can be made of Berkeley and his defence against them. I shall deal first with the problems of Space and Time, because they are central, and if Berkeley were as near to Hume as he is generally supposed to be, he could have no theory of space worth looking at, as Hume had none, and as Lord Russell found when he began to work one out

[1] See also Ch. VIII on *Siris* as well as the following.

on Humean lines in *Our Knowledge of the External World* (1914). Next and closely related is the Problem of Induction, already mentioned, which might appear to be as acute for Berkeley as for Hume. Then comes Berkeley's own discussion of criticisms made by his contemporaries.

SPACE AND TIME

If Berkeley evaded these problems rather than solved them, he is in no worse position than most philosophers, who are likely to go on evading them till the end of time (and space). Berkeley argued against Newton, that all observed motions are relative, as is all observed rest. He even challenged the validity of the experiment with the spinning bucket.[1] We need not at the moment go into this very difficult question. It may suffice to say he would not have quarrelled with Leibniz's theory of Space. He also said that there are no absolutes at all within the realm of physics.[2] He would also have been pleased with the modern view that space cannot be absolutely empty any more than it can be absolutely full. Nevertheless for a science of physics to be possible there must be one Space, universal, embracing equally all physical things, bodies, processes or events, so that all bodies are spatially related to all other bodies, and at measurable distances, however small and however large. Berkeley did not explain in so many words how this could be according to his theory; and for a visualist like Hume or Lord Russell no explanation is possible. The consistent visualist has to finish up as a solipsist with an entirely private egocentric space, which cannot be Euclidean or anywhere near Euclidean, in fact cannot be metrical at all. Not only was Berkeley not entirely visualist but the fundamental premiss of his philosophy was 'In God we live and move and have our being.' His second premiss is naturally that 'we' who 'live and move' are human persons. The two are linked by the doctrine of the Incarnation. There is no solitary bodiless cyclops. Our *ideas* come from a common source, are spatially extended, some are shared, though some are private, and among those *ideas* is a specially

[1] Cf. Newton's *Principia*, Def. VIII, Scholium; Berkeley's *Princ.*, § 114, and *DM*, § 62.
[2] Cf. Karl Heim, *The Transformation of the Scientific World View*.

important group, partly shared, of our bodily posture and move-ments. These are prior to our knowledge of lifeless bodies[1] and of their relations to our own bodies. Visual experience, because it comes second not first, then ceases to be private and egocentric.

The bodiless cyclops is a fabulous monster, not even a myth; there is nothing to be learned from him. Something can be learned from the rock barnacle, who is real, and depends upon haptic experience to make a livelihood by catching small fry with his numerous limbs which are well adapted for this function. We can assume that his space is ego-centric, or somato-centric, perhaps gastro-centric, because he is fixed motionless to his rock and has no other senses of importance except those needed for his special kind of haptic experience, or fishing. Men are different. Even the totally blind can move about successfully and they move in a gravitational field, which is an aid to movement, not a hindrance. It is the gravitational field which gives men their orientation, so human space is neither ego-, somato-, nor gastro-, but geo-centric. This is true primitively and quite apart from astronomical theory. Those who also have sight to help them are no different, except that their world is expanded. No fundamental obstacle for Berkeley arises here. But we must go one step further.

§4 THE PROBLEM OF INDUCTIVE GENERALIZATION

Spatial and temporal relations tend to display a certain kind of continuity, or, better, continuance or continuing. They provide both the togetherness (contiguity) and the separateness (distance) of everything. We can distinguish from among looser and more casual aspects of the world definite *continuous historic routes of occasions* (A. N. Whitehead's phrase); each of these is distinct from others and each has a collective character, as a *route*. Some of these routes are produced by our own activity, some are just presented to us, but the most conspicuous are joint products. Every scientific experiment is such a joint product. Some historic routes turn out to be so uniform and so enduring, within the time scale of

---

[1] There may be no lifeless bodies as the philosophy in *Siris* would seem to imply. However that is a speculation that can perhaps be dispensed with. There seems to be no inherent contradiction about an angelic will and in-telligence linked through a spiritual body, but this again is a speculation that can perhaps be dispensed with.

ordinary human interest, that optimistic observers turn them into the old corporeal substances, by a bit of exaggeration here and there and a touch of mythology.[1] The later physicists are more sceptical than the older common-sense enthusiasts, but are not without their own mythology of 'Constants of Nature' and 'Conservation Principles'; though if challenged they would confess that nobody can discover by measurement quite how constant or quite how conservative. Berkeley is on very strong ground here.

Apart from spatial relations and, specially, certain kinds of metrical relations there is little in the world that is not loose, transferable and adjectival. The sense qualities, *green, cool, soft* in themselves carry no suggestion for or against there being any link between them. But given the substantive name *grass* there appears to be such a link and substantive names suggest continuity and stability. Most civilized twentieth-century persons when they hear the name 'grass' think of grass lawns and take them to be more or less stable features of the environment regardless of the fact that such stability as they have is the product of continual human toil and sweat. The life of a lawn left to itself is nasty and short, even if not solitary, poor or brutish (unless under very exceptional 'natural' conditions, as in estuaries where the tides do the work of cultivation).

Nevertheless the very beginning of any empirical investigation is very much as Hume says; it starts from adjectives or qualities, as loose as you like; and it is hard to see how mere accumulation of instances can make them any tighter. Hume is mainly right but exaggerates and mythologizes a bit. He did it usefully in his day against former opposed exaggeration and mythology by the old upholders of causes and substances, or worse still of Substance in the singular and Causality in the abstract. Berkeley does not mythologize, has a firmer grasp of the role of spatial relations in experience and of the rudiments of physical science.

It is fatal to deal with inductive arguments entirely in abstract terms, as if they were formal arguments. For empirical investigation is itself a physical process; it requires the actual handling of bodies, and depends for its value, if it has any, upon what bodies they are and how handled. Let us consider an example which,

---

[1] For instance, 'The Eternal Hills', when every geologist knows they are either being heaved up or worn down; for the changes are more perpetual than the hills.

though fictitious, applies to many kinds of actual investigations. Robinson Crusoe on his desert island, though he took care to salvage all available stores from the wreck, knew that to keep alive for any long time he should investigate the food resources of the island, more especially which parts of what plants were nutritious, which poisonous, which neither. He had to start from the basis of Hume's dictum that until you actually examine the plants that are there you have no information at all; any leaf, fruit or root may in principle possess any of the three different characters. But Crusoe's quest would have been hopelessly long and difficult had plants, men (and other animals) been random, *casual* aggregates instead of belonging to species, which are *causal* aggregates. Also Hume's other dictum that the guiding relations to consider are those of resemblance and contiguity, is too vague to be useful. Resemblance needs to be specific, of the kind which causes members of the same species to resemble each other and differ from members of other species. Again, Hume's contiguity needs to be taken as causal, that is to say tangible, even if invisible. Lastly, though 'nutritious' and 'poisonous' are plain adjectives they cannot be dismissed in the ancient fashion as attributes of substances, they are causal relations between bodies, between the bodies that are absorbed and the body that does the absorbing. Contiguity in this case is of a very special type that has two opposite forms, one promoting life, the other destroying it. Crusoe had to conduct (not without risk) a series of experiments in absorption, and they had to be systematic. Random eating of whatever lay handy would take too long and tell him too little. If I remember rightly, there were goats on the island, and once Crusoe had got on to speaking terms (if I may so put it) with them they would be very helpful. Goats are inquisitive, will try almost anything once, and even come back to ask for more. They have very tough constitutions. So much for the potential absorbers, beside himself. As for the absorbees, the plants, Crusoe required some knowledge of botany, at the farmers', gardeners' and housewives' level, as to what a plant species is and a plant-life history. Every specimen of one species (with rare and generally obvious exceptions) has many characters which distinguish it from specimens of other species and these characters are linked in an orderly way; the order is physical and causal. Modern taxonomy, morphology, physiology, and ecology can say much more in greater detail than the rudimentary sciences of Crusoe's day, but he knew quite enough to see that the causal links between specific characters of plants and animals were the kind of links that the science of physics deals with in a general way as the biological sciences do in a special way. In the very process of collecting specimens, preparing them by cooking, drying or other ways, tasting them himself, feeding them to the goats, watching the results, he was acquiring rudiments of several sciences about causal interrelations of many things. Before long the success of his investigations would become obvious; the goats and he would be growing fat. We can now define nutrition in quite general terms applicable to any kind of living organism, past, present and future; it is a process by which one set of bodies are absorbed into the interstices of other sets of bodies, by means of which the latter set grow, develop and complete their life cycle.

In conclusion, we can discover what bodies are doing and what is being done to them, directly by handling these bodies, indirectly by handling other bodies, and both because our own behaviour is causal in the secondary sense. Just looking gets us nowhere; even just talking is slightly better because it is a sort of indirect handling of bodies.

There is a great deal here that should worry visualist philosophers, but nothing to worry Berkeley.

§ 5 BERKELEY'S REPLIES TO CONTEMPORARY CRITICS

In his *Principles* Berkeley answers a number of objections made by contemporaries. Most of them are the stock misunderstandings that have been trotted out ever since, but for all that a number of important questions are raised, and worth discussing.[1]

Objection 1. 'All that is real and substantial in Nature is banished out of the world; and instead thereof a chimerical scheme of ideas takes place.'

This is the other Dr Samuel Johnson's famous refutation put into words. Objections 10, 11, 12, 13, are the most important

---

[1] What follows is not an exposition of Berkeley's replies, which the reader is supposed to have before him, but a comment on them to endeavour to indicate where Berkeley's real difficulties lie. For the early intelligent objections see two letters from Samuel Johnson (U.S.A.; not the Dr Johnson of the famous 'refutation'), *Works*, vol. II, pp. 267 ff.

special cases. This, the general vaguer form, springs from vulgar metaphysical prejudices or ancient folklore, whichever you like to call it; namely that if we find constancy or uniformity in the world it is constancy of stuff, because stuff is real, indestructible and an absolute, while ideas or their relations are flimsy, ghostly things that cannot be really real, permanent or enduring. Twentieth-century physical science has almost entirely got away from this prejudice or folklore, and is very nearly or even entirely Berkeleian about stuff. The whole business of physical science is to deal with what can be observed in order to discover constant relations or uniformities among observables, and not to impose absolutes on the world. *Stuff* is not observed, nor *matter* nor even *ether*. All this is very bleak and unsatisfying to common sense which likes its universe stuffy.

Apart from vulgar prejudices there is something more serious at stake. If sense experience alone can provide *a* criterion, or worse still, *the* criterion for judgment of truth and error in science, it is a criterion with grave disadvantages and no 'objectivity' about it, as most understand objectivity.

In the first place, past experience is no longer with us and has to be recovered through human memory, which is fallible. Even when reinforced through all the apparatus used by historians and legal experts memory is still not completely reliable. Present experience is seldom doubted during the time it lasts, but is transient and not always to be repeated when most needed. However vivid and convincing while it lasts, an experience may be repudiated the minute it is over, as is a nightmare, because it contradicts other past experience and newer experience. Future experience, so much praised by logical positivists while they lasted, is worse, it is surmise, guesswork, speculation. Even those who used to be logical positivists have now lost faith, finding that the future did not come up to youthful expectations. Thus past experience is the best that is left.

If, to the question: 'Why should we accept proposition *p* as true?' the answer is: 'Because Mr A, the leading authority, vouches for *p*', that at least makes sense. But the answer: 'Because *p* corresponds with Reality' is nonsense, unless somebody or other is prepared to vouch for this alleged correspondence. Mr A can explain: 'My acquaintance with reality through sense experience, which is all I have, in this matter of *p* is considerable, varied, entirely consistent and all points to the truth of p; whereas any suggested alternatives such as q, r, s, etc. are guesswork or rest on single quite uncorroborated bits of evidence. Moreover, you need not take my word for it. Ask Messrs B, C, and D; and if they fail to convince you, go and look for yourself.' Berkeley has already outlined the notion of corroboration in *NTV*.

However, people want an 'objective' criterion, universal, utterly trustworthy, so invent a pseudo-Platonic heaven or refrigerator constructed of corporeal substance or other materials to store it in, out of harm's way. Offhand, it looks so very rational to ask for an infallible criterion; for if there is none, what is the use of reason?

Berkeley in dealing with this objection confesses to making a change in terminology, but the change is not a trivial one; it is a challenge to deep-seated prejudice, as Berkeley discovered before long.

Objection 2. 'There is a great difference betwixt real fire and the idea of fire, betwixt dreaming or imagining one's self burnt and actually being so.'

In common usage the word 'idea' is not used of actual experience, but is used mainly where the speaker has doubts and refers to what he takes to be a faint copy of a 'real original'. Hume took over the common usage and sharpened it into metaphysical dogma, which got him into serious difficulties.[1] Berkeley did in fact minimize the distinction of common usage, and in the long philosophical run was right not to go the way of Hume, however plausible it might appear at first sight, for Berkeley left room for *apperception* (see above, Ch. III, § 4) and could make his own distinctions (see above, the answer to Objection 1). Common usage depends on a Hobbist or Lockean confusion; namely that 'real' is equivalent to 'outside the percipient's body' and this is equivalent to 'outside his mind'; while 'inside the mind' is equivalent to 'inside the body' and that means 'not quite real', 'subjective', or 'imaginary'. (If you prefer, put

---

[1] Over belief, in *Treatise*, Bk I, because he could not make up his mind whether it could be an *impression* or had to be just an *idea*, and if so, what did it copy? In Bk II it was because he had to give some emotions and feelings the status of *impressions*, as they were the moving forces in human action, and then could not see how to distinguish merely remembered feelings from actual feelings.

'brain' in place of 'body'.) Common usage is here, as usual, inconsistent. In the case of pain, at least, it admits that something can be real and yet inside the body (or brain or mind?).

Berkeley's retort (I need not here rate his argument higher) takes advantage of the confusion and inconsistency. He says: 'If real fire is very different from the idea of fire, so also is the real pain that it occasions very different from the idea of the same pain; and yet nobody will pretend that real pain either is, or can possibly exist, in an unperceiving thing or without the mind' (§ 41).

In discussing this, the first point is that the psychology of pain is a most awkward subject; those who touch it touch fire. However, let us be brave.

As already said (Ch. III, § 3), what is violently obtrusive in experience, specially if unpleasant, is accepted as true or real, during the time that it lasts. Afterwards, on reflection, it may be rejected as imaginary or false. While you dream that you have been flung out of a top window of a tall building and see the pavement rapidly approaching, you have no doubts at all; but then you wake up sweating, and possibly shrieking. A few seconds later, as soon as you are fully awake, you dismiss the whole episode; because the dream experience is not corroborated but contradicted; you are not falling through the air nor crashing on the pavement; you are in bed in a dark room and nothing seriously wrong is happening or going to happen.

If a drop of liquid falls off something which you think is very hot, you draw your hand away feeling a sudden stinging sensation and say: 'I've been burnt.' If some minutes later you see a blister on the place, not only you but the other people there also see it, and your statement is confirmed as a true statement. You did not imagine you were burnt; you were really burnt. On the other hand it may turn out that it was not a drop of boiling water but of freezing cold water. The immediate sensation might be just about the same, you might say you were burnt, but afterwards there will be no blister and afterwards you (and your friends) will discover that the vessel is very cold not very hot. Corroborative evidence about what goes on at the surface of our bodies or in their near neighbourhood is easy to get, and opinions about it can easily be made reliable. What goes on inside our bodies usually, of necessity, remains uncorroborated, though something can be done

H

about it, as for instance when a doctor is examining a patient and saying at intervals: 'Does that hurt?' 'Does this hurt?' But it is common clinical experience that many patients feel no pain when all the indications are that they 'ought' to feel pain; while other patients feel pain, sometimes acute unendurable pain, when all the indications are that they 'ought' to feel no pain.

Let us go now to the opposite end of the intensity scale; very faint sense experience is generally, and should always be, suspect. It leads to many common errors and illusions, and in the more bizarre kinds of experience to what are called hallucinations. When you are walking in semi-darkness and nothing is seen distinctly, you cannot be sure whether what you see ahead is a manor, a cow or perhaps a fixed feature of the landscape, a big tree a long way off or a small one nearby; or possibly, if you are frightened, nothing at all; you may be just 'imagining things'. In a good light you recognize things correctly, you can pick out those commonly used visual signs you look for. Berkeley has a very good answer as against the learned, but not a simple one and it requires an understanding of *NTV*, which only a few of the learned have troubled to acquire.

As against the vulgar his position is more difficult, for he could not expect them to understand *NTV*. He did, however, claim to be more nearly on the side of the vulgar. Berkeley considered that he was a realist on the subject of sense perception, as Hobbes, Descartes, and Locke certainly were not. He may have been right to suppose that the vulgar were more realist than these members of the learned, but unhappily the vulgar have swallowed or always had far more of these three thinkers than is good for them. (See also under Objection 13.)

Berkeley knew, as Hume did not, that the difference between the 'real' and the 'imagined' or 'feigned' is not just given to us with each item before our minds but has to be discovered by examining carefully the relations between items. The 'real' has order, consistency and fullness of content that the 'imagined' has not.

Objection 3. 'We see things at a distance and therefore not in the mind.'

This is a confusion that has been sufficiently indicated already. These first three objections rest on common confusions embedded in common verbal usage which Berkeley asks us to drop. The next one is different.

Objection 4. 'Everything at every moment is annihilated and created anew.'

This is a perversion of common usage intended to put Berkeley in a false position. When I shut my eyes I see *nothing*, when I open them in daylight I see *something*, therefore by the mere fact of opening them I *create* something or other, *if you care to put it that way*, and by the mere fact of shutting them I *annihilate* something or other, *if you care to put it that way*. The difficulty is entirely *created* by your putting it that way, and can be *annihilated* by not putting it that way. Berkeley does not create any difficulty, but, as a Christian, he would be bound to say that such language is blasphemous; men move things from place to place but create nothing and annihilate nothing.

Berkeley at this point refers to *Princ.*, §§ 3 and 4. He also puts his point admirably in § 23, which is worth quoting even if familiar:

§ 23. But say you, surely there is nothing easier than to imagine trees for instance, in a park, or books existing in a closet, and no body by to perceive them. I answer, you may so, there is no difficulty in it; but what is all this, I beseech you, more than framing in your mind certain ideas which you call *books* and *trees*, and at the same time omitting to frame the idea of any one that may perceive them? But do not you your self perceive or think of them all the while? This therefore is nothing to the purpose; it only shows you have the power of imagining or forming ideas in your mind; but it doth not shew that you can conceive it possible, the objects of your thought may exist without the mind: to make out this, it is necessary that you conceive them existing unconceived or unthought of, which is a manifest repugnancy. When we do our utmost to conceive the existence of external bodies, we are all the while only contemplating our own ideas. But the mind taking no notice of itself, is deluded to think it can and doth conceive bodies existing unthought of, or without the mind; though at the same time they are apprehended by or exist in it self. A little attention will discover to any one the truth and evidence of what is here said, and make it unnecessary to insist on any other proofs against the existence of material substance.

He then points out that Locke's philosophy is in a more awkward case than his own.

However, objection 4 remains one of the favourite refutations of Berkeley and causes critics to break into poetry, or at least into limericks.[1]

Objection 5. 'If extension and figure exist only in the mind, it follows that the mind is extended and figured.'

This objection belongs to seventeenth-century metaphysics and few now would raise it. Descartes made it his basic presupposition that bodies occupy space and do not think, while minds think but do not occupy space, thus making any connections between minds and bodies inconceivable, leaving his successors to struggle with the problems raised. Among these was Henry More, a friend of Newton, who put forward the daring hypothesis that the mind of God occupies or comprehends all space or that space is, as Newton put it, 'the sensorium of God'. Such a theory was shocking to Berkeley, who was more Platonist and more Cartesian than usually supposed, and anxious not to be implicated. His answer is simple, in Scholastic terms, and a masterly compromise, if you approve of it, an evasion, if you do not. I doubt whether any philosopher can do much better. Three minor points however should be mentioned.

i. Locke would have chuckled at the statement itself: 'Those qualities (extension and figure) are in the mind only as they are perceived by it, that is not by way of *mode* or *attribute*, but only by way of *idea*' (§ 49). Is not this Locke's distinction between Primary and Secondary Qualities of Sense? For example, a red colour is in the mind 'by way of mode or attribute', but its triangular shape 'by way of idea'. Berkeley never claimed that either were mental, only that they were *not* material or substantial.

ii. A number of early twentieth-century critics (e.g. G. E. Moore, 'Refutation of Idealism', *Mind*, 1903) accused Berkeley of failing to make any distinction between the two aspects of perception, the perceiv-ing and the perceiv-ed. Can he have read the passage in *Princ.* (§ 45), or understood §§ 89–91? He may perhaps be excused for failing to understand the entries in *PC*, at that time printed in wrong chronological order.[2]

With Moore the distinction between -ing and -ed seems to be

---

[1] [Compare A. A. Luce, *The Dialectic of Immaterialism* (London, 1963) for a different analysis of Objection 4.]

[2] See Nos. 429–429a, 474–474a, 535, 546–546a. The first of these states Berkeley's full doctrine, 'To be is *percipi* or *percipere* (or *velle* i.e. *agere*).' The first part should never be quoted alone. [The second part was introduced by

entirely visual. The distinction which Berkeley requires should not be stated visually but in terms of articulate speech. Let us suppose that A is speak*ing* to B and B is hear*ing* him. There are two distinct mental activities, both properly expressed by the present participle active, though the sender of the signals, A, is active relative to the receiver, B. The past participle passive can refer only to the signals (σ) which are not parts of the minds of A or B now, even though the code (σ) was once previously agreed on by them. σ is, as Berkeley says, senseless, unthinking, doubly passive. In purely visual terms there is no such distinction as Berkeley requires. If, as Moore supposes, what is look-*ed* at is non-mental the look-*ing* must be non-mental also, for it is bodily posture and movement. Moore is left with Hobbist phantasms.

iii. Granted that it is the function of the mind to *compare* the sizes of fleas and elephants and to *decide correctly* that the latter are bigger, not *incorrectly* that the former are bigger; is it helpful to add the comment that the mind can do it because it is in some way intermediate in size between the flea and the elephant? This is the kind of answer that Hobbes would have to give if pressed, and so would Hume. Both have been refuted in advance by Plato's *Theaetetus* (184C–185E). Can we rest content with Plato's answer, that the mind can do it because it has no size at all of its own?

Objection 6. 'That there have been a great many things explained by matter and motion; take away these and you destroy the whole corpuscular philosophy and undermine mechanical principles.'

This brings us back to the source of Objection 1; but special pseudo-scientific folklore, not general folklore. I take 'corporeal philosophy' to mean physics in general and not the atomic theory. Berkeley's reply repeats that the doctrine of corporeal substance is not an explanatory principle in science nor in any way useful. The actually used explanatory principles do not conflict with his own philosophy; i.e. the general rules by which sensible relations of sensible bodies signify other sensible relations of sensible bodies.

Objection 7. This objection arises out of the reply to 6 and raises a new, more difficult point: 'That it is absurd to take away natural

---

Berkeley in a footnote; the brackets have been introduced into the text by the editor so as to bring out the force of Berkeley's important gloss. See also on this subject, p. xiii above, especially footnote 1.]

causes and ascribe everything to the immediate operation of spirits.'

Berkeley's reply introduces valuable but dangerous advice: 'We ought to think with the learned but speak with the vulgar.' (The opposite policy is much favoured and still more dangerous.) The advice is dangerous because the learned, though differently and each according to his metaphysical bent, do at least attempt consistency, while the vulgar never bother about it and blithely cling to contradictory beliefs. Berkeley has to expound an explicitly theocentric theory derived from some of the learned in order to attack an explicitly atheistic theory derived from others of the learned. It is not easy to persuade the vulgar that the two are contradictory or that a few contradictions do any harm.

The *De Motu* puts Berkeley's answer better than anything he says here in *Princ.*; but he makes a valuable comment on the use of language in this connection. The most convinced Copernican still talks about the sun 'rising' in the morning and 'setting' in the evening.

Propriety being regulated by custom, our language is suited to the received opinions, which are not always the truest. Hence it is impossible, even in the most rigid philosophical (i.e. scientific) reasonings, so far to alter the bent and genius of the tongue we speak, as never to give a handle for cavillers to pretend difficulties and inconsistencies.

Objections 8, 9, 10, 11 introduce a number of allied topics, which might all be headed 'More errors about scientific knowledge'. I venture to reclassify them; there are more complexities about the problems of matter and motion than appeared when Berkeley first dealt with them. Berkeley falls foul of certain nearly universal beliefs of mankind (Objections 8 and 9). This, I think, has to be accepted as a historical fact. My experience in trying to introduce his theory to University students, is that some 90 per cent of them make no serious attempt to understand him, but reject him offhand because of their beliefs. Some 1 per cent or so take to his views, equally offhand, or, more politely, instinctively, and cannot understand any other view. The remainder, not a very big minority, can consider both sides carefully, with understanding, and then reject or accept, after this consideration.

Thus it is necessary for Berkeley to be able to maintain that the common belief that the ultimate origin of the order and regularity of the natural world must be 'some senseless unthinking being' (§ 54) and not an Intelligence or Will is muddled and self-contradictory, however many believed it and go on believing it. Majorities, however large, prove nothing; if they could, experience would not teach us effectively and science would be impossible.

So far as this parish and the half-dozen neighbouring parishes extend the earth *is flat*, and to this day maps of them are drawn on that basis (§ 55). Ordinary vulgar thinking extrapolates this parochial judgment to the whole earth and goes woefully wrong, until the minute scientific minority are allowed to bring wider and newer experience to bear on the subject, to put the majority right, even if they resist for hundreds of years.

Berkeley is also one of another minority, this time of philosophers, in realizing that those who oppose majority views as erroneous, have a duty to show how the majority went wrong, and to show that their new theory can explain the error out of its own resources, without introducing extra hypotheses *ad hoc*. This is done most effectively where the error, as in the flat earth, comes from taking notice of part of the evidence and ignoring the rest of it which happens to be less conspicuous to those who make the mistake. Thus we mistake what we see in a mirror for 'reality' as long as we fail to see the mirror itself, but having seen that we make no mistake, apart from a possible lapse of memory.

Berkeley's position is complicated because in his view the learned are immersed in worse errors than the genuine vulgar; and not only is ordinary experience misinterpreted but science too. He thus has four controversies on his hands; against vulgar pseudo-experience and vulgar pseudo-science and also against learned pseudo-experience and learned pseudo-science. (Only an Irishman would undertake such a job.) A point that eases Berkeley's task is that the vulgar, even if unanimous, are not consistent, and the learned, even if consistent, are not unanimous. Berkeley's metaphysics is one of Will, not Stuff (vulgar), nor Substance (learned); while all the vulgar and most of the learned assume Will to be capricious or else conventional. But Berkeley has in view first the Divine Will that creates the whole world, not at all the human will when it is in conflict with the Divine. Berkeley has on his side the Hebrew Prophets and a very few of the Hellenists; but with them he holds that only Will and Intelligence (cf. *DM*, §§ 32 ff., on

Anaxagoras) can create order or law, and without it there is no *rerum natura* at all. Further he holds that the nature of things is not concealed from us, but directly revealed through sense experience, more especially through experience enlarged and interpreted by science, when the pseudo-part is dropped out. There is some excuse for vulgar errors because of the limitations of vulgar experience, but none for the learned errors of those who 'have first raised a dust and then complain that (they) cannot see' (*Princ.*, Intro., § 3).

The examples that Berkeley uses are those of the spherical form of the earth, its diurnal rotation and orbital motions. If these are really inobservables and if Berkeley accepts the current scientific theories about them then this is a specific and serious challenge to his philosophy. The three questions, however, cannot be treated *pari passu* and Berkeley's statement about the earth's motion is too brief, vague and visualist; also definitely misleading, in one respect.

About the figure of the earth Berkeley is in no difficulty. For once, the learned are unanimous and opposed to the vulgar on grounds common to them and Berkeley. The flat earth has never been observable except in the purely parochial sense already mentioned, and has been pure folklore, never scientific theory at all; indeed, the exact contrary. The spherical earth is *the* basic theory of astronomy, geography, geodesy, and the art of navigation. The oceans and continents have been explored by means of it and the stars mapped. Its beginnings can be found in the visual observation of the curvature of the sea, to be seen on any hilly coast on any clear day (e.g. almost any Mediterranean coast on most Mediterranean days). This is only slight curvature, which by itself signifies hardly anything, until it is worked out and extended systematically, precisely and completely for the whole of the earth's surface by measurements of the altitudes of the same stars when seen from different places and other astronomical measurements. When the measurements were sufficiently complete no figure except a sphere (with certain very small deviations) remained possible. What makes this science not folklore is system, precision and completeness. It is theory and not direct observation, but with observation keeping always close to theory, and no inobservables unless we suppose merely parochial observation from a merely inland parish. There are also the undoubted facts that nobody reached any edge where the sea met the sky, nor fell off on reaching the Pacific Ocean; but these are incidentals.

Given that the earth is a sphere, the scientific question, whether the visible diurnal rotation of 'the heavenly bodies' is their own rotation, or else that of the earth, cropped up and was discussed indecisively from the fifth century B.C., almost up to Berkeley's day. It was not Copernicus but Newton with the help of Kepler who gave the decisive answer, decisive because not in visual terms but dynamic, and, as I insist on adding, haptic terms. (Einstein did not make a scrap of difference, in spite of what excited and visualist journalists said in 1919 and 1920.) When Berkeley wrote, it is likely that not all the learned yet accepted the earth's diurnal rotation. (I can imagine Dean Swift objecting.)

All this preliminary is to emphasize that in Berkeley's day the problem of obtaining further evidence for the earth's rotation was still a live one; now it is as completely settled as any can be. It is not that any genuine man of science would object to more evidence, only that if it agrees with the old he is a bit bored by it; if it disagrees he will not accept it without very stringent enquiry into its *bona fides*.

Berkeley's statement is: '. . . if we were placed in such and such circumstances, and such and such a position and distance, both from the earth and the sun, we should perceive the former to move among the choir of planets, and appearing in all respects like one of them . . .' (*Princ.*, § 58). He is, unfortunately, thinking mainly if not entirely, of orbital motion; but diurnal rotation has to be established first before the question of orbits arises at all. Many people today, as in his day, would take him to mean: 'If we could go up in a rocket in the right direction we should then see the various bodies of the solar system twirling round, as in an Orrery or Planetarium[1] and the earth twirling among them.' As visualists they would approve and think the question settled.

Of course, it is possible that a rocket with the necessary apparatus could be landed on the moon, take a film of the earth's surface for a few hours and televise it back. Then if there was not too much cloud and surface features were clear enough, there would be new visual evidence of rotation. If anybody thinks that that would be better than existing evidence he should keep his

---

[1] The dynamics of such a model are entirely wrong. It is meant for visualists.

thoughts to himself. In any case he would not venture to set his watch by what he saw.

In short, the eighteenth century should not have been waiting for a sputnik, but for Foucault and his pendulum, whose experiment was done in 1851, at a minute fraction of the cost and at no risk. Or rather, there was little need to wait at all. Already from the time of Newton's *Principia* a new body of dynamic evidence was accumulating and accumulated all through the nineteenth century (quite apart from Foucault) and I doubt if it has yet stopped. All of it confirms the rotation theory and none goes against it. There was Newton's explanation of the earth's equatorial bulge, of the *Precession of the Equinoxes*, as well as his beginnings of the theory of the tides, the dynamic consequences of the earth's rotation relative to sun and moon. Bradley's discovery of *Aberration* in 1724 and later of *Mutation* was helpful, if less directly. To continue the general story; the nineteenth century produced a more complete and satisfactory tidal theory, it also plotted out systematically the ocean currents and air currents. All these currents if they last long enough and travel far enough tend to have a curved path, as they should on a rotating, but not a stationary surface.

The general dynamic consequence of the earth's diurnal rotation at its surface has been stated, i.e. that all freely moving bodies follow curved paths, whose curvature can be calculated, where similar bodies would follow straight paths on or near a stationary sphere with a similar gravitational field. The problem of deciding between the alternatives is a practical one of finding or producing such bodies. It is quite possible that Archimedes, who knew more than he wrote and far more than has come down to us, guessed this principle and looked round for freely falling or floating bodies to demonstrate it. He knew about the balance, which moves freely in one plane. He may have done some experiments with the pendulum, which is closely related to the balance, and got so far as to decide that only a very long, slow-moving pendulum would do, since the air resistance would be negligible and it would swing freely for a very long time. In later centuries many seem to have tried dropping stones from the different sides of towers with no results, but the possible effect in a short drop is very small and swamped by irregular effects of air resistance.

I should not bother with imaginings about Archimedes were it not clear that many people in later days pondered on such lines;

but they came up against two practical problems they could not solve which were finally solved by the help of unforeseeable inventions, quite irrelevant to the paths of freely moving bodies.

The first is, how are we to find a place from which to suspend a very long pendulum? It must be quite steady and hang in a place free from draughts and other mechanical disturbances. Archimedes put it, laconically, 'ποῦ στῶ;' No suitable building existed in his time, but a century or two afterwards architects learnt how to build domes and the Pantheon at Rome would have served, as the later Pantheon at Paris served Foucault. The solution of the second problem had to wait longer; that of how to make a string on which to hang the pendulum bob, long enough, strong enough and flexible enough. This had to wait first for the invention of a musical instrument, the pianoforte, and then for longer, stronger and more uniform strings to string it. No catgut nor the older steel wire was good enough. This last problem was solved by nineteenth-century drawers of steel wires, who could make them of almost any length you could ask for. Foucault managed with a bit more than 200 feet.[1]

Though Foucault's experiment was not the unique and finally decisive demonstration of the earth's rotation that some have thought it, it was an important event. It was quite easy to understand, needed no difficult mathematics and was more direct than any other evidence before 1851. Even the most bigoted visualist could not seriously misinterpret it. Moreover, and this is the most important point, Foucault did not merely vaguely expect the plane of swing of the pendulum to shift somehow, but calculated in what direction and how fast; i.e. clockwise and one complete revolution in 32 hours (to the nearest whole number). That is what the pendulum did.[2] He did *not* find that at Paris it took 36 hours to complete a revolution, and then have to explain away the discrepancy by ingenious hypotheses. In that kind of way it was decisive and final, but it remains one item in a large number of different and independent bits of evidence, all corroborating

[1] Thus Music has come to the assistance of her sister Astronomy, as foretold by Plato and Pythagoras.

[2] The formula is that at any given latitude the shift per hour should be 15° multiplied by the *sine* of the latitude; thus it should be nil at the Equator, exactly 24 hours at North and South Poles.

one another, all of them things happening at the surface of the earth and none requiring aid from sputniks.

There is nothing inobservable about the earth's rotation nor contrary to Berkeley's principles; it makes its presence seen and felt wherever and whenever anybody has set about observing the consequences of that presence under the right conditions. On this topic Berkeley makes his one serious blunder, and most conspicuous lapse into visualism. There is no need to go on to deal with orbital motion where his position is very slightly better, and visualist errors not so fatal.

Berkeley was weak on dynamics as is seen in his comments on Newton's argument about the spinning bucket (*Works*, vol. II, p. 92n.; *Works*, vol. IV, p. 48, see above p. 88) which fall below his normal standard of clarity. Something needs to be said about this. Newton was a pioneer using dynamical or haptic arguments in a predominantly visualist and unsympathetic world. It was not only Berkeley who failed to understand his highly condensed statement. His point is more easily put in modern terms; but let us start with his bucket of water hanging on a rope and set spinning by twisting the rope. Once the water is got spinning at uniform speed the surface is found to be depressed in the middle to a uniform extent. But before it was set spinning the surface was flat. This can be observed from outside the bucket, but equally well from within, e.g. by an intelligent minnow or by a water spider on the surface. No outside information is needed. It is not necessary to know whether the solid wall of the bucket is spinning or the walls of the room. A uniformly rotating body has a special structure and symmetry of its own, which a non-spinning body does not possess. Consider a 'freely' spinning sphere, the 'natural' and only astronomically important case, or else a flywheel on a machine, or the special case of the gyrostat, discovered by Foucault. The structure and symmetry is determined by Axis and Equator; the first is stationary, the second has the maximum rotatory speed. All rotating parts are subject to stress and/or acceleration. For any one part there is another corresponding part with an equal and opposite stress or motion. In short, the rotating body has a supply of potential energy of its own, which no non-rotating body possesses. This can be most dramatically seen (occasionally) in flywheels which are set spinning too fast and burst, less dramatically and more instructively in the gyrostat which resists any attempt to change the orientation of its axis. There is something absolute about this axis, that is why I emphasize the words, *structure, own, store of energy*. For physics, there are three different kinds of body; i. the plain particle, which is not interfered with, is either at rest or moving with uniform velocity, and is indifferent which; ii. the accelerated particle which is being interfered with; iii. the freely rotating body, which is not now being interfered with from outside, and is not a particle if by 'particle' is meant something with no apparent or significant structure or energy of its own.

In the modern world the human body is often subject to quite large accelerations in buses, trains and aeroplanes, when starting, stopping or turning corners. The accelerated motions and/or stresses can be *felt*; and by the *feel* their direction correctly judged and their intensity (roughly). Neither Berkeley nor Newton enjoyed these modern advantages. They were confined to experience of ships at sea, which is more confusing than instructive.

We can now deal briefly with Objections 10 and 11; that Berkeley's theory 'is inconsistent with several sound truths' in (i) philosophy and (ii) mathematics, nor can it explain (iii) 'that curious organization of plants' nor (iv) 'the admirable mechanism in the parts of animals'.

(ii) needs separate treatment elsewhere in connection with *The Analyst*. (Cf. below, pp. 131 ff.) As to (i) 'philosophy' here means physics and if it can be taken quite specifically to be Newtonian physics, as expounded by Newton, then Berkeley has no quarrel with him except where he lapses from his own principles. Newton accepted the general rule that observed phenomena must be explained, where explicable, in terms of other phenomena observed or observable, and that 'hypotheses' are to be reduced to the minimum needed as working tools. But other natural philosophers were less cautious than Newton and a great deal of Berkeley consists of direct criticism of them. So far as botanists and zoologists can abide by the Newtonian rules of philosophizing, Berkeley has no quarrel with them, and notes quite correctly the different status of zoology and botany.

By the early eighteenth century animal physiology had made some progress and Berkeley could use the artificer analogy quite properly about functions of animal organs. Early progress in knowledge depended very much on human analogies. Harvey could explain the pumping function of the heart because men had made pumps. The working of animal sense organs and animal muscles was understood because of direct analogy with human sense organs and direct experience of human locomotion. Not so the early eighteenth-century botanist; he could admire aesthetically the 'curious organization of plants', but lacking human analogies had scarcely an inkling of its functions. That had to wait, mostly till the nineteenth century. On the whole the biological science of Berkeley's day provided evidence of the uselessness of inobservables and of 'hypotheses' about them.

The greater part of Berkeley's reply to Objection 12 is directed against Malebranche, and does not concern us here. But the Objection at § 82, not numbered in the text, is a theological one and has to be considered, if quite shortly.

Berkeley was accused of being unable, on his principles, to accept the account of the Creation in the Book of Genesis, and of probably explaining away the 'miracles' of the Old and New Testaments; a dangerous accusation in his day because that was just what some of the learned were busy doing, and what the vulgar, along with others among the learned, strongly objected to. The issue here was specially confused and complicated. If however Berkeley is a genuine realist about sense perception and the vulgar are also realists, and if he can persuade them that God's Will is the sole creative 'force', then there is no difficulty for him in Genesis, much less over 'miracles'. Berkeley points out (in effect) that the Scriptures are not written in the language of Hobbes, Descartes, Locke or any other philosopher, nor do they embody any of their doctrines, but in the plain, simple 'realist' speech of the vulgar, who also accept the mysteries of religion and are not so presumptuous as to explain them. It is the learned, specially the philosophers, who create difficulties, the kind of creation they do best. Granted Berkeley's contention above, he has a very good case. If it is not granted his position is not so happy, but that of Hobbes, Descartes or Locke is worse.

§6 GENERAL SURVEY OF REDUCTIONIST CRITICISM OF SCIENCE (i)

We are here concerned to attempt a more general conclusion about Berkeley's critique of scientific method, but not about the general metaphysical problems facing him (whether he looked at them or not), nor popular misunderstandings of him. His answers to contemporary objections have, however, brought up some important considerations. I summarize them in my own order.

i. How can future experience which does not exist (yet) and cannot be predicted be used as a criterion of truth and falsehood? Note that the attempt to predict the future has from time immemorial been the professional job of the soothsayer, the first and most fraudulent of all professions. Genuine empiricists have never had any dealings with any such professionals, knowing that truth cannot be bought, only falsehood. Yet empiricists are in an awkward position. To the obstinate critic or doubter the final retort has to be: 'All right, if you don't believe me, then go and look (or seek) for yourself, you will find it is as I say.' Then the critic asks, quite reasonably: 'Tell me how to look (or seek)?' If the seeking is just a matter of using existing techniques he can be told and only requires the caution: 'Learn the technique properly, don't come rushing back to report your first premature efforts.' Here there is no difficulty. But if new techniques or tools for observation can be invented, as they generally can be, no soothsayer can tell us beforehand what they are going to be. Even the most hardened professional fraud has never tried this game.

This is a sad state of affairs, but it is the state of affairs. Not Berkeley only but all genuine empiricists have to face it, because they put their faith in evidence and not in guesswork, professional (soothsayers') or amateur. Faith in guesswork poses no difficulties, that is what is wrong with it.

ii. If you are a Humean and a visualist, there is nothing in your world to talk about but loose adjectives, beside them only the useless pronoun 'I', and no useful substantive nouns. Are substantive nouns nothing but linguistic conveniences? Is Berkeley's polemic against corporeal substance and other occult entities an attempt to live in a Humean world? I should answer both questions with 'No'. Berkeley did have occasional lapses, but was not a Humean, not even half way to one. It is the other way round. Hume fell into the pit Berkeley was climbing out of. That should be quite clear from NTV and the later TVV.

There can be no kind of scientific knowledge without *continuants*,[1]

[1] W. E. Johnson, *Logic*, vol. i, 1921.

because without them there is no constancy; there are no general rules, no measurements, no standards, no criteria. Without *continuants*, there might be adjectives of sorts, but no useful ones, e.g. no *equal*, no *unequal*, than which nothing can be more adjectival, more empirical or more necessary. But they belong to the realm of haptic experience and the haptic world springs from the contact of two *continuants*, the bodily 'me' and 'my environment', which is both obstacle and opportunity. What Berkeley asks for is that *continuants* and their continuing should be manifest in or through sense experience, not hidden.

iii. Now comes the real difficulty about hypotheses, peculiar to Berkeley and the reductionist or phenomenalist approach to physical science, and Berkeley is even more suspicious of hypotheses than Newton, admits no absolutes and, at least by implication (*DM*, § 66), only approximations, no exact laws. He does admit mathematical hypotheses which exist by definition or convention (*DM*, §§ 40, 67), but what are these?

For example, is *mass* an occult entity or a legitimate mathematical hypothesis? Would Berkeley reduce dynamics to kinematics? If *mass* is admitted what about *energy*, in its nineteenth-century form?

As at least a mathematical convention, i.e. something you put in to make your equations equate properly, even the most fanatical kinematist has to admit *mass*. But surely it is something more than this? Is it not what you discover about the sensible world of bodies by the use of the balance? Do you not find also that the results you get with spring and torsion balances agree as closely as you can measure with those of the ordinary beam or gravity balance? If corroboration is the test, here is all that can be asked for. Similarly, when you correlate kinetic energy with heat energy, and also chemical potential energy and electrical potential energy after the method of Joule, you get good agreement, not so easily nor so accurately as with *mass*, but quite well enough.

What is wrong with occult entities and superfluous or purely speculative hypotheses is that they do no work in any actual process of investigation; they are passengers, not members of the crew and in bad weather are liable to get in the way. Newton's corpuscular theory of light and Huygen's wave theory in their day were equally passengers, but Thomas Young could make his

wave theory do useful work immediately, for he could measure
the wave lengths of light, and his work led, almost immediately,
to the invention of the spectroscope by Fraunhofer, which was
(apart from electro-magnetic instruments) *the* great new invention
of the nineteenth century, and the new chemico-physics.

Newton and Berkeley are pioneers of what is conveniently
called phenomenalism in physical science, and it must be noticed
that they were both in their different ways truly interested in
phenomena and reliable observers. This has to be said because too
many who have written about science in recent years are more interested in *abstract ideas* than phenomena.[1]

Newton is one of the great experimentalists. He knew that
before you begin you must have adequate tools and if they are not
ready to hand you must make them, and may even have to invent
them. Then you must not expect to be successful unless you know,
or, more likely, have painfully learnt, what to do with them. In
other words you must ask the right questions or you will get the
wrong answers or no answers. Lastly, among the necessary tools
are theoretical tools as well as those you work with your hands,
the means for interpreting and calculating. Again you may have
to invent these.

No such claim can be made for Berkeley, but he was the very
opposite of the 'idealist' of popular fiction, with his head in the
clouds, ignorant of where his feet are taking him. He was emin-
ently practical-minded, observant, with wide interests (see the
Life by A. A. Luce, and specially his economic interests and influence on Adam Smith: see below, Ch. VII, § 7). The failure of his
Bermuda scheme was not the failure of a woolly-minded 'idealist'
as many have imagined.

As I have said, Newton and Berkeley were pioneers of reductionism or phenomenalism in physical science in an age which
needed this kind of corrective discipline (cf. Descartes's speculations about cosmic vortices; below, p. 114). They advocated
the elimination of inobservables, occult entities of any sort, and
superfluous hypotheses. And they practised what they preached.
Berkeley in *NTV*, Newton in nearly all his published scientific
work, and where he appeared to lapse from the straight and
narrow way Berkeley criticized him severely. They both understood the limitations of phenomenalism. They did not suppose

[1] I ask pardon for some repetition of Ch. II, § 2.

I

that all hypotheses could be eliminated and pure uncontaminated phenomena intuited by themselves; they did not suppose that what was good so far for physical science must be equally good for everything else.

In *NTV* Berkeley initiated the basic research on the test of truth and falsehood in sense experience. (Basic researches are seldom first in chronological order.) He pointed out that the various items of experience are signs of other items, past, present or future, by means of which we can guide our activities so that where different signs appear in close succession or simultaneously, all pointing in the same direction, we can take them as reliable guides in that direction to further experience which we can use to our advantage. Solitary or uncorroborated signs we may ignore without much risk. Here is the foundation of experimental method, for by our own activities we can set the sign series going. So far as the argument of *NTV* goes, it is concerned with short term and habitual experience, with what happens to everybody, everywhere, every day, or even every hour, and with the imminent future not the distant; with crossing the road without getting killed by the traffic, or even with standing still without coming to harm.

This is the beginning, but is not enough for science, which has to take account of the rare and distant as well as the near and familiar, which also calls for precision and measurement not only vague estimates or guesswork. It is not enough to observe that A is bigger than B, we need to know how much bigger. Berkeley very properly emphasizes the most continuous and most useful of all corroboration, that of the visible with the tangible.

Newton's experiments on the decomposition of white light and the spectral colours are an example of the next most basic stage, where geometry and measurements come in, but the very minimum of theoretical apparatus, as well as of physical apparatus; namely a narrow beam of sunlight, a glass prism and a white screen. The most instructive illustrations in connection with the argument of *NTV* are in fact experiments, but a sufficiently *perceptive* reader (emphasis on 'perceptive') could do without them by merely attending to what was going on round him. Though plenty of people noticed that glass prisms produced pretty colours, none of them got much further, if any further, till Newton deliberately assembled the right things in the right place at the right time, and *made* the observations by making them observable. Nobody before had asked the right question.

People have often asked why Newton never observed the Fraunhofer Lines, nor anybody else, not even Thomas Young, till they were observed by Fraunhofer himself. The answer is that Newton's prism was almost certainly a crude affair optically, he had no lens to focus the rays, and his slit was too wide. Fraunhofer, a professional instrument maker, had first to produce an instrument of precision and to answer the question which Newton had no need to ask: 'Precision for what?' In short, Newton in the 1660's was long before the time. He had made observations, arrived at a simple general conclusion and then could go no further with his methods, whereas Fraunhofer and his contemporaries could, thanks to Young's theory.

Even more premature than Newton was Pythagoras with his discovery of the mathematical ratios corresponding to the harmonic intervals. This was in principle a more excellent feat of phenomenal science than Newton's, though less fruitful in its consequences. Pythagoras made a generalization correlating three fields of sense experience, not just two. Again, nobody could use it in the sixth century B.C., not indeed till the seventeenth century A.D. and again for lack of theory, namely the wave theory of sound. Here let me insist again that the wave theory of sound is useful only because it is a theory about observables, namely wave lengths of sound, as is Young's wave theory of light. His theory remains that, even though we still use the ray theory, without Young, and the quantum theory, which Planck added on to 'complement' Young's theory.

However, let us come back to Berkeley, Newton and Pythagoras, from whom we have the phenomenal basis of the whole of physics. I mean that between them they have shown how to ask precise questions about actual mechanical tools and also theoretical tools, so that a precise and quite general answer can be obtained. For the general and long range predictions of science these special tools are needed but not for short range and more particular predictions about each perceptual situation as it arises; Berkeley's subject in *NTV*. We can make quite sure enough that *this* bus now turning *this* corner will miss us by a decent margin, without any of the apparatus of scientific investigations, technical or theoretical. To make sure where the various bodies of the solar system will be in five years' time or else how to pump the water out of a deep mine, we do need them—pure science and technology should not be considered entirely apart.

§ 7 GENERAL SURVEY OF REDUCTIONIST CRITICISM OF SCIENCE (ii)

There can be no simple, above all no final answer to any question about the future which always remains unknown as long as it is future; this includes the future of science. There always have been and probably always will be two opposed schools of thought about the value of the theorizing which accompanies scientific investigations. There are the reductionists who accept too little, a small select group who all say much the same about rash speculation. On the other side are the *fantastics* who claim too much; a very large assortment of very diverse opinions varying from genuine discoverers to sham ones. For the most part reductionists have been mathematicians thinking in terms of strict proof and economy of means, or else sceptical onlookers, not discoverers. Our two under discussion are exceptions, and I shall return to them shortly. The present-day fantastics are mostly and conspicuously technologists; that was not so in Newton's or Berkeley's day, for technology then was a meagre affair. The fantastics were then mainly Platonists of sorts; not so harmful as technologists, if sometimes more fantastic.

Newton was a reductionist against his will, because his contemporaries would insist that his phenomenalist account of the spectral colours was an investigation into occult causes of light and colours. Some made the same mistake about his Law of Gravitation, while calmly accepting Cartesian fables about vortices carrying the planets round in their orbits, so compelling Newton to devote a whole book of the *Principia* to refuting them —a very valuable book too, for its positive content as well as its negative argument. Reductionist checks are often badly needed.

Berkeley, I think, was reductionist by temperament, but he was also a discoverer, in *NTV*. He does appear to overdo his reduction in defining and restricting mathematical hypotheses (*DM*, §§ 66, 67). If by 'the natures of things' he means assumed occult causes or essences, then certainly mathematical hypotheses can and should be framed without them. But if, as he suggests in § 67, they are to be purely formal, depending only on arbitrary definition or convention, and if similar results can be attained by different hypotheses, then he is thinking of the kind of hypothesis that provides logicians with amusing toys, but not with the working hypotheses of the physicist. If he means no more than that, provided the numerical result of measuring an entity is the same, it makes no difference what you call the entity, there is no objection. I must, however, insist that mathematical hypotheses are concerned with what it is you measure and how, and in that the physicist needs complete freedom to *try* every device he can. If the one he chooses is wrong he can find out by trying and failing, and in no other way.

Berkeley at this crucial point in his text is not clear. If working scientists had taken the extreme kind of reductionist advice, then most of post-Newtonian physical science would have been smothered before birth. As it was, Mach's reductionist criticism at the end of the nineteenth century, had the chemists paid any attention to it, could have murdered a fine and lively science.

On the other hand, Berkeley was correct in pointing out that premature seventeenth-century speculations about what was later called *energy* were idle verbiage *at the time*; but after a century and a half *energy* could be and was defined and measured. The concept, if I may be allowed a horrid pun, could then perform useful work.

If experiments and theory are to be useful, not idle, then the system of mechanics requires *conservation principles*, i.e. definitions of things, processes or conditions, which we cannot alter whatever we do or however we do it. Descartes's instinct led him right in supposing that there should be some mathematical *function of motion* that is always *conserved* in all operations. He was premature in seizing on the first that came into his head, without testing it (perhaps he could not), nor trying any alternative. He supposed that the simplest function, directionless speed, was conserved, and it gave him an apparently neat solution for his problem of how the mind (which does not move) can interact mutually with the body (which does nothing else) by supposing it to alter the direction of motions without their total speed. Descartes's theory was very pretty, but could not be used; it was and is idle. Incidentally, nobody has shown by any positive test that his view of body-mind interaction is false. Nobody in the seventeenth and eighteenth centuries could do better than Descartes, nor yet worse.

To return to conservation; the nineteenth century acquired the technical apparatus from various sources and the theory along with it, also from various sources. They learnt what it is that the thermometer measures, and could define *heat energy*; they learnt about chemical and electro-magnetic *potential energy* and transformations between these and *kinetic energy*. Above all they had the steam engine which put to them the most searching questions about how *heat energy* can be turned into *kinetic energy* of a useful sort and how it cannot. (Does 'cannot' here mean 'never' or just 'very seldom'?)

All this was made clear in course of time; the eighteenth century had not yet acquired the tools for asking the questions or finding the answers. Time and observation alone can tell us which seed is dead and which is not yet ready to germinate.

Energy provides a useful *conservation principle* which goes a very long way, further than the nineteenth century could see. But it came with difficulty. There is another which came almost too easily so that it was hardly noticed. Newton just assumed it, as did Galileo, perhaps Archimedes, and it was left to Lavoisier (1789) to make the first serious empirical enquiry as to whether or how far it held or not; this principle is the conservation of mass, without which chemical analysis would never be quantitative at all. Recently it has been assumed that separately neither principle holds exactly, an assumption or mathematical hypothesis which has had quite remarkable consequences for practice and theory. Lastly, conservation principles are one type of what have been called *Postulates of Impotence*,[1] and of these the seventeenth and eighteenth centuries had no definite knowledge.

To come back to Newton, his notion of *force* might be called *the* (not *a*) *non-conservation principle*, namely that which distinguishes a system of bodies that is not interfered with, a *closed system*, from one which is an *open system*. Force can be made manifest in acceleration and measured, or else, in special cases, in stress or pressure. It is, for physics, *the* causal process; thus within the Newtonian system, there is no need, indeed no sense, in looking for causes of causes, as Berkeley maintained, in *DM*.

However, Newton himself realized that his own system was not complete. His Law of Gravitation provided all that the

[1] See above, p. 90, and my *Studies in the History and Methods of the Sciences*, (Edinburgh University Press, 1958) pp. 123 and 199.

astronomer then required for calculating acceleration, but said nothing about many small-scale terrestrial processes which make some bodies stick together and some fall apart, and specially nothing about chemical composition or decomposition, 'elective affinities' as he called them. He could discover nothing about them in spite of long and strenuous efforts, as he confesses in the long Query added to the 2nd edition of his *Opticks*. He had neither the technical nor the theoretical apparatus even to begin the work. The work began at the end of the eighteenth century and during this present century has gone a long way, since the structure of the atoms of the different chemical elements has gradually and in part become known. Could Newton possibly have guessed that one indispensable instrument for all this work was going to come from his simple experiment on the colours of the spectrum?

Any *a priori* general conclusion about reductionist criticism of science has to be very modest, because almost any speculation may look useful at first, even be useful. Only by taking a speculation seriously, working it out, then trying it out, can it be discovered to be useless. We are never compelled, though, to take it so seriously that it distorts our observations. All imaginative speculations (or models), such as science has to use, tend to be distorting and contrasting media—minute philosophy.

Theological speculation is different and has different criteria, temptations and risks.

VI

ARGUMENTS FOR FAITH IN GOD

§ 1 The Argument in *Alciphron*

THE defender of Christian faith has to meet attack from three different directions, fortunately for him incompatible, since the less scrupulous and less intelligent attackers often dodge from one to another. The first two are hardly more than rhetorical gambits and of course never put simply and brutally, as I intend to do here. The first is: 'I neither know nor care anything about God. *I only ask to be left alone.*' It was a new idea in the eighteenth century and Lysicles, who brings it up in *Alc.* (*Works*, vol. III, p. 163) does not make much of it. The nineteenth century invented a name, Agnosticism, which made it popular. The only genuine idea contained in it is in the words italicized. But they also contain the genuine difficulty. Nobody wants to be left alone except on special occasions, for special purposes of his own, at his own request; certainly not entirely always and for ever. Everybody, at times, is glad to have got himself born.

The second position of attack is plain atheism, which means: ' I know all about the whole universe, for I have examined it carefully from top to bottom. I have found no God there at all.'[1] Many nineteenth-century physicists or chemists claimed that their physics or chemistry had proved this very point, just as the eighteenth century claimed that the Newtonian system had. The experience of the last half century has produced more caution and less confidence about top or bottom.

The third position, which again I put frankly and brutally, is: 'I have no use for your Christian God, thank you, I have a more convenient one of my own.' This is Alciphron's position in the dialogue and the rival religion he professes is the popular caricature of Shaftesbury, who it must be confessed lent himself to caricature, but had many followers and indeed he crops up in recognizable form in many modern writers, who call themselves Humanists or even Scientific Humanists. Lysicles's more frivolous view owes more to Mandeville, who probably wrote with his

[1] Contrast Psalm CXXXIX, first 8 verses.

tongue in his cheek, but has long been forgotten, and even his ingenious economic fallacies are now seldom heard. However, these two contemporary forms of idolatry provide Berkeley with his opening. For his strategy was not passive defence but counter-attack (the military metaphor is his own; *Alc.*, *Works*, vol. III, p. 143). In most of his works, as I have mentioned, he is attacking some form of idolatry popular in his own day which interfered with an understanding of and obedience to God.

Those who sympathize with his strategy are placed in some difficulty. The idols that men have worshipped are innumerable, changing and conflicting. It seems wrong to deal with a few only, but nobody can hope to deal with all individually one by one, nor together collectively. However, let us first have a glance at history. Some very obvious forms of idolatry are relics of ancient forms of religion and ancient codes of morals, not all of them entirely false or bad; also ancient caricatures of religion and morals, which are distinctly worse. But there are also modern idols, modern forms of magic and witchcraft, and caricatures of things that may once have been genuine. The idols that were new and fashionable in Berkeley's day have led to still newer ones in our day, for as plants and animals and men evolve, devils evolve too. Those idols that are born of the human imagination are dangerous, perhaps more dangerous than any actual creature that God creates; for figments widely believed in acquire a power of their own; e.g. witchcraft is fraudulent, but where people believe in its potency it is potent, and it can actually kill them.

The Hebrews, thanks to their Prophets, beginning with Moses, escaped from the heavy yoke of ancient polytheism, learning, though painfully and gradually, of man's own true nature from God who created men in His image. Polytheism in its old and obvious forms is the reverse process by which the human imagination concocts idols in the image of men, animals and even lifeless things; and this goes on still in ever more subtle and elaborate forms.

One must not ignore the fact that theology begins with myth from which it tries to disentangle truth. This is just as children are taught by means of stories and first by means of make-believe ones, only later by means of true ones. The ordinary twentieth-century man believes implicitly all the myths of contemporary science in the hope that his descendants may learn better ones.

But in the meantime the process of education of man or, more simply, revelation to man has not ceased, though it reached its culminating stage nearly two thousand years ago. I need not here repeat what is said in summary form in the preface to St John's Gospel and in the opening words of the Epistle to the Hebrews. This is not to say that all other religions are false or useless, only that they are subject to greater limitations. You can walk on crutches, and sometimes you must if you are to walk at all, but under more normal conditions you do not need them. Nor is it to say that professing Jews and Christians never lapse into idolatry; quite the contrary. A large part of the teaching of the Old Testament and the New Testament is taken up with pointing to lapses and warnings against them. As I have said, the Devil evolves along with everything else. He is not so foolish now as to go about like a roaring lion. That was good enough to frighten desert nomads; now he uses more civilized methods.

Some may object to this wide use of the term 'idols' but there are good precedents. St Paul speaks of 'covetousness which is idolatry', an ancient idol that has never fallen out of favour. Francis Bacon uses the term very aptly to name a number of errors, intellectual as well as moral. Thus I need not apologize for using the term to cover all those errors of intellect and will by which we put our faith in creatures, including mere creatures of our own imagination, the lowest of all, in place of the one Creator. We are idolaters when in defiance of Plato as well as Moses we pay too much respect to the transient in place of the eternal, to effects in place of their cause, to shadows in place of substance, to parts in place of the whole, and, most frequent of all, prefer things which contain no image of God to persons who do, however distorted that image may be. This is not a complete list but full enough to indicate a precaution to be taken, in considering those of the contrasted terms which are spatial and temporal. Hours are not better nor more important than seconds, nor yet are millions of years, though they go on longer still; nor are kilometres better or more important than millimetres, nor yet light-years though they are bigger still. Worship of mere size is a strange, new and deadly kind of idolatry, from which the most benighted savage and the most superstitious rustic was entirely free in former times. It has been claimed that mathematics is the only science that has never done any harm to anybody; perhaps even mathematics has become corrupted.

Now a word about atheism. The 'foolish man' of Psalm XIV said in his heart: 'There is no God', and if he said it and then did no more he might be harmless, however foolish. But the man of Psalm X also said: 'Tush, God hath forgotten: he hideth away his face, and he will never see it.' He was dangerous and an idolater, who thought he could cheat God, perhaps with the help of some old-fashioned idol; perhaps he was the modern type who deceives himself solely by his faith in his own cleverness. The first weakness of the traditional forms of argument for the existence of God is that they carry no weight against the idolater, who has already convinced himself of the existence of his own idol by the help, perhaps, of his own caricatures of the ontological, cosmological and teleological arguments. Of course it would not be difficult to restate the traditional forms so as to begin with a refutation of caricatures, after the Scholastic fashion where you establish your thesis by refuting antitheses. But when that is done they will look like an attempt to establish a better idol in place of worse ones. This is clearly not a good method, even though the history of theological controversy may sometimes show it at work. The suggestion, however, brings out a second weakness that is actually present in the traditional forms. Discussions about idols are properly conducted in terms of I–It, because idols are mere objects, even if they are real objects, not figments. God is only to be discussed in terms of I–Thou, for we carry on our human discussion in His presence, and our discussion is in vain if we forget this. There is no discussion *of* God, that is not an invocation *to* God, like the discussion, if it can be so called, of Elijah with the priests of Baal. Certainly, Berkeley took his own discussion in this way. Unless I am much mistaken, St Anselm intended his ontological argument to be taken this way.

'The argument for the immediate providence of a Deity' (title page of *Dia.*), as Berkeley expresses it, needs to be put first in general terms to apply to common human experience and then there is room for special arguments about the particular providential interventions in human affairs to which Jews and Christians bear witness. That witness, however, is feeble if there is no comprehension of the immediate intervention of God available to everybody and anybody here, now, always and everywhere. All religious observance begins with an invocation—'Where two or three are gathered together in My Name, there am I in the midst of them.' Honest work is not so frequent as it should be, and when work is really honest it is done as in the presence of God. For most of us the pricking of conscience is the first clear acknowledgment of God's presence.

None of these examples is quite general enough for the purpose of Berkeley's argument; they all imply some sort of prior knowledge of God. Moreover, genuine worship, honest work, pricks of conscience are not quite universal in human experience.

There is, however, a difficulty about many kinds of very common experience. The sun shines equally upon the just and the unjust, as the rain also falls; but the unjust man always complains that he gets either too much or too little, even the just man is not too sure, while the self-righteous man takes his different and self-righteous view. But there are constant and common factors in sense experience about which differences of opinion are hardly possible, at least among ordinary people, not blind or deaf or otherwise handicapped.[1]

Now one further preliminary word. There is a pseudo-Platonist lurking in the hearts of most of us who considers the senses to be low and vulgar, hardly to be mentioned in polite society. Let us brush him aside, and go straight to the argument as it appears in *Alc.* in its simplest form, where reference is made directly to *NTV*, while the immaterialist part of the argument is not introduced. It is a change of tactics from *Princ.*, not of strategy. The argument by way of immaterialism is stronger, one would think, but had turned out to be unpopular and is not so simple.

Our daily life in the world, of avoiding injury, obtaining food and shelter, communicating with our friends, depends upon our learning in early life and continually using the universal, natural sign language of the senses. We have to know and use the prognostic signs of sense and specially of sight, the most far-reaching and comprehensively prognostic. Our use of this system, for it is systematic, is habitual, therefore normally unnoticed as being merely a use of signs and not intuition of causes, essences, necessities. But anybody who takes the trouble, as Berkeley did in *NTV*, can discover for himself that learning is needed and that things can, in exceptional cases, be different. Berkeley stresses, rightly, the relations of sight and touch, which are the most

[1] Even those both blind and deaf can acquire, with help, the necessary experience; cf. Helen Keller.

conspicuous and continually used, but others are also instructive.[1]

Euphranor, in the dialogue, claims that 'God speaks to man in the same clear and sensible manner as one man doth to another'. Alciphron will admit no other manner as satisfactory. 'I am for admitting no inward speech, no holy instincts or suggestion of light or spirit. If you do not make it plain to me that God speaks to man by outward sensible signs, of such sort and in such manner as I have defined, you do nothing.' Note that the criteria of divine utterance which Alciphron rejects are those which most people accept and those he accepts were hardly thought of till Berkeley produced them.

At any rate, Euphranor replies as requested. 'Light and colours, with their several shades and degrees; all which being infinitely diversified and combined, form a language wonderfully adapted to suggest and exhibit to us the distances, figures, situations, dimensions and various qualities of tangible objects: not by similitude nor yet by inference of necessary connection, but by the arbitrary[2] imposition of Providence, just as words suggest the things signified by them.' Note again, Euphranor has not said that he too rejects any appeal to 'inward speech, holy instincts, suggestion of light or spirit'. The language by which God chooses to speak need not be always one and the same for everybody on every occasion. But Alciphron has chosen his criterion and must abide by it.

A portion of the discussion is missing from our present text, which should come after Crito has spoken (*Alc.*, Dialogue IV, § 15–end) and before the three rejoin Lysicles at the tea-table. I venture to interpolate some of the missing passage:

Alciphron. I have been silent, Euphranor, while you have been answering Crito's questions about the strange doctrines of this Mr Berkeley; not for lack of interest, but because of distressing thoughts. I could find no fault with your reply to my challenge to show that God makes his presence known to us directly through our senses, as when one man speaks to another; yet I could not at once accept it. Now I am certain that I never can; and must explain.

We might all of us be in the predicament in which you state and accept. Any or every smallest idea that comes into the mind might be a

---

[1] Cf. above, Ch. III, § 2.

[2] 'Arbitrary' means 'willed', not 'irregular'.

command or prohibition or warning direct from God. At this moment He might be urging me to act in this way and not in that, at the peril of my soul. The supposition is intolerable, I protest against it, and ask for protection. A mere pagan god might leave me alone or be content with trifling ceremonies, but not your Christian God, who you say is perpetually at my elbow. I ask for a screen to protect me and so I think does every ordinary man of the world. If you call such screens 'idols' you are welcome but do not attempt to remove them.

The old pagan philosophers provided several such screens. The best of all is the doctrine of Substance expounded in its pristine and full-bodied form by the great Parmenides. His Substance is one, indivisible, universal, unchanging: a screen against all contingencies. The feebler doctrines of plurality of substances are confused, complicated, inconsistent, uncertain; I need not linger over them. Of the Substance of Parmenides I can only say, 'It is, as it is'; and that is all I need to say. I cannot say, 'It changes.' That is precisely what I do not wish to say. If I am momentarily deceived by any appearance of change I know that even that appearance is reversed by an equal and opposite appearance. This, the noble doctrine of *isonomia*, has been revived by one of our deepest modern sages. Truly and in reality nothing ever happens, nobody acts, decides, even thinks, nobody is held responsible or praised or blamed; all is as it is.

This I say is the complete and perfect doctrine. But if you are too weak for it you can have others. I cannot accept all Mr Berkeley's teaching, if I heard aright; but I have no need to quarrel with his view of substance and can use it to my purpose. He condemns recent theories about substance but his condemnation does not affect me. He says that substance is senseless, stupid, inert; let it be so. I do not pretend to see or touch substance, nor yet imagine it. I need it only as a screen against what I might imagine; and the more senseless, the stupider, the more inert the better.

Even more useful to me is the doctrine of a young man whom I met in France recently. He is a Mr David Hume and he allowed me to peruse some of the MSS. of a book which he is writing. He claims that substance, in every sense of the word, ancient and modern, is to be considered to be a fiction. We all feign that substance exists because by so doing we make the world appear to be more uniform and regular than anything which untouched experience actually shows us. This kind of feigning is a universal human habit. When we examine our mental life carefully we find we have the habit, are using it continually and no effort of mind can prevent us doing this, except momentarily. There is no habit more useful to man than to be content with habit and look no further. Mr Hume provides me with a screen almost as good as that of Parmenides, and easier on the mind. I am not afraid of the word 'fiction'; I do not expect eternal truth. I am afraid of perpetual responsibility, for I want peace and quiet. As long as habit and fiction can give it to me I shall ask for no more.

But enough of these grave, disturbing topics. We need something lighter to discuss over tea.

This is what the plain man would say if he could bring himself to understand the paradoxes of the philosophers before jeering at them. On the other hand there is another story to tell, far nearer to Berkeley's and far removed from that I have put into the mouth of Alciphron.

Berkeley's view is, in short, that experience is given to us by God for learning and for going on learning, not for taking a rest all the time and sticking to habits whether good or bad. This is precisely what the great scientific discoverers have done. The great discoverers are very few and must not be confused with the little discoverers who are many and talk louder, nor the hangers-on who are more numerous still and talk still louder. The great discoverers know that each new discovery is a revelation from God and a work of art. It carries no ordinary signature, so that snobs and popular journalists do not recognize that it is a work of art. The connoisseurs, though, do and have no hesitation in naming the Artist, whose style is unmistakable. Note that this is not the old artificer metaphor. It is not that of a hireling doing routine or repetitive 'jobs' just well enough to get his wages. It is creation in the sense of making something out of nothing or producing a unique life out of death. What is more, the discoverer knows also that only a small part has yet been revealed, even more is still to be discovered. The greatest of all the fallacies of the little discoverer is that the work of discovery has been almost completed (thanks to his valuable help) and only details remain to be filled in. It would be nearer the mark to say, as Newton did, that discovery is hardly yet begun. Three more centuries have revealed more and left still more unrevealed.

Berkeley's procedure and conclusions do not exclude any part of experience, not the most extraordinary, nor the most private, nor the entirely unique, but he does not begin with these. He begins at the other end with what links all these together, which nobody can reject saying: 'I know nothing about that or anything of the sort. It may be just a private whim of yours or of some of your friends.'

The method is comparable to Euclid's. He says: 'Here is one specimen of a triangle; it might be any one, but here *it* is before you and you can see for yourself that *it* has such and such properties. If you have any doubts, try another, or another. Now universalize what you have discovered, for here are instances of universal order.' In Berkeley's argument the order is that of Providence, in providing certain basic conditions by means of which we can keep alive.

One final point about Berkeley's conclusions is needed to show how he differs from nearly all his contemporaries. Even Leibniz acquiesced (though it must have gone against the grain) in the idea of a Creator who had done all the creating long ago and just left behind a Pre-established Harmony. For Berkeley God is now and everywhere actively creating (*Alc.*, *Works*, vol. III, p. 160). The harmony which a conductor can produce by means of his orchestra and their instruments is not produced instantaneously nor once only, nor once and for all, but is being produced anew during each performance. Note again that this is not the false *artificer* analogy but another, though still an imperfect one. It could be slightly improved if we assumed that the conductor was also composer and also could leave the players to improvise occasionally. Thus no performance would be a repetition, but each one a new work.

§ 2 IDOLS OF SUBSTANCE AND OTHER IDOLS

The seventeenth century, more than any other age since Thales is said to have said 'Everything is water', was the age of metaphysics of substance, cf. Gassendi, Hobbes, Descartes, Spinoza; naturally it was followed by that of the critics of substance, cf. Locke, Berkeley, Hume, Kant. Since then nobody who considered himself a philosopher has had a good word to say for substance. Apart from all this process of the *Zeitgeist*, Berkeley was by nature, as I suspect, more Hebraic than Hellenic in his thinking. His cosmology, so far as he made it explicit, is one of Wills, not of things, nor of stuff. He has therefore a certain affinity with Leibniz, who was a substantialist of a very peculiar sort. The real world for him is spiritual, as for Berkeley, and the corporeal is no more than phenomenal, there are no atoms, no void, no plenum either. Apart from the special topic of infinitesimals, and Leibniz might have compromised on that, there is nothing in Leibniz to worry Berkeley; it is a pity they never met, and that Leibniz, at second hand, supposed he was just concocting paradoxes.

As to substance, the first point to make is how much it hindered theology, as indicated by the words I put into the mouth of Alciphron above (p. 124). The second point is that in any of the ancient forms it was not necessary or even useful to science, early or late.[1] What all science requires both early and late is a clear distinction between what, in any investigation, is to be taken as *continuant* and what in contrast is to be taken as *occurrent* (W. E. Johnson, *Logic*, I, 192). The distinction is not absolute but relative to the investigator's purpose, context, and instruments. A *continuant* is for him anything relevant, which is always there and to be relied on not to vary significantly on the time and space scale he is using. For primitive astronomers earth and sky are prime continuants; next come the fixed stars, once it has been sufficiently established by observation that they are recognizable and do not vary in number and relative position; next come the planets (sun, moon and five others) whose changes are confined to locomotions among the fixed stars, locomotions which can then be investigated to see whether they follow rules. No occurrences can be reduced to rule at all until they have been referred to continuants.[2]

No *continuant* need be assumed to be everlasting or absolutely stable, and modern physics is pretty clearly showing that none is. All that is required is considerable constancy for a considerable time, enough to be able to recognize without ambiguity and clearly distinguish between occurrents and continuants. This rule applies more especially to the instruments used. These, if rigid, must be entirely continuant, no significant movement must occur among their parts during the process of observation; or, if by any chance they do, must be subject to effective control by separate observations. Instruments with moving parts are both continuant and occurrent, and subject to a similar rule, *mutatis mutandis*. For example, all astronomical instruments are subject to small systematic errors. These have to be observed carefully, plotted out, all

---

[1] For the question of *chemical substances* see below, Ch. VIII. They are in any case *species* first and *continuants* second.

[2] Note that in ancient times comets and meteors, in the modern sense, were referred, not to the *heavens*, but to *sublunar* regions to which clouds belong.

observations corrected for them, and they should also be checked at intervals.[1]

Consider also a different kind of example. A physiologist (A) who is studying the functions of muscles of animals, takes the bones to be among the *continuants*, the muscles themselves, within limits, as *continuants* and the muscular movements as *occurrent*. Physiologist (B), who is studying processes of growth, takes both bones and muscles as *occurrent*, but the whole animal as a sort of *continuant*. The difference between (A) and (B) is mainly a matter of time and space scales. (A) will use a time scale of seconds (between 1/1,000″ and 1,000″), which will accommodate the muscular activities of both mosquitoes and tortoises. His space scale will be of centimetres, with a similar margin, or a bit longer on the large scale if he is dealing with human athletic efforts. (B) generally needs a longer time scale, though not so much longer for the growth of microscopic organisms, quite a lot longer for the growth of men or forest trees. Moreover different scales call for different instruments.

There is nothing here to disturb either Newton or Berkeley, nor that requires more than Kant's 1st and 2nd Analogies. Sooner or later however the 3rd Analogy must come in, and incidentally it is to that Category of Reciprocity that we should look to deal with any difficulty over *chemical substances*, which are first and fundamentally Aristotelian *species* (see Ch. VIII below, and my *Studies in the History and Methods of the Sciences*, pp. 104-5).

There is no scientific excuse for taking the category of substance (nor that of cause) any further than stated above. Nor is there any excuse from any other source. Cosmologically they are subordinate categories, and theologically of the second degree of subordination unless used for idolatrous purposes.

Quite apart from legitimate metaphysical purposes mentioned above, the eighteenth century was the period of maximum substance idolatry. More particularly the whole idea of Providence and of everything with which the teleological argument should be concerned was degraded and made vulnerable to Hume's criticisms in *Dialogues concerning Natural Religion*. God the Creator had been turned into an *artificer*, one who manipulates pre-existing material, moving things from one place to another

[1] Probably more of the astronomer's time is spent observing the tricks of his instruments than observing the heavens.

place, but never *creating* anything. A very interesting point about *Timaeus* is the way in which it shows Plato already entangled in, yet struggling against, the *artificer* theory of cosmology (or cosmogony if you like), in the fourth century B.C., while Christians of the eighteenth century A.D., who should have known better, never put up a struggle at all.

Worse was yet to come. An anthropomorphic *artificer* had been invented to take the place of the Creator, but no sooner invented than forgotten in favour of a mechanomorphic idol, a machine that makes itself or else needs no making at all for it just grinds on for ever and for ever. Descartes had warned them. If there was a machine the physicist will observe it, and the geometrical and mechanical relations of its working parts; but while it is at work he will never observe any *artificer* at work on it. No human machine is self-maintaining, much less self-designing, self-constructing, self-starting, self-controlling. It used to be supposed that for a machine not to be self-maintaining was an accidental defect of design or craftsmanship, as if it were understandable that a cheap alarm clock should not be self-maintaining, but surely Harrison's chronometer must be. It would be a lesser error to argue the other way about. Because an alarm clock is inaccurate, cheap and mass-produced it is not worth maintaining; as soon as anything fails you scrap it and get a new one. But a good chronometer is well worth the labour and cost of maintaining and many have been maintained with loving care for a century or more.

The most striking feature of machine idolatry is that the idolaters are equally ignorant of the nature of God and of machines. It is inherent in the humanly available materials and mode of construction that machines with metallic moving parts wear out; friction, play and backlash are processes inherent and not accidental. (Presumably this applies *mutatis mutandis* to electronic machines, even if they take longer to wear out. See note below, p. 130.

To sum up: no machine exists, much less works, without its special human satellites to design, make, start up, maintain in working order, control and finally scrap it. Machines are parasites of man; despite all the latest superstitions, men have to do all the thinking for them and do it beforehand. What has just been said answers questions about 'living machinery' in principle. If carefully interpreted, this is an apt and penetrating metaphor. No completely autotrophic organism, such as a green plant, whether microscopic *alga* or forest tree, is itself, taken as whole, in the least like a machine, but any one of its functionally distinct and separable parts or organs (i.e. instruments) is machinelike and is also parasitic on the rest *qua* whole organism, not just part. Consider *one* separate green leaf operating as an organ. Consider also that in a few, but only a few species, a separated leaf can be planted out as a 'cutting' and produce a new plant. Those plants and animals that are naturally parasitic in habit are all machinelike, because parasitic. Lastly, and this is the nasty part, all animals are parasitic on green plants if not on one another, and of all animals man is the most fatally destructive parasite. This should suffice to indicate the limits within which machine analogies can be properly used for cosmological and theological purposes.

We can now, in the twentieth century, treat substances and machines with more than Berkeleian scorn for we know more about them.[1]

In *Alciphron* Berkeley deals with the fashionable idols of the 'bright young people' of the early eighteenth century, who were remarkably like their successors of the 1920's and 1930's. Lysicles and Alciphron could then be found in Staff Commonrooms at Oxbridge, Redbrick and other universities as well as in lower haunts. They quoted or misquoted different authors but their

[1] Human machines are all made from different materials on a different scale of dimensions suited to these materials, as compared with plant or animal machinery. The man-made chronometer is a much simpler machine subserving one function only; the smallest single muscle fibre, of microscopic dimensions, is a more complex machine subserving other functions besides motion and on the whole self-maintaining. (Examine a live cyclops, or one of the common marine copepods under the microscope, and you will see single muscle fibres at work.)

The electro-magnetic and mechanical toys (I use the word 'toy' deliberately) which have been recently demonstrated imitating animal behaviour are crude caricatures that would not for one moment deceive a biologist, and no different in principle from the 'automata' that amused seventeenth-century princes. To pack into one of them all the functions to be found in one cyclops or many much smaller living creatures, would need a building as large as a house and quite mobile. The man-made machine cannot be on the small scale of the living organism because of its different materials, and also because the rule for man-made machines is 'one bit of structure for one function', while the rule for living organisms is 'many functions for one structure'. On Laplacean idols see my *Studies in the History and Methods of the Sciences*, p. 199.

idols were much the same, and their criticisms of Christian belief and practice identical almost word for word with those of the original 'minute philosophers'. This is because they suffered from the same 'poverty of imagination and narrowness of soul' (Berkeley in *Essays in the Guardian*, 1713, *Works*, vol. VII, p. 183). The particular theories of Mandeville, Shaftesbury or others, now forgotten, are not very important, any more than those of their modern equivalents. The point that needs to be noticed is that newer 'minute philosophers', in every age, tend to resemble either Lysicles or Alciphron. The first is too superior to listen to any Christian (or bourgeois) talk about moral right or wrong; the second lives a much superior, more moral life, which dispenses with slavish obedience to any external authority, human or superhuman. Lysicles is convicted of ignoring ordinary common knowledge about social and political life, anything more abstruse would be wasted on him. Alciphron has to be taken more seriously, but his moral optimism is shallow and he has to be shown that God's authority is not what he supposes and is neither merely human nor yet merely external. No further discussion of *Alciphron* is needed here; we must pass on to the idol of *The Analyst* for brief comment.

The Analyst, besides being a criticism of mathematical theory, is an attack on the Righteousness of the Pharisees of Science, then appearing for the first time in history (though I should not be greatly surprised had it been anticipated in the ancient world.) At any rate a few of the men of science were then beginning to say that their morals were too pure to allow them to mix with the riff-raff of Publicans and Sinners who called themselves Christians. There is a pleasing irony about the eighteenth-century situation. Berkeley, the mere Christian theologian, succeeded in pricking the super-Pharisees, the mathematicians, in a tender spot and also started a new development of an ancient controversy.

Unfortunately, Berkeley wrote in English for a British audience, not in Latin for a continental one. He therefore attacked Newton's *Fluxions*, not Leibniz's *Infinitesimals*. (There is no difference in method except in notation; Leibniz's, the easier to use, is now universal.) Now Leibniz had faith in his infinitesimals, a metaphysical faith about space, time and motion, in terms of which he would have defended himself, or one of his followers might. In such a case Berkeley would have been called on to produce his own metaphysical faith, perhaps in *minima sensibilia*, and the battle might have been fought out. It never has been. Newton's British followers were not interested in metaphysics, nor was Newton. It is almost certain that Newton in his early days considered his *fluxions* to be no more than a useful labour-saving dodge, to discover mathematical relations rather than to prove them. In the *Principia*, where proofs were required, he used older more orthodox methods. Had he been tackled early, before the controversy over priority between him and Leibniz, he would probably have agreed to most of Berkeley's argument, so far as Berkeley actually put it into print. It was Newton's followers who supposed the method to be exact and to provide fully satisfactory proof. As the battle was not fought out, we do not even know whether Berkeley would have stuck to the *minima sensibilia* of his early days. Nevertheless he did succeed in making some of the British mathematicians begin to think and to realize that their faith in Newton (or Leibniz) was faith and not reason.

Men of science have mostly been rashly optimistic about the precision, generality and reliability of their own methods and theories, and few have been as cautious, cold-blooded and sceptical as they make themselves out to be, except about other people's methods and theories.[1]

Galileo was a better theologian than those who attacked him,[2] but quite a bit of his scientific faith was rash speculation and provided useful weapons for his opponents. Much of Descartes's physics was not only rash but totally unfounded speculation. Plenty of examples could be quoted from three subsequent centuries, specially the twentieth. To come back to the mathematicians. The mathematician at work is one man, the mathematician talking about his work is another, one often involved in loose metaphors, slang, and generally careless in his use of language. Moreover he has no private infallible criterion by which to test the validity of his methods. He has to try them out on familiar material and simple cases and see whether they always produce the expected result. A new mathematical argument which, when first used, appears to show that Achilles never over-

---

[1] Cf. M. Polanyi, *Personal Knowledge*, 1958.

[2] Cf. his letter to the Archduchess of Tuscany, English Translation, Thos. Salusbury, 1661, Pt I. There is a modern reprint of a large part of Salusbury's text by R. Ulich in *3,000 Years of Educational Wisdom*, 1954.

takes the Tortoise has to be looked at with suspicion, until you can get it to give you a more orthodox answer.

What is more important for our immediate purpose is that Berkeley was the first to puncture the Pharisaical conceit, moral and intellectual, of certain scientists.[1] Swift, of course, tried to do it in his account of 'Laputa', but had not himself the necessary information.

APPENDIX TO CHAPTER VI

Note on the relation of Berkeley's argument to the three traditional types.

Berkeley leaves little room for the cosmological type as found in St Thomas or the eighteenth-century metaphysicians, for it is based on the categories of substance and cause, and is thus irrelevant to Berkeley's cosmology so far as we can see it in his earlier works. He could have gone further than Kant who only condemned their use outside the sphere of natural science, but Kant when he said it had already stripped them of all or nearly all that Berkeley's objected to.

As to the ontological argument, Berkeley is clearly saying, 'Consider those things in your experience whereby you are able to keep alive from day to day and hour to hour without ceasing; and now behold the work of your Creator.' He does not say, 'Behold your Creator.' We must distinguish at the very least between *Natura naturans* and *Natura naturata*, or else fall into hopeless pantheistic confusion. The works we behold; the Creator we do not. Granted that, then the argument is ontological, in intention, however different in form from St Anselm's. All the being of God that can be present to us is present always, whenever and wherever we look; and 'look' may be taken as literally and also as metaphorically as you like.

Again, the works of God which we see are providentially ordered *for* us and not *by* us. Here is the teleological argument stripped of the encumbrances of substance, artificer and artifact.

[1] [For an elucidation of *The Analyst* and its problems, see J. O. Wisdom's three articles in *Hermathena*, nos. 54, 57, and 59 on 'The Analyst Controversy'. See also for a more general discussion G. J. Whitrow, 'Berkeley's Critique of the Newtonian Analysis of Motion', *Hermathena*, no. 82.]

VII

MORALS, POLITICS AND ECONOMICS

§ 1 BERKELEY'S OCCASIONAL WORKS

'Whatever the world thinks, he who hath not much meditated upon God, the human mind and the *summum bonum*, may possibly make a thriving earthworm, but will most undubitably make a sorry patriot and a sorry statesman' (*Siris*, §350).

MOST academic persons, and clergy too, who write political pamphlets or essay political journalism, show themselves second-rate politicians writing in a second-hand manner, below usual academic standards. Berkeley's occasional political writings are different. I say 'occasional' literally; they were produced for some specific occasion, addressed to a particular audience, to persuade or advise for a specific purpose. He did not talk down to his audience, the favourite academic vice, nor take them for earthworms, the favourite political vice; rather, he endeavoured to promote meditation such as that of the chapter heading.

I shall comment at some length on the early essay *Passive Obedience*[1] (1712, Three Discourses in Trinity College Chapel), then, briefly, on the *Essay towards preventing the Ruine of Great Britain* (1721) and *The Querist* (1735), often reprinted and widely and profitably read. These comments will be preliminary to those on *Siris*, Berkeley's last work, which brings together in a fashion all the different strands of his thought. It has been neglected and despised because its language has become unfashionable; yet it is worth trying to understand.

The first of the three writings named is a discussion of the principles of moral conduct, couched in general terms, based upon a careful drawing of distinctions, not using models, illustrations or parables, nor yet an appeal to authorities. It is the kind of

---

[1] [It is a pity Ritchie did not go on to comment on Berkeley's *Discourse addressed to Magistrates and Men in Authority*. A powerful defence of intellectual censorship, it illustrates strikingly the side of Berkeley with which Ritchie is concerned in his analysis of the passive obedience discussion. (Vol. VI, Luce–Jessop edition, pp. 201–22.)]

argument to be found in University teaching of ethics and political theory; and it was addressed in the first instance to an academic audience, not to the general public. Its general theme is the Socratic one, that it is better for a man to suffer injustice with patience than impatiently to inflict injustice. It is concerned, however, with one special kind of injustice and that the burning topic of the day, in Ireland and other parts of the British Isles, namely whether or not rebellion can be morally justified.

The time was 1712, the place Dublin, the audience Irish, mainly Protestant and for the most part young. The primary sovereign authority ('government' for short) was that of Queen Anne in Dublin, but she also had another Government in London; she also had not very long to live. The first problem was who was to succeed her? the second was, how? So far as laws can settle these things it should be George, Elector of Hanover. There was another claimant, called, according to your political views 'The Pretender' or 'The King over the Water'.

§ 2 ANALYSIS OF BERKELEY ON PASSIVE OBEDIENCE

[Here Ritchie intended to quote from Professor T. E. Jessop's analysis of the doctrine of passive obedience in vol. VI of the Luce–Jessop edition. In order to elucidate Ritchie's discussion, the Jessop synopsis of Berkeley has been transcribed in full—vol. VI, loc. cit., pp. 8–11. This extensive quoting is justified from Ritchie's point of view, in that it brings home to the modern 'liberal-minded' reader what 'illiberal', anti-Lockeian theory is like, and how reasonable it can be.]

ANALYSIS OF THE ARGUMENT

I. Non-resistance to the supreme civil power is an absolute obligation. §§ 4–32.

i. Civil loyalty is a moral duty. §§ 4–25.

(a) The moral end—§§ 4–7. The moral rules or laws of Nature are to be discovered by reason. Reason proves the existence of God, and it follows from His nature that His will is our law. Since the purpose of His will cannot be His own good, it must be the good of man, of all men everywhere and in all ages. This, then, is the moral end.

(*b*) The means to it—§§ 8–14. That end is not of itself a sufficient guide to action, for none of us has enough knowledge or wisdom to foresee what particular decisions would lead to it. Even our best impulses cannot be trusted uncontrolled. The means to the moral end can be certainly known only as general rules, discoverable by reason, and never to be deviated from by private judgment of the relation of the particular case to that end.

(*c*) Loyalty is such a rule of reason—§§ 15–20. Like justice, chastity, etc., it has a necessary connection with the moral end; it is, indeed, the fundamental rule or duty, since it is the condition of ordered society, within which alone the remaining moral duties can be discharged. The relation of subject to law, being thus not accidental but essential and therefore universal, needs to be governed by a general moral law.

(*d*) Three objections against loyalty as a moral duty—§§ 21–5. First, civic disobedience is not felt with the repugnance which moral vices evoke. True; but feelings, being the result of the accidents of our upbringing, are not the criteria of what is morally good or bad. Secondly, civic obedience rests on a social contract, the breach of which by the ruler makes rebellion lawful. No; such a contract is not expressed or implied in any constitution nor is it involved in the notion of political society; and in practice the regarding of rulers as deputies would lessen respect for law and tend to destroy the social tie. Thirdly, political government is man-made, so that the measure of submission to it is an affair not of moral but of civil law. No; loyalty to an institution that, though man-made, makes man, is not a merely conventional obligation.

ii. Negative moral precepts are absolute—§§ 26–32.

Positive moral precepts, not all being applicable in a given situation, and often not one of them being fully applicable, leave room for discretion; but negative precepts can in fact always be obeyed, and ought to be, since vice is unconditionally wrong. The moral order, like the physical, would not be an order without general laws. It cannot be objected that even so private judgment must still come into play, in judging the criterion and content of moral laws—for these are matters of reason; or that the moral end, in instances where a general precept would have consequences inconsistent with it, should itself be made the direct rule of action —for what makes an action obligatory is not its probable tendency to the general good, but its being in accordance with a law that is necessarily implied by the concept of the general good, and therefore a law of Nature, and therefore an expression of the will of God, and therefore unequivocally binding.

II. The grounds and reasons of the contrary view. §§ 33–40.

i. Self-preservation is the first law of Nature.

Yes, but as a law of fact only, not of duty. If it were the latter, it would sanction all sins—which is absurd; and no negative precept is to be broken to observe a positive one, i.e. evil may not be committed to produce good.

ii. The public good is the measure of civic obedience.

This point has already been answered.

iii. No civil power can rightly have unlimited control over the life of any man.

True; but it follows only that resistance to an unjust ruler does not wrong the ruler. A wrong is done to God, since a negative rational law is broken.

iv. Non-resistance would be slavery.

No; no more than is the subjection of our passions to reason, this and civic obedience being the condition of our humanity.

v. Tyrants are wicked.

Of course; but the purpose of passive obedience is to honour not them but a law of God.

vi. Since active obedience is limited, why not passive obedience also?

Because positive and negative precepts are not on the same footing: the former can commit us to a wrong act, and the latter cannot.

III. Objections against non-resistance on the ground of its supposed consequences. §§ 41–56.

i. A law that brings suffering on the innocent cannot be God's law.

But such an effect is not a necessary one, the purpose and natural tendency of the law being otherwise; but an accidental one, due to the violation by the ruler of other moral laws. Besides, God rights the wrong in the next life.

ii. Unfailing submission would only encourage tyranny.

No; if a ruler is good, he will not become a tyrant, and if bad, being ruled by self-interest he will be aware that his subjects would be goaded by excesses into defending their interests—a lesser crime all but necessitated by his greater one.

iii. By precluding redress the law of non-resistance makes oppression all the more intolerable.

But rebellion, whether successful or no, produces enormous suffering; and it ignores the possibility that, under Providence, the tyrant will be either converted or removed by death.

iv. Are there not exceptional instances in which rebellion is right?

No; rebellion is a sin, and a sin can never be right. If exceptional oppression should occur, the ruler's ministers would be morally obliged not to execute the decrees.

v. The only obedience incumbent on rational beings is rational obedience, resting on the recognition of the suitability of the laws to the public good.

But most men are not qualified to examine and judge the laws.

vi. Complete submission would place men in a position worse than the anarchy from which politically organized society is the rational escape.

No; anarchy is worse.

vii. Must we submit even to usurpers and madmen?

No; this is excluded. The law of non-resistance applies only where there is a rightful ruler. This is a limitation of the law only in the sense of being a definition of it. Like all other negative moral laws, once the sphere of its application is defined, it allows of no exceptions under calculation of inconvenient consequences.

§ 3 WHIG AND TORY THEORIES

Berkeley makes it clear in his Preface and opening paragraphs that he is opposing certain popular doctrines: i. that submission to government is to be measured and limited by Public Good, for which government is instituted; ii. that subjects may resist even by violence, if public good plainly requires it; iii. more, that they ought to resist because to promote public good is a universal obligation.

These three propositions belong to the Whig type of tradition, or Utilitarian theory, or the doctrine of Natural Rights.[1] They all assume that the individual citizen is able to predict the civil consequences of his actions; a very rash assumption.

Berkeley also emphasizes that he opposes the extreme Whiggish view of Conditional Obedience, 'I obey the King's or Magistrate's commands, when I approve of them, otherwise not.' He also makes it clear that he opposes basing loyalty purely on prudence or expediency, as Hobbes does (up to a point).

It can be seen in the course of discussion that Berkeley also opposes the Tory doctrine that we can distinguish between an authority which is *de jure* even if not *de facto* and one which is only *de facto* and not *de jure*. Berkeley had to be careful not to invoke Hobbes in support, but he explained his position in a letter to Percival (*Works*, vol. VIII, pp. 21–3). Berkeley is expounding a moderate case, Tory rather than Whig. His advice is intended for both Tories and Whigs and mainly for Protestants, but there is nothing that he could not have said to Roman Catholics and Priests, whom he did actually write to publicly in 1745, when he was Bishop of Cloyne and the Young Pretender landed in Moidart.

The points which he had to establish are two. The first (*Passive Obedience*, §§ 4–26) is that passive obedience, submission to the commands, which can be enforced, of the constitutional and legal government through its recognized officials is a moral duty which is required of all citizens on all occasions. More than this is not required, neither expressed approval nor active assistance. The second point (§§ 26–32) is the more interesting philosophically as bringing out a neglected distinction between what Berkeley calls *negative* duties, of which this is one, and *positive* duties. The generally recognized negative duties are to refrain from acts of

[1] Cf. D. G. Ritchie, *Natural Rights*, 1895.

violence, fraud, deceit and other malicious acts against persons. These duties are universal, absolute, admit of no exceptions and apply equally to all persons, at all times, places and occasions, and without regard to probable consequences. Positive duties vary from person to person, occasion to occasion, and depend upon consideration of consequences. For example, while the last five of the Ten Commandments are purely negative, the Fifth is positive. Each son or daughter has positive duties to his or her father and mother, which are different according to age, particular needs and particular circumstances, and are in this way hypothetical. Those who have no parents have no duties; those who have no children have no claims. A child who is crippled or blind cannot nurse a sick parent; he or she must find some other way to perform their duty. Similarly a citizen's positive duty to assist the government depends upon his normal functions in life and his skills; the physician's duties are different from the lawyer's; the blind or crippled cannot be asked to assist the police in dealing with offenders, though all are asked to pay their taxes. Even the commonest positive civic duty, to serve on juries, is hypothetical; 'when called upon'.

What was most novel and unpopular about Berkeley's view, in his day and his country, was his inclusion of passive obedience to government among the negative duties, familiar and generally acknowledged by all, even when disobeyed, such as the last five Commandments. Irish Whigs would mostly have repudiated any definite moral obligation to Tory governments, perhaps even to Whig governments. Irish Tories, Roman Catholics, or peasants who had not yet reached these subtle eighteenth-century distinctions, would almost certainly hold the traditional view of personal loyalty to King, Feudal Superior or Clan Chief, or just family loyalty. These loyalties are exclusive and particular, but also total and not to be separated into positive and negative parts.

§ 4 THE DOCTRINE OF NATURAL LAW

The basic assumption from which Berkeley starts is that there are general moral laws which are discovered by the natural intuition of human reason, or, if you wish, by observation of God's world. This is the ancient doctrine of Natural Law to be found in Aristotle, the Stoics, especially Cicero, and the Scholastics; even, in a special form, in Hobbes; also in Locke, though Locke began also the deviation into a new doctrine of Natural Rights. Berkeley chooses to call them Laws of God, as many others before him, and as his whole system of thought demanded. This way of stating them was also congenial to any Irish audience, Protestant or Catholic. Berkeley explains that our human reason can find Moral Laws in the natural world only because the world is governed by a Creator, so that processes of that world lead to ends which can be seen to be good.

On the other hand we have no *general* insight into positive ends or purposes, into which our use of means is going to lead us. At the most we can make some probable predictions about the particular consequences of individual acts of our own, relating to individual persons we know and with whom we collaborate directly (e.g. those specified in the Fifth Commandment).

The most illuminating way of explaining the difference that Berkeley's theistic treatment makes is to compare his account with Hobbes's. Hobbes emphasizes the Law (or Laws) of Nature and his attempt to formulate them (if plural) is quite as good as, if not better than, any up to his time and many since; but for him the laws are purely hypothetical until something has happened to actualize them. He might have used his psychological terminology and called them 'phantasms'. What has happened is the Original and, once made, indissoluble Contract, which has created the body politic, commonwealth or Great Leviathan. This is a purely human act by a hypothetical multitude, who previously did nothing but prey upon and destroy one another, to hand over all that they possessed (with one solitary exception which they could not hand over) to one of their number to use henceforth on their collective behalf.

Now, if a young would-be rebel had come to Hobbes for his advice, the advice would have been as definitely 'No' as Berkeley's, and much grimmer. Hobbes would say, 'You have suffered no injustice at all, me lad, and can suffer none at the hands of any actual government or its agents; see my *Leviathan*, Pt I, Ch. 15, and Pt II, Ch. 18. You now propose to do the greatest possible injustice, because rebellion is the road to anarchy, and anarchy is worse, as you would realize if you used your reason, than the worst possible government. You may have been unlucky in the particular agents of government you came up against, but you will be unluckier still when there are none to come up against. You should grin and bear it. If you are a theist you have a consolation, that although agents of government cannot be unjust yet they can be iniquitous and God will punish them in Hell for it. If you keep quiet He will not punish you.' Though Hobbes is as materialist, rationalist and hedonist as could be wished, he also professes to be a theist and a Christian, to the great annoyance of all later materialists, rationalists and hedonists. But his theism comes only at the end of his political theory, not at the beginning, where it would have fitted better.

The one exceptional right which Hobbes says no man can hand over to the sovereign power of the commonwealth, is the right of self-preservation. However, it should not be called a right (*jus*) in the sense in which Hobbes defines it, much less a law (*lex*) in the sense in which he defines that; it is an animal instinct, urge or habit, as Berkeley points out. Many who have respected law have in fact handed it over, as did Socrates. This exception does not make things any more comfortable to the rebel or the would-be rebel. It only means that governments anticipating trouble from the rebellious provide armed guards to arrest them (*Leviathan*, Pt I, Ch. 14).

A further peculiarity of Hobbes's theory remains to be mentioned. In a general way it is correct to call Hobbes a hedonist, because he knows of no human ends or purposes except for each to seek his own individual pleasure and avoid his own individual pain or misery. But this does not admit of any summation or accretion of pleasures or pains, each of which is what it is at the time it is felt and exists only for the individual who feels it when he feels it; sympathy and benevolence are psychological *simulacra*. Thus there is no *summum bonum* but there most definitely is a *summum malum*, namely death, which comes sooner or later to each one of us separately. The sooner the worse, hence our supposed inalienable right to make it come later.

Berkeley did not mention Hobbes; nobody did in those days who argued against him, neither Locke nor Butler, for example, and nobody argued for him. Hobbes was a red rag to every political bull, Whig or Tory, English, Scottish or Irish.

§ 5 THE REPLY TO HOBBES

The moral and political theory of Hobbes is ferocious, crude, exalts the place of mere self-preservation, reduces happiness to illusion; it is rigid, artificial and has all the vices of the Great Machine Theory of the Universe, for it is part of it. It is expounded in terms of imaginary insensible entities (or 'phantasms'). It turns moral laws into replaceable machine parts, either in full working order and quite rigid or else completely broken. In one thing though Hobbes is perfectly correct. There is no secular *summum bonum*: we should not pretend to have insight into it or knowledge about it. We do have some insight into a *malum*, or *mala*, and among them death, which for the secularist only is the final and worst. From this point Hobbes begins to go wrong.

Survival is not itself a good or end, it is a means. Those who survive do so because they possess a skill which, with a little luck to help, postpones an evil, death, the 'last enemy', not the first, for that is what may be called compendiously, *ill-will*. It has many forms, from simple direct passion to hurt, or malice, to more elaborate kinds of ill-will, such as covetousness, which can amount, as St Paul says, to idolatry.

This is where Berkeley comes in. He needs no 'phantasms', or imaginary machines. (Actual machines are human toys.) For him as for the Hebrews, the universe consists of Wills, cooperating or conflicting. Human wrong-doing, or sin, comes from human wills trying to act in opposition to God's will. Though God's will cannot be finally defeated, these sins make a difference in the world and we are witnesses of their effects because directly or indirectly they hurt us and people known to us. Indirectly too we have some inkling of what God is doing to counteract these evils. Berkeley too can leave room for chance in his cosmology, which most of the Greeks (but not Aristotle) had denied, and unfortunately many Christians too. He did not say much about this, not even in *De Motu*, for it was a dangerous doctrine and he would have had most of the men of science snapping at his heels as well as the bishops; but not I think Butler, an important exception.

The sole basic insight or knowledge that we can apply to the world is that already known to Hobbes. Chaos with violence is destructive of life at any level ('Nature red in tooth and claw'). Therefore morality begins by replacing chaos with order and by precautions to avoid lapsing back into chaos. We can hardly doubt that some degree of order causes less misery and less destruction of life than no order, even if it may still cause some by chance or else by the uncontrolled malice of some people. Nor can we doubt that God's will is a will for order in the first place. But in the second place and beyond the level of Hobbes's argument, we can distinguish human acts that are positively benevolent from those that are malevolent positively or negatively (negligent). But, as Berkeley says (*Passive Obedience*, § 13, see also *Works*, vol. VI, p. 23n., for Butler), both benevolence and malevolence are themselves *passions*, though not just animal behaviour. We can hardly accuse the cat of malice towards the mouse, and it is absurd to suppose that the spider is being malicious to the fly or even to the husband she devours as soon as the nuptials are over; though she does seem to be something of a Hobbist. As mere chance tends to destroy any kind of order, so we can observe that human malice deliberately sets out to destroy human order more completely and quickly. Human order means co-operation, justice and mercy, in a word, harmony. Harmony is not only destroyed by physical violence but by fraud, deceit and every kind of false dealing. Thus we can and should accept the obligation to refrain, first of all, from such violations of order and we cannot exempt ourselves from the negative duties without claiming to be subhuman or else superhuman. All this can be concluded by the light of reason or by observation of the world or both together.

Berkeley calls our general duty to refrain from malicious acts and intentions *negative* duty, to distinguish it from our *positive* specific duties to perform particular benevolent acts towards particular persons as and when special opportunities arise. Such terms are convenient but too simply arithmetical. Berkeley's full view is St Paul's, whom he often quotes, that God the Creator and Maintainer of the world is perpetually bringing order out of chaos and doing it in a regular way, the regularity of which we can see for ourselves, if we only care to look at past events where consequences have worked themselves out and so that a pattern has become now manifest which before was hidden. We have this historical hindsight, but we have no foresight at all. We do not know what the consequences of present events will be, except on a very small scale and for trivial events. God's work in this world is not yet complete and though it cannot be fully frustrated it is temporarily hindered by evil human action and primarily by human neglect of this simple and obvious duty of not interfering where interference is quite obviously wrong. Men constantly act under the illusion that they can put one wrong right by doing another. God can put wrong right, but men suppose they know better than God and can do better.

Having made his distinction and set out the political aspect of our negative duty Berkeley had completed his first task, and cannot be blamed for not going on to expound a theory of positive duties, perhaps an impossible task, certainly a very complicated one and hardly even attempted since Plato's tentative efforts in *Sophist and Statesman* (before he was distracted to other subjects). Had Berkeley been asked, I suspect he would have replied that there can be no general precepts for positive duties, only examples, which each must interpret for his own circumstances and follow for himself as best he can.

Berkeley had undertaken, however, a second task which needs brief comment; namely to meet objections to his view likely to be made by his contemporaries. Of these only II, i and ii, and III, i and vii, call for any comment (see analysis, pp. 137–8 above). The first of these, a Hobbist argument is nowadays very popular but needs no more comment than on pp. 142–3 above. The second is a Utilitarian argument, but it applies properly only to positive obligations and not to any general negative obligation. In any case the positive consequences of positive action are not in *general* humanly predictable by any human agent.

The third to be considered, III, i, is the most important and difficult for Berkeley or anybody else to deal with.

The justification of *law*, which is general, not particular, nor individual, is that it tends to produce happiness or welfare *for the most part*, but in a world where evil acts are being done or attempted contrary to God's will and His law, happiness or welfare is not always nor necessarily secured. To go back for a moment to the argument of II, ii, also. If a policeman has been bribed to arrest me unlawfully and I resist him with violence, I do no wrong to him *personally* for he is wrong already, but I do wrong to the *law* which he (though corruptly) represents, so I ought to submit quietly and invoke the law to put things right, not take it on my own shoulders to try to put right a wrong by doing another

wrong. On the other hand, if the corrupt policeman tries to get
me to help him to arrest somebody else I am quite right to refuse
him. I am then wronging nobody, not the law nor him, and my
conscience is clear whatever the after-effects may be. In neither
case do I need to take account of after-effects, nor can I do so
rationally, for I do not know what they will be; all I know is that
the law has to be respected, even when its agents are corrupt. I
must not try to make exceptions for my own supposed benefit,
but should accept the incidental suffering that may come to me
and which is not the intention of the law.[1]

I have tried to put the case for Berkeley as nearly as possible in
Hobbist terms, appealing only to the principle that any law is
better than no law, and that if the law has been broken once to
break it twice is another step to anarchy and in no way strengthens
the law. But all special Hobbist mechanical subterfuges only make
things more complicated and indirect, and are no improvement on
Berkeley's argument in terms of God's will.

Berkeley did not rest his argument on the authority of the
Scriptures, and he was dealing with the problem of threats of
armed rebellion, not with the much commoner and (in the modern
world) often more serious threat of tax dodging. I am free however to refer to the N.T. story of the tribute money (St Mark XII,
13–17). The Jews' objection to paying taxes to Caesar was not
merely Jewish covetousness. They could claim with a considerable show of reason that it could not be God's will nor God's law
that they, the Chosen People, should pay taxes to idolatrous and
blasphemous foreign conquerors; and that God would surely
approve of their rebelling if opportunity offered. They would, of
course, add the usual formula, that if God did not know of their
distress He could not be all-wise, if He knew and did not interfere He could not be all-mighty, or if He knew and refused He
could not be all-righteous. This is relevant to Berkeley's Ireland
of the eighteenth century, because it was not a well-governed
country and Berkeley never said it was, any more than did his
friend Jonathan Swift.

Now for the last objection, III, vii. Berkeley says I must never
try to evade my negative duties by making exceptions for my own
benefit or for the sake of supposed benefits to come, but I do need
to define the limits of my obligations. As my obligation is to the

[1] Cf. Socrates in *Apology*, 32 A–E.

law as such, or to an actual and operating government even if imperfect, whether that of Caesar in Palestine in A.D. 30 or Queen Anne in Ireland in A.D. 1712, it follows that if and when government has broken down or is breaking down obligation ceases and I have to make up my mind to the best of my ability how to act or refrain from acting. The examples considered are where a usurper has seized power or power is failing by coming into totally incompetent hands. It is impossible to avoid speculating how Berkeley would have considered the outbreak of the English Civil War. Was that a case where there was no rebellion, but a schism between the two powers, King and Parliament, so that a man could choose to take arms for either party with a clear conscience?

Hobbes thought he could join his moral and political theory on to his theory of the physical world and erect one great edifice on one insecure foundation. Of course he could not; the cracks were too wide and the whole affair too crazy. Berkeley's moral and political theory, so far as he chose to develop it, is aligned simply, naturally, without effort with his theory of the physical world. His economic thought too fits in perfectly easily, so far as it goes; but time was not yet ripe for anything more than rudiments of theory. Had he been able to go further, he would have had to elaborate and explicate his scanty references to chance as a factor to be reckoned with in human affairs. For instance, the process of economic exchange is made to work by betting on future probabilities, and not upon any laws of nature other than the laws of large numbers. Those beginning to venture on insurance business in his times were gradually discovering something about them. However, no eighteenth- and hardly any nineteenth-century thinker was yet prepared for the effort needed to throw away the relics of the Machine theory, except Berkeley alone, who did not have to throw anything away.

§6 'THE BISHOP IN ORATORY AND LABORATORY'[1]

In the previous sections I brought in Hobbes, dragged him in, some will say, since Berkeley does not refer to him; but his moral theory has to be taken seriously and should be quite intelligible even in these illiterate days. Hobbes's theory is wrong only because his view of human nature is wrong, and that only because

[1] Luce: *Life*, p. 189.

he left out one thing, the voice of God or 'the moral law within', by reason of which men possess some freedom and are not entirely governed by fear and greed, as Hobbes supposed. I begin this section with a contemporary, who was mentioned by Berkeley in several places, a very minor figure, yet much discussed in his own day, namely Bernard Mandeville. He did, I believe, perform one service to mankind because his economic fallacies roused Berkeley's interest in economic theory, that is to say in what produces health or disease in the body politic and what are the incentives for individuals. Economic fact already interested him, as appears in his Italian travel diaries of 1717 (*Works*, vol. VII, pp. 193 ff.). Berkeley makes fun of Mandeville (the proper treatment), but only for his perverted hedonism, which Berkeley counters with the simple distinction between 'natural' and 'fantastical' pleasures—leaving Joseph Butler to provide a more adequate psychological analysis of pleasure.[1] Note that Butler is only incidentally interested in pleasure and what he says is by the way, but possibly all that needs to be said.

Now as to Mandeville himself. His first doggerel verses, *The Grumbling Hive* (1705), were clever, trifling and well worth the pennies eagerly paid for them, a gross caricature, but recognizable. Sophisticated people love to be told that the more viciously and extravagantly they behave the happier they and all the rest will be. Mandeville should have stuck to verse. Instead he spun out his meagre stock of ideas into a big volume of ponderous and pretentious prose, which some readers have taken as seriously as he himself did. He made one observation of some validity; namely that hypocrisy has its social uses among imperfect, competitive, imitative human creatures; but that is because, as Mandeville did not say,[2] it is the homage that vice pays to virtue, without which virtue might vanish out of the sight of most of us.

But Mandeville's most influential effort, of which traces still survive, was his economic theory that reckless expenditure and reckless speculation together make for prosperity. The world learned the fallacy of this theory once again in 1929–30, as it did earlier when the South Sea Bubble burst in 1720. Berkeley saw that Mandeville was an economic fraud as well as a moral one, but that he posed a theoretical puzzle as well as perhaps instigating

---

[1] *Fifteen Sermons*, 1726, especially VI, X and XI, also Preface.
[2] [It was said by François, Duc de La Rochefoucauld (1613–1680).]

a moral disaster. So began his education in economics, by making an acquaintance with facts. Fortunately for him there were no books.

The primary bases of material prosperity are hard work, in order to produce enough, then careful spending and the least possible waste. Nevertheless these alone, without adequate distribution, are very little use; there has to be exchange and even in the smallest, most primitive society some transportation. All the usual means for procuring these involve speculation and tend to foster extravagance, not thrift. Even Plato saw something of this. The most primitive City of Pigs depends upon exchange, and then ordinary human greed and extravagance tend to turn it into the Fevered City, which has more wealth of a sort but fewer real merits (*Republic*, Bk II). Plato's elaborate advice about what to do next has never been taken except once, in part, by the Jesuits in Paraguay, who were not permitted to continue, perhaps because they had thought of something that Plato and Aristotle would both have despised. While for the most part excluding money transactions they raised a valuable 'cash crop' for export and might have established a world monopoly.[1] Aristotle is not helpful either (*Pol.*, Bk I). He knew, what the world later forgot, that

i. wealth or prosperity consists solely in the production and use of useful commodities and human services connected with them, and ii. that money, i.e. silver, gold or even paper (had he had any) is not wealth because its sole use is to be a medium of exchange of those things that do constitute wealth. Aristotle, however, cherished unworthy suspicions about the process of exchange and thought there was something wrong about producing anything for the express purpose of exchanging it for something else. If all products were works of art there would be some weight in this suspicion. We think ill of an alleged artist who composes a piece of music, writes a poem or paints a picture solely in order to sell it for money. But fresh loaves and salt fishes, ploughs and bedsteads, kettles and pots are only very occasionally works of art, and no disgrace should attach to the man who makes them for sale or even to the man who buys them to sell again. Exchange is a necessary part of distribution and a man can produce far more loaves, fishes, ploughs, bedsteads, kettles or pots in a lifetime than he can ever consume. Aristotle was not at his best over this, nor

[1] See R. B. Cunningham-Graham, *A Vanished Arcadia*, 1901.

yet about usury, which has, within strict limits, its proper function in facilitating exchange and even production. But his two first truths are important, and the age of Berkeley had to struggle to rediscover them.

The *Essay towards preventing the Ruine of Great Britain* (1721), like the earlier *Guardian* essays was addressed by Berkeley specifically to a London audience, then still dazed by the catastrophic end of the South Sea speculative orgy and needing the solemn warning at the end that covetousness can be the worst idolatry.

The essay contains the two Aristotelian truths and also a third one that commercial speculation can be and often is nothing but gambling, namely trying to get something for nothing at somebody's expense. It may easily be worse than private gambling because on a larger scale. Nobody was ever much the worse for playing Ha'penny Nap or even putting a shilling on a horse, as long as he confined his efforts to ha'pennies and shillings. For all that, commercial speculation, unlike card games or backing horses, can have a legitimate function, indeed may be necessary and entirely morally defensible if it does facilitate exchange of goods and production of goods; if it does render a service and does benefit both parties to the exchange. These, though, are formidable 'ifs'.

Berkeley's economic advice at this stage was sound but went no further than Aristotle, nor did he go further in *Alciphron* though there, in the second Dialogue, he polished off Mandeville's economics as well as his morals. Yet during the interval Berkeley's education in economics was going ahead and went on to its final stages at Cloyne, when he was Bishop.

Popular caricatures of 'idealism' suppose that the cure of souls to which a bishop is committed can be entirely divorced from the cure of bodies, but that was never any part of Berkeley's 'idealism' (nor of Plato's 'idealism', nor yet of Hegel's if we accept the view of his most sober interpreter, Bosanquet; nor yet of the 'idealism' of the Gospels). Before souls can be cured, bodies have to be fed, clothed, housed (economics), and in such a way as to protect them from death by disease (medicine). Moreover what governments can and cannot do turns upon economics. If the Bermuda scheme which Berkeley conceived and promoted was a failure, it failed because the politicians failed to keep the promises they made of economic help. In part at least that was because they failed to learn the economic facts before making the promises. It was their business, not Berkeley's, to learn the facts, and he, who did take the trouble, did it rather late. Bermuda was impossible because of the economics of transport. Few people had supposed that Andrew Marvell's account was precise:

'Where the *remote* Bermudas ride
In th' Ocean's bosome *unespy'd*'

They were a very long way from the centres of population, and hardly any ships ever sailed that way. People had looked at small-scale maps, the only ones available, and supposed to supply a more scientific kind of information than poets do. But the maps did not say how many days' sail Bermuda was from Baltimore or Boston, nor how many ships went there *per annum*. Berkeley quickly discovered the mistake when he reached the New World; he made himself acquainted with the Universities already established or projected, and their chief needs. He devoted all the resources he had at his command to supply these needs, where they were most urgent. He gave encouragement and skilled advice. He also gave what young educational establishments always need most—books, properly selected. He was one of the very few from the Old Country who thought well of and acted kindly towards the Colonies of North America, and there he has never been forgotten.

In America Berkeley learned about economics in another way; he bought a hundred acres of land and farmed them. I strongly suspect that Mrs Berkeley instigated this venture, and she almost certainly ran the farm. (In ancient Greece the art of economics meant the management of the household, which included farm and workshop.) This first farming venture was done in the encouraging conditions and environment of the New World; that was just as well, for she and the Bishop had to start again in the Old, under the most depressing possible conditions, six years later.

The colonists of Rhode Island and the neighbourhood were vigorous, enterprising, hard-working, prosperous and, in those days, far from uncultured; the community contained neither idle, spendthrift rich nor idle, thriftless poor; two of the many plagues of Ireland. Rhode Island was even free from sectarian strife. It was a model of the virtue of the doctrine of 'laissez faire, laissez aller'. This, remember, originally was meant as a warning to politicians: 'Do not interfere ignorantly with production, transport or distribution'. It was nineteenth-century British politicians who translated it as 'Dolce far niente' and only applied it to themselves. But, earlier, most of the Irish, high or low, had translated the Italian into both Gaelic and English, as meaning 'Let things produce themselves'.

Now before we go further, what did Berkeley's contemporaries who knew him well have to say about his character and capacities? Luce (*Life*, 1949, p. 193) quotes the comment of a friend of long standing, Thomas Blackwell, made shortly after Berkeley's death.

'I scarce remember to have conversed with him on *that art*, liberal or mechanic, of which he knew not more than the ordinary practitioners. With the widest views he descended into minute detail, and begrudged neither pains nor expence for the means of information. He travelled through a great part of Sicily on foot, clambered over the mountains and crept into the caverns to investigate into its natural history, and discover the causes of its volcanoes; and I have known him sit for hours in forges and founderies to inspect their successive operations.'

Luce summarizes (*Life*, p. 189) his activities at Cloyne.

Neither his episcopal duties, nor the domestic and social round monopolized Berkeley's time; nothing could narrow his horizon. Buildings of very varied types, representing very varied activities, clustered close, as they still do, at the round tower of Cloyne. The cathedral, the bishop's palace,[1] shops and cottages—there they are, in a small compass, symbolizing a wider field. They all were his concern and interest, and the manifold needs of Cloyne, spiritual and physical, were for Berkeley an epitome and focus of the needs of Ireland.

He set up a spinning-school at Cloyne for the children, and a house of work for sturdy vagrants; he provided winter relief and employment on a large scale; he sowed hemp; he sowed flax; he encouraged home-spun; his sons might employ a Cork tailor, but he wore Cloyne-made clothes and Cloyne-made wigs; he fostered the fine arts; he planted myrtles, one of which remains to this day. He drew off an infusion of tar, and made a medicine. He took up his pen and wrote the *Querist* and *Siris*. All these varied activities must be taken together and kept together, and projected on a national scale, if we are to understand Berkeley and measure his episcopate aright. They sprang from a social creed which was part of a widespread and much-needed move-

---

[1] The cathedral is smaller than many English country parish churches and the palace than many English vicarages; see illustrations in Luce's *Life*.

ment for an improvement of the conditions of Irish life; they were phases of an economic nationalism that was temperate and reasoned, but organized and determined.

The best known of all this group, who were, I would venture to suggest, the best as well as the first of the Irish nationalists, was Swift the great Dean of St Patrick's. Luce (*Life*, p. 190) claims William Molyneux (of *Molyneux's question*) to be the earliest and he names several friends of Berkeley; he also recommends a study of the articles and advertisements in the *Dublin Journal* of the late 1730's and 1740's to give an impression of the background of Berkeley's *Querist* and his life at Cloyne.

One further point, on two occasions Berkeley published an open letter addressed to Roman Catholics; he was probably the only Protestant Bishop who would have done it, or could have done it with any chance of success. The first was to all the Roman Catholics of his Diocese, published in 1745 along with one to his fellow Protestants and warning all of the dangers of dragging Ireland into another futile Jacobite rebellion. The second letter of 1749 (*Works*, vol. VI, pp. 225–49), a long explanatory one, is the important one for my purpose. It was addressed to the Roman Catholic clergy of Ireland, 'Reverend Sirs', and headed 'A Word to the Wise'.

Berkeley urged them, as part of their pastoral duty, to inculcate the virtues of industry and thrift. 'In this fertile and plentiful island, none can perish for want but the idle and improvident. None who have industry, frugality and foresight but may get into tolerable, if not wealthy circumstances' (p. 240). He knew that injustices were produced by bad laws (not all of them invented by the wicked English) and by bad landlords (not all of them bad) and he went so far as to say that some landlords were 'vultures with iron bowels' (p. 243). But Berkeley was sure that these were not the main determining causes of the combined idleness, poverty and dirt in which far too many of the Irish lived. Indeed, a mild climate and fertile soil was in itself a snare. A fortnight's work in spring to plant potatoes, a fortnight in summer to dig peat, ten days or so to lift and store potatoes in the autumn, was very nearly enough for a man to keep a family of four or five alive —in a favourable year. In a favourable year too, the potatoes were as safe in the ground as anywhere else, and only needed to be forked up from day to day to go straight into the pot.[1] The household work of his wife did not go much further than to keep that pot boiling.

Berkeley cites the example of countries no more, perhaps less fertile, where no such dirt and poverty are to be found as in Ireland; but where 'A tight house, warm apparel, and wholesome food are sufficient motives to labour' (p. 241).

> But alas! our poor Irish are wedded to dirt upon principle. It is with some of them a maxim that the way to make children thrive is to keep them dirty. . . . Were children but brought up in an abhorrence of dirt and obliged to keep themselves clean, they would have something to do, whereas now they have nothing (pp. 242–3).

Many modern readers, brought up to believe that denunciation is a sacred duty at all times, think that Berkeley was too mild, here and elsewhere, in denouncing the political injustices that prevailed in Ireland; but denouncing was not his way; besides Dean Swift had been at work already, and left little unsaid; every literate Irishman knew it. Here are two examples, quoted in Luce's *Life* (p. 190): 'By the laws of God, of nature, of nations, and of your own country, you are and ought to be as free a people as your brethren in England'; and 'I confess myself to be touched with a very sensible pleasure when I hear of a mortality in any country parish or village, where the wretches are forced to pay for a filthy cabin and two ridges of potatoes treble the worth.' These have their value in their time and place, but more permanently valuable is the voice of Berkeley (on the same page of Luce), 'To feed the hungry and clothe the naked by promoting an honest industry (is) no improper employment for a clergyman who still thinks himself a member of the commonwealth.'

§7 ECONOMIC THEORY

The final stage of Berkeley's economic education was his life at Cloyne from 1734; and more especially the famine period, 1739–41, which showed the extreme process of economic disintegration and provided also for medical education. The famine came suddenly with severe early November frosts ushering in a hard long winter. Practically the whole potato crop was destroyed—a forerunner of a different and greater disaster a century later—certainly

[1] See R. N. Salaman, *The Potato*, 1949.

all those that remained in the ground, and probably few that had been lifted fared much better. The next two years were also bad ones from other causes. Food was very scarce, many were very ill-nourished and the usual outbreak of epidemic diseases followed. Though severer than most, this famine should be reckoned an 'ordinary' one (see note at the end of the chapter), such as throughout all recorded history, could be expected every few years in the less fortunate places or every few decades anywhere. They were too frequent and too familiar for 'ordinary' historians to take notice of them as such, though they might receive passing mention as related to wars, civil strife, or unusually destructive epidemics. Moreover, 'ordinary' people, including ordinary kings, politicians and priests, took no action about them except to leave the famine area, if they could, or else to speculate in the food market, if they could not. I emphasize the term 'ordinary', because in these times and places where they have ceased so many have never heard of any Irish famine except the Great Famine of 1845–9. (How many Scots, for example, have heard of the 'Seven Ill Years', which decisively changed the course of Scottish history at the turn of the seventeenth to eighteenth centuries and provided Scotland with most of its population of Tinkers, apart from the few real Romanies?) The Irish famine of 1845–9 was anything but ordinary, the first and last of its kind in history.

But as to ordinary famines; even if nobody did anything about them, yet famine could, from the earliest days, be reckoned culpable negligence of a sort. In ancient Egypt, Joseph showed how a strong and efficient local government could forestall one locally and without the aid of any modern facilities (*Genesis*, Ch. XLI, vv. 47–9). Alas, there have been too few Josephs and not many strong and efficient governments. Foresight of any sort is very rare and lethargy very common. The idea of storing surplus food obtained in good seasons to tide over the bad seasons that are bound to come sooner or later, does not need any dreams; only good political sense. But it is very expensive. It is expensive today with all modern technical and technological resources, and even more so in earlier times without them, when only a few kinds of food could be stored at all, at great cost in wastage and at considerable capital cost. The many 'Pharaohs who knew not Joseph' have a first-rate excuse on grounds of cost. Yet storage was relatively easy in Egypt for its main crops were dry seeds easily stored in a dry climate. Ireland was less lucky. Its mild damp climate, which makes its grass grow all the year round, also encourages *fungi* and other destructive pests to keep at work all the year round. Already in Berkeley's day potatoes were the largest crop, a good crop from many points of view including nutritive value, but one of the worst for keeping; frost destroys them, warmth makes them sprout and in any ordinary Irish weather *fungi* attack them. Undoubtedly, the cheapest policy for men and pigs is to eat them as quick as they can, keeping only enough seed potatoes for next year. This is not, however, the policy that averts famine when bad years come round.

The traditional outcome of ordinary famines, where there was no such observer as Berkeley about, was just that the very young and very old tended to die while those in between very often survived somehow or other, some of them apparently not much the worse for their experience, and when food became plentiful again they forgot about it. Far more deaths were due to epidemic diseases than to direct starvation. These might continue for a long time, and might include any of a large number of infections. Conspicuous among these and recognizable in ancient accounts of pestilences are the louse-borne infections, Typhus and Relapsing Fever, and Bacterial Dysentery, or Typhoid Fever, which is mainly water-borne.

It was only in the seventeenth century that a few towns in the most advanced regions began to keep mortality statistics of any sort. Before the nineteenth century, when people died in country places only their near relatives and neighbours knew of it. (That is probably true today in China and Russia, where there are no reliable statistics about anything that *has* happened, though plenty of ideologically inspired guesses about what is going to happen.)

At the moment I am concerned with famine solely for its bearing on Berkeley's interest in economic incentives. The importance of famine conditions is that they tend to disintegrate the structure of normal economic relations, thus to remove incentives to and rewards of industry, frugality and thrift. When you have no food left to eat, no seed left to sow for next harvest, to stay on your farm, where there is no work you can do, is certain death. To wander off begging at the roadside is more profitable. Some passers-by are sure to be better off; you may even reach a place where normal life prevails. In the meantime you cease to bother about work, at least for today; you may find congenial company; and the more ragged, filthy and diseased you are, the more immediately profitable your new calling.

Nevertheless, there can be no such thing as a complete, self-supporting community of beggars. Even beggars know that, if they remain sane and if they expect their appeal to be effective. 'Give me food (or money) so that I may beg for more tomorrow', is less effective than 'Give now, so that tomorrow I can work instead of begging'. I am, of course, not dealing with the subject in twentieth-century but in eighteenth-century terms as Berkeley and Adam Smith had to, in a society where the typical productive unit was still the family farm and family workshop (with a few hired hands), as it had been in Aristotle's day. Long-distance ocean transport had made a considerable new technical contribution, but so far mostly, indeed almost entirely for high-priced commodities of small bulk, including human passengers. The big changes began with Watt's steam engine and after 1800.

Obviously, conditions that are too hard produce no incentive to nor rewards from industry. Equally, conditions that are too easy do not, e.g. the traditional life of Pacific Islands in Trade Wind latitudes. Also persons of extreme temperament find no conditions to provide incentives; those who are natural idlers, spendthrifts, or misers who direct their energies in the wrong direction: there are also those who are dedicated to ends which are uneconomic, though they may be worthy. The poet or painter starving in his garret is the stock example and the inventor starving in his garret is an equally good and genuine example.

Berkeley's *Querist* takes us a good deal further than his *Ruine of Great Britain* and quite definitely in the direction of Adam Smith's *Wealth of Nations* (1776).[1] Let me consider for a moment one example, that of exchange, for Berkeley is concerned with refuting Mandeville, as well as with the troubles of Ireland. Without the process of exchange, production would be confined to the

---

[1] [It might be worth noting that, in certain respects Sir James Steuart's *Principles of Political Œconomy*, 1767, appear to be nearer to Berkeley than is Adam Smith. i. Berkeley, like Steuart, saw that, in certain circumstances, there was a case for protectionism. Steuart, for example, is prepared to defend, in reference to Ireland, some of the mercantilist theories of Berkeley's friend, Swift (*Principles of Pol. Oec.*, vol. 2, pp. 131–3). ii. Berkeley, like Steuart, was very interested in John Law, and his financial policy in regard

particular needs of the particular producer and his family. A's exchange of goods with B can be profitable to both directly, also indirectly, through other exchanges between many other persons, thus exchange is profitable generally, under certain conditions, though not entirely universally nor necessarily. Berkeley himself would have pointed out that the same is true of the laws of physics which, under certain conditions, hold very generally and with a high degree of precision, but not universally nor necessarily. The only important difference lies in the conditions, which in physics are simple, very precisely known and hold very widely, while economic conditions are complex, not precisely known and narrower. One man's private vice may easily in special cases be of public benefit to many. The consciously fraudulent quack doctor (witch or medicine-man), if clever, does actually cure a number of patients, and perhaps it is better to have him at work than nobody. Yet we all believe that he does not cure quite as many as the honest physician, even if rather stupid, and therefore on the whole we are better without the quack doctor. We believe this on general grounds without any very definite statistical evidence. Clearly, statements about conditions are difficult.

Still, it seems possible to make some statements about what conditions are needed to make exchange processes profitable all round and generally. At any rate, let us try three; even if there are others that need to be stated too. There should be i. a free market, ii. a stable currency, iii. enough of it. These are all parts of a more general expectation that neither unforeseen accidents, nor rascally acts of private persons or politicians, are likely to rob people of their fair rewards. Then, having said all this, we are left with the questions: i. What makes a market free and whose business is it to make it so? ii. How is currency kept stable and whose business is it to keep it so? iii. Who is to judge and how does he judge how much currency and of what denominations is going to be required? Lastly, exchange conditions depend in a complicated way on transport conditions. The ancient way is for the farmer's wife to walk ten miles into market with her two pounds of butter and

to French Banking (Berkeley, pp. 163–7, vol. VI, of the *Works* and Steuart, *Principles of Pol. Oec.*, vol. 4, pp. 316–87). In the case of both men, this interest in credit control went hand in hand with a belief in a certain measure of state-intervention in economics.]

dozen eggs and sit there till she has sold them; very good for gossip, not efficient economically. For all this read *The Querist* and later works, but not earlier works.

There is no need to say more here about this unusual and fascinating work, *The Querist*, except to mention Arthur Balfour's observation that it constitutes a special form of literary composition, rhetorically effective, with a poetry and humour of its own. Socratic questioning is also rhetorically effective and also has its own poetry and humour; nevertheless the two forms are surprisingly different.

M

VIII

SIRIS

MEDICINE, ALCHEMY, AND THE THEORY OF THE GREAT CHAIN OF BEING

BERKELEY was appointed Bishop of Cloyne in 1734 and began to publish *The Querist* in the following year. There was nothing to hinder this quick response in economics. Irish conditions were much as they had been in earlier years, though now he saw more of poverty and at closer quarters. He was already more competent than any politician in London or Dublin to compare Irish conditions with those elsewhere. He was not faced with any hostile vested professional interests. He had yet to experience famine conditions; but they came soon enough in the winter of 1739–40. This was just an 'ordinary' famine, but severe, and followed by the usual sequel of epidemic infections. These probably decided him to trespass on the sacred medical ground and do it publicly with an *apologia* to the intellectual world of his day. All this took time, but *Siris* appeared by 1744. It enjoyed considerable popularity, as did tar-water, and met with only a few grumbles from physicians and druggists who complained that he was taking the bread out of their mouths. The medical profession, though not very scientific according to twentieth-century views, was very jealous, also very theoretically-minded and often philosophically competent. This is enough to account for the fact that *Siris* consists mainly of philosophical discussion, and contains no case histories and no statistics. Berkeley had, however, another and harder problem to face than convincing the medical profession that there might be a theoretical justification for tar-water. He had to explain to the whole of a peculiarly obstinate generation that the cure of bodies was not so remote from the cure of souls as most educated people then supposed. Descartes and Hobbes, in agreement for once, had done their work only too well. Any account of health and disease couched in general terms and not explicitly mechanistic would be taken to smell of magic, witchcraft or other outmoded superstition; this in spite of the fact that magic and witchcraft always have been quasi-mechanistic, if not totally so.[1]

It was perhaps unfortunate that Berkeley felt that he could satisfy the learned world of his day with nothing less than a comprehensive theory of the nature of health and disease and therefore a complete metaphysical or cosmological system. But it was certainly sheer bad luck that the only supposedly scientific ideas available for him to start from were already obsolescent and were couched in terminology of extreme obscurity, soon to be entirely forgotten. It must be remembered, though, that he did not say, 'Here is the one true doctrine of health and disease, with metaphysics to correspond.' All he said was, 'Here is an ancient and respectable kind of doctrine, after the manner of Plato and Aristotle, which has the advantage of being theistic, even if imperfectly, and by which you can escape from the terrors of the Great Machine theory.' He could have added, 'It is the best I can provide at the moment, if you insist on having a metaphysical system. You may remember that Plato, badgered by disciples in his old age, gave them *Timaeus*, a cosmology after the Pythagorean fashion, thus impaired by use of the Artificer theory, and solely in order to keep them quiet.'

Strictly, there is no cosmological justification for anybody who hands to a sufferer two ounces of something to drink, whether it be a Fellow of a Royal College of Physicians or an old wife who has made an infusion of herbs, except to say, 'If you don't drink this you will almost certainly drink something worse instead.' The first and the last word in Surgery and Medicine rests with Ambroise Paré, the 'father' of military surgery: 'I dressed the wound; God healed it.' Hippocrates, though after the manner of the Greeks, would have agreed, as would Pasteur and Lister. More about theory will come later, but now as to Berkeley's practice.

In speaking about his experience of the use of tar-water Berkeley says (*Siris*, § 72):

It may with truth be affirmed that the virtue of tar-water extends to a surprising variety of cases very distant and unlike. This I have experienced in my neighbours, my family and myself. And as I live in a remote corner, among poor neighbours, who for want of a regular

---

[1] Lynn Thorndike's *History of Magic and Experimental Science* adds eight large volumes of confusion to this difficult topic; but does show that in early times few knew which they were doing and probably some do not yet know.

physician have often recourse to me, I have had frequent opportunities for trial, which convince me it is of so just a temperament as to be an enemy to all extremes.

In more up-to-date terminology, it is a useful prophylactic against a variety of common infections when taken regularly in the place of water or other drinks, likely to be already infected and certainly not antiseptic.

He could have spoken more strongly about the conditions he had to face. There were no doctors at all in rural Ireland in those days, and famines were frequent. Had there been any doctors, they could not have done better than any man or woman of sense would. Most would have done much worse, for violent, painful and noxious dosings were only very slowly giving way to the advice of Sydenham and a few other humane and enlightened practitioners. In any case adequate knowledge of infectious diseases lay more than a century ahead. By tradition the peasantry, if not content with magic from the local witch and whisky from the local still, would look to 'the big house' and specially the lady of the house to minister to their ailments.[1] These ministrations would be quite as scientific as those of the medical profession, would be on the whole sympathetic and certainly better than even white magic or black market whisky.

Berkeley had found tar-water, a traditional Amerindian remedy in use in North America, had improved the method of preparation, used it in his own house and gave it to all who asked, under conditions totally different from those now existing on either shore of the North Atlantic.

Tar-water is not poisonous in moderate or even quite large quantities, not even nasty, can be easily prepared and preserved in any kitchen, from common ingredients to be bought in any seaport at trifling cost. It is a mild antiseptic and can be safely used internally or externally. No patient young or old, whatever his condition, is likely to be the worse for it. Luce mentions (*Life*, p. 204n.) that in the nineteenth century, when people were beginning to understand that typhoid is a water-borne infection, many continental hotels served *l'eau de goudron* at table. This was almost certainly prepared exactly according to Berkeley's pre-

---

[1] We must not imagine Mrs Berkeley sitting knitting in the drawing room, but rather employed outside in the kitchen garden or on the Glebe land.

scription, the *aqua picis* of the old editions of the British and many other *Pharmacopeias*. *Pix liquida*, or Stockholm tar, still appears in the British Pharmacopeia, for use in making ointment.[1]

Whatever his claims or theory look like now, Berkeley's practice —and Mrs Berkeley's—were true Christian charity bringing hope and comfort to those otherwise hopeless. Not all medical practice is as good as that and much present theory will look worse than Berkeley's in 200 years' time.

Before going further with theory it is worth while having a look at a little medical history and first of all at the predicament of the physician at all times.

Most people recover from most diseases, or more accurately, everybody recovers from every disease except one, the one that kills him. Recovery is a natural process, native to every living organism. Medical and surgical practice can aid this natural process but do not originate it.[2] Death is also a natural process, natural to later life, which skilful medical practice can make less miserable and less painful, but also, unfortunately, can prolong unduly or shorten unduly.

The living organism possesses some machine-like characters, but is more than any man-made machine. Of all human organs the heart is most machine-like, for it is a pump, and the mechanical principles of pumping are seen at work in it as clearly as in any man-made pump. Against that it is self-operating (if normal), self-regulating (in large part), self-maintaining and self-repairing. No man-made pump is like that and none is ever likely to be. A careful engineer fits a stand-by pump to use occasionally and exceptionally when the main pumping machinery is being cleaned,

---

[1] The conspicuous diseases of famine times were probably: i. Typhus, ii. Relapsing Fever, both louse-borne, iii. Typhoid or Bacterial Dysentery, iv. Scurvy; this is according to reports of the Great Famine of the 1840's when diagnosis was much better and about which there is documentary information. Tar-water would not be much direct help for iv. For i. and ii. it might give some protection from infection if used to wash the skin; even more if anybody thought of washing clothes in it. Against iii. it would be of considerable use, like *l'eau de goudron* on the table in a hotel. Used habitually it might give protection against infection for smallpox, for which it was originally recommended in North America.

[2] The distinction between medicine and surgery is clumsy but sometimes corresponds with an important decision. Is a gastric ulcer to be treated only by foods and drugs given by mouth or is the patient to be cut open and the ulcer cut out?

repaired or renewed. Such a human device is useless in a living organism, in part because every organ in it has several functions, not one only; even more because it is work that makes an organ grow and keep alive; if it stands idle for more than a short time it begins to waste away. Nevertheless surgeons (Greek for 'artificers') can carry out certain repairs on the heart in a very machine-like way, and do it by fitting in temporarily a machine of human manufacture to do the pumping. These are preliminaries to indicate what medicine and surgery can and cannot do, however skilled and scientific. The improvements between the mid-fifth century B.C., roughly the time of Hippocrates, and the mid-twentieth century A.D. have not altered the position except in matters of detail.

The life of an organism is not like the prime-mover[1] of a machine such as the explosion in an internal combustion engine or the steam pressure in a steam engine. Life is a divine gift, or to use a more appropriate metaphor, it is a loan from God; for after a time it has to be returned, and human life is needed as an instrument to obtain the supreme gift of Eternal Life. It is through living organisms of every sort that God creates order of any sort out of chaos. All organisms, however, are subject to accidents or diseases which reduce orderly or harmonious process to less orderly or more chaotic process. Though recovery from disease is natural, as has been said, it is not always complete and after a time there is a cumulative effect of diseases and accidents of all sorts, through which organisms begin to die; after a few minutes if they are bacteria, small fungi and protozoas, after hundreds of years if large forest trees, after about 70 years if men, or perhaps 73·5 years where some modern actuaries now put it.

The physician who is treating diseases of children or young people in the prime of life should forget that all are going to die and should only consider that they have not yet fulfilled their purpose or their promise, whether God's to them or theirs to God, we need not at the moment decide. At any rate the physician, who need not be a theologian further than the Hippocratic Oath requires, should assume that they can recover from their diseases

---

[1] Aristotle is accused of calling God the Prime-mover. What he meant was difficult to say in Greek, which had no word for 'Creator'. Κίνησις included both locomotion which is not initiative and initiation which need not be locomotive.

at least sufficiently to fulfil that promise or purpose, so that his task is to help to restore them to health as quickly and completely as he can, and never hinder in any way. He should tell them so quite explicitly, if they need to be told. The first things he should do concern their physical state, for it is by physical means that he begins. Patients should be kept warm, quiet, restful, with food and exercise moderated according to circumstances. This prescription has to be put in carefully qualified terms without which every physician might just give a good stiff injection of morphine and have done with it. More good and less harm has been done by intelligent nursing than by removal of portions of the body, large or small. One further point; the physician's most difficult task is with neurotics who fight to be allowed to remain ill, for their disease has become their dearest possession.

So much for the treatment of the young and normally healthy, up to middle age, 48, 49, 50, according to taste, after which health is the exception rather than the rule, and the patient is going gradually downhill, first physically, then mentally. Nothing that any skill or science can do does more than postpone the end; and enable the patient to recover sufficiently from one disease in order to die later of another, in a few years or a few weeks. With such patients physicians face their most difficult and unwelcome tasks. Many must wish, on many occasions, that the stiff dose of morphine might solve their problems. The physician should never hold out false hopes, and be very economical with the lies he may have to tell. But he must never say, 'You are dying', unless and until there is definite need for it and to the patient who is prepared for it. After all, and on any reckoning and any philosophy of life, many people who are past 60 years or 70 years, or even 80 years, still have their greatest work before them. This is seen most clearly in the realms of art and learning, including, surprisingly, the military art, and, less surprisingly, the political art.

All this in the last three paragraphs is well known to genuine Hippocratics, outside as well as inside the medical profession, and was known to Berkeley. But Berkeley knew something more too; namely that God is health to all the living while fully alive; and God is also peace to the dying.

The spectacular new drugs of the last 30 years or so have not altered anything fundamentally. They mean that far fewer are killed off young and in full vigour, and far more arrive unimpaired at middle age. For those who do so, the expectation of life is better than the Psalmist's 70 years of age, possibly a trifle over the 73·5 already mentioned. The credit for improvements even within the medical field is not entirely due to spectacular drugs, it is due to vast numbers and kinds of improvements beginning almost in Berkeley's lifetime. The credit does not go entirely to the medical profession, either. As Berkeley well knew, the death rate is increased by bad political and economic conditions; and these are greatly improved, since his day. Good civil servants administering good laws save vast numbers of lives, even if indirectly, unromantically and unseen.

The great weakness of eighteenth-century medicine was in methods of diagnosis rather than in lack of drugs. Most medical men then imagined that there were a few general types of disease which would yield to treatment by a few types of drugs.[1] Old Greek dogmas about physiological or pharmacological opposites were accepted along with some new ones (e.g. *Siris*, §§ 86–106). Alchemical theories were applied to explain actual or imagined properties of drugs, and Newton's authority could be quoted in favour of alchemy (e.g. *Siris*, §§ 126, 130, 133, 134, 148, 165, 221). If Berkeley's discussion in his book appears to be confused, the confusion was not put in by him; he found it there. He did take the trouble to consult the best and most recent authorities that he could find.[2] At least he recommended something harmless and not very disagreeable to drink; this can be said of only very few of the remedies prescribed in his day by qualified or unqualified practitioners. His objections to the misuse of alcohol for the sake of supposed therapeutic virtues make good sense, and are far ahead of his time (*Siris*, §§ 107–9).

This brings us to the once famous Brunonian System of Medicine with which we can profitably compare the theorizing of Berkeley. Dr John Brown (1736–88), M.D. of Edinburgh, put forward the theory that all disease is either too much tension or excitation (*incitatio*) in the body, or else too little. So far Brown was reproducing ancient Greek theory, as we still do when we

---

[1] Exceptionally, van Helmont (1577–1644) held that diseases are specific, each calling for specific treatment.

[2] E.g. Boerhaave's *Elementa Chemiae*, 1723. See *Works*, V, p. 233, for passages quoted.

speak of climates as 'bracing' or else 'relaxing'. His proposal for treatment, however, was more drastic than anything Hippocrates would have cared for. For over-excitation Brown prescribed opium in liberal doses; for under-excitation, alcohol, also in liberal doses. The theory was strongly opposed, but also found many adherents. It is reported that in 1802 discussion between Brunonians and Anti-Brunonians in the medical school at Göttingen rose to such a pitch that there were riots in the streets.

The story of C. F. S. Hahnemann (1755–1843) and his Homoeopathic System of Medicine is well known. His arguments and evidence are certainly no better than Berkeley's, and yet his system had a very considerable vogue throughout most of the nineteenth century. Indeed it is well within the last 100, or even 50, years that a priori theorizing about disease has finally been discredited, and it is admitted that there are many diseases, that they are different, that they and their characters have to be discovered by observation, as also the appropriate methods of treatment.

The Brunonian System now sounds utterly absurd, but in its day there was something to be said for it. It was based on some empirical evidence and in its way scientific. Certainly the simple remedies proposed could be put to the test of experiment and shown to be right or wrong. It had the bad luck to be mostly wrong, though not entirely. Some ailments are connected with or possibly caused by some kind of over-excitation. For them treatment by sedative or narcotic drugs is useful and opium, or a derivative, is still used for this purpose, though more cautiously, one hopes, than by Dr Brown. Still, this kind of treatment is palliative rather than curative. Other ailments, perhaps more frequent, are connected with some kind of under-excitation. There are some special types of exciting drugs which can be used in special cases (e.g. in hypo-thyroid conditions). It is extremely doubtful if there is such a thing as a general excitant. Certainly, alcohol is not that. It is of the nature of a narcotic, as large doses indicate clearly enough; though in smaller doses it appears to excite after a fashion (e.g. it makes people talk louder but talk less sense). So far as the Brunonian System depends upon any general theory, philosophic or scientific, its position is very weak. Some quasi-mechanical theory postulating unobservable hypothetical mechanisms is involved.

For the Homoeopathic System it is hard to find any justification at all. It seems to be based on malobservation and very rash philosophizing of a sort that can survive because experience neither refutes nor confirms it. If a drug A in large doses produces symptoms in a normal person similar to a disease X, and a drug B symptoms similar to Y, there is nothing except belief in sympathetic magic, or perhaps anti-pathetic magic, why A in small (or any) doses should cure X, and B cure Y. No decent empirical evidence has been produced to show that this kind of thing happens. Hahnemann's starting-point, that quinine produces in a healthy person a 'fever' like malaria, is just bad observation. The minute doses habitually used by homoeopathic practitioners are not likely to have any positive effect at all. The doctrine that the more diluted the drug the greater its potency is pure fantasy.

The great successes of early homoeopathic practice are unquestionable. The homoeopaths kept their patients quiet, gave them something to cheer them up, and for the rest left them alone to recover. Their allopathic rivals killed off their patients with strong poisons and acts of violence, bleedings, purgings, and burnings. The same success could have been attained on strictly Hippocratic lines; the characteristic homoeopathic doctrines were irrelevant.[1]

These instances are quoted to show that Berkeley's arguments were no queerer or weaker than others of the age before the rise of scientific medicine in the mid-nineteenth century, however queer and weak they may sound now. What makes his arguments doubly puzzling now is that they are expressed in terms of alchemical theory, now entirely forgotten and never intended even by those who devised it to be readily understood. Alchemy was based partly on fraud, partly on fantastic speculations of a pseudo-mystical kind, and partly also on genuine but misunderstood technique and genuine empirical evidence. I have tried to explain how alchemy became transformed into chemistry in *Studies in the History and Methods of the Sciences*, Ch. VII. Given the *provisos*

---

[1] This is not to say that Hahnemann was a quack, or bad, or stupid. He was among the first to investigate the pharmacological properties of drugs, using one substance at a time and examining its effects systematically. He did not do it very well but he made a beginning. He had very enlightened views about the treatment of the insane and the possibilities of preventive medicine.

discussed above in Ch. V, § 2, there is nothing which Berkeley wished to say that is not open to him in modern terminology.

In addition to alchemy, however, there is the ancient cosmological system on which its concepts were based, this is the theory of the Great Chain of Being. The central doctrine, which forms the basis of alchemy, is summarized in a sentence quoted by Berkeley from one of the *Hermetic* works:

All parts of the world vegetate by a fine subtle aether which acts as an engine or instrument subject to the will of the supreme God.[1]

There is an exclusive implication here, that there is no other engine or instrument. To complete the outline we must add that there is held to be one universal substrate. This, in Aristotelian terms, would be in itself formless and is informed and transformed by means of this same *aether* to a lower or higher degree of perfection, the result being all the variety of things we find in the world. On this theory what we call physical processes represent the lowest stages in the scale of forms. They are not, however, totally inanimate; physical change is taken as an inferior kind of growth or decay. Animal processes and transformations represent higher stages; human intelligence and will higher stages still, but not the highest. The neo-Platonists expounded an elaborate form of the theory, but it belongs also to Stoic and Aristotelian tradition, as Berkeley points out. He could, had he known about it, have pointed to a very interesting and special development of the theory by his contemporary Leibniz. If we wish, we can add to the list a twentieth-century version, A. N. Whitehead's cosmology.

As long as the ideas belonging to this type of philosophy are restricted to conscious or organic life there are few real difficulties. Trouble begins if they are applied to the lifeless physical world also; certainly in the older versions. The special qualifying concepts to be found in Leibniz and Whitehead go some way towards avoiding it. If earlier exponents, up to Berkeley's day, were incautious about the distinction between the animate and inanimate, there was as yet no very obvious reason for caution.

---

[1] *The Asclepian Dialogue*—probably fourth or fifth century A.D. That minerals grow in the earth, while plants grow and live, animals grow, live, and feel, was still current doctrine in the eighteenth century. It was held by Linnaeus (1707–78).

Analogies based on observation of transformations in the organic world seemed impressive and might quite well have been valid. There was nothing in Newtonian physics to show they were not, and Newton himself accepted them.[1] *Prima facie* the whole of the natural world is full of transformations which might well be due to the operation of an indwelling spirit or creative agent. There is nothing obvious to show that fire and light and especially the sun's activity are not of this sort. Even Lucretius, who as Atomist and Epicurean, should have repudiated all such notions, believed in a creative transforming power in the material world—*natura daedala rerum*. Indeed, would-be materialists constantly have recourse to a subterfuge of this kind.

The crucial question is that of transformation or of transmutation. The alchemists saw it everywhere; the nineteenth-century chemists said it never occurred anywhere, so far as they could discover. Technically and within the limits of their own science they were right, but it took them a long time to show that they were right; only the new operational concepts and methods could show that the alleged alchemical techniques were illusory.

Since Lavoisier (to name one pioneer only), chemical processes have been reduced to mechanical terms based upon the doctrine of conservation of mass, and transmutation doctrine has been found superfluous. The strength of the new chemical theory is that it is grounded on simple successful technical operations, on what the chemist actually does with his hands. Alchemical theory ignored existing technique or misinterpreted it, or imposed impossibly difficult operations. For all that, when the caterpillar turns to chrysalis and then the butterfly emerges, there is genuine transmutation. But that is not done by any human craftsman working with his hands. It is done by God, or if you prefer a more obscure kind of metaphysics, by *natura daedala rerum*.[2]

The new chemical theory made it possible to see the yawning gap in alchemical theory, and made it necessary to take chemical change as a mechanical process; but it did all that in virtue of introducing a new and difficult concept (or doctrine), that of a very large number of distinct substances each with its own specific

---

[1] See *Studies in the History and Methods of the Sciences*, pp. 101 ff.

[2] Please note: i. the craftsman's hands are too big and clumsy; so, necessarily, are his machines; ii. Daedalus is a fable, unless he was just the first sculptor who carved statues with two legs separate.

properties. The concept was used by Archimedes, is implicit in atomic theory, but was ignored until reintroduced by Boyle. It was not understood or widely accepted till the end of the eighteenth century.[1]

Berkeley's special theory to explain the virtues of tar-water (with the minimum of obsolete terminology) begins with the view that heat, light, and especially the light of the sun are formative or creative natural powers, modes or phases of the universal 'aether', the 'plastic principles' of Cudworth's philosophy. The power of sunlight is exhibited in the growth of plants. Of all plant tissues and products, resins hold more of the inherent virtue of sunlight than any other part. Berkeley, though he does not say so explicitly, probably believed this because resins burn more fiercely than other plant products and also possess an aromatic smell. It was one of the alchemical doctrines that the 'essence' of plants is to be found in aromatic or sweet-smelling constituents, especially when these are volatile and can be concentrated by distillation (cf. the term 'essential oil' still in use). Resins as such are indigestible, but in tar-water their essence or virtue is extracted in a palatable and assimilable form. Thus tar-water makes available for the healing of the human body the power of the sunlight, assuming that the animal organism is analogous to the vegetable. The theory depends also upon another assumption that there are transferable qualities, essences or virtues, transferred by quasi-mechanical processes, but no distinct substances with specific properties.

The explanations in *Siris* are in quasi-mechanical terms and some critics have held that this kind of explanation is incompatible with Berkeley's earlier views. This criticism is based on a misunderstanding of Berkeley's attitude towards scientific explanation and theory, though he stated it sufficiently in the *Principles* and very clearly in *De Motu*. His attitude was reductionist, as explained above, Ch. V, § 2.

Neither in *DM* nor *Siris* did Berkeley deny the value of the ordinary type of mechanical explanations and mechanical theories within certain limits and for certain purposes; provided, that is, they did some real work, simplified, clarified, and suggested new things. If they can be kept within such limits, he is justified on any view and there is no radical inconsistency with his earlier

[1] See *Studies in the History and Methods of the Sciences*, pp. 103–5.

expressed views. When Berkeley attacked any theory, including the Cartesian or Lockean theory of corporeal substance, it was on the grounds that it did no work or was self-contradictory. His view is explicitly stated in *Siris*, § 295:

> From the outward form of gross masses which occupy the vulgar, a curious inquirer proceeds to examine the inward structure and minute parts, and, from observing the motions in nature, to discover the laws of those motions. By the way, he frames his hypothesis and suits his language to this natural philosophy. And these fit the occasion and answer the end of a maker of experiments or mechanic, who means only to apply the powers of nature and reduce the phenomena to rules.

I quote half the paragraph here; the rest later. Ordinary positivists, and others too of different persuasions, have supposed that these rules, laws, or hypotheses were complete, self-sufficient, and legislated for the whole universe. On the contrary, as Berkeley says, they amount to no more than *a* natural philosophy, and they are useful for certain technical purposes. He goes on:

> But if, proceeding still in his analysis and inquiry, he ascends from the sensible into the intellectual world, and beholds things in a new light and a new order, he will then change his system, and perceive that what he took for substances and causes are but fleeting shadows; that the mind contains all, and acts all, and is to all created beings the source of unity and identity, harmony and order, existence and stability.

In other words, scientific theories are technical and secondary; they should not conflict with the first philosophy of mind and of noumena, and if they are strictly empirical they never will.

Berkeley found such a philosophy ready to hand in the theory of the Great Chain of Being. It provided a repository of first principles which could at least be recommended, and also certain general suggestions as to secondary causes (rather too much of this, as we can see now). For actual accounts of secondary causes he looked to the empirical sciences, and he himself was not committed *a priori* to any one way in which they might develop.

In general, poor scientific theory is better than none. It is true that theories can be so bad that they conceal facts, but it is their business to help to reveal them. Without any theory at all there would be no criteria of relevance or irrelevance, of compatibility or incompatibility. If there were data they would have no significance, they would point in no direction; they would be like the experiences of a dream. The genuine empiricist is not the man who starts without theories, for he would never start at all. He is the man who uses his theories as tools for examining facts and submits his theories to be judged by facts; not *vice versa*. According to these tests Berkeley comes out very well; and he did take the trouble to consult the best authorities of his day. Only he was not very lucky in the scientific theories he found ready to hand. Two centuries earlier his plight would have been worse, for then medical diagnosis was done with the help of astrology, and in economics nobody would have known what he was talking about.

It was still customary in the eighteenth century to mix up the categories of matter, life, and mind, of the physical, biological, and mental (psychological if you like). In the realm of physics this is an error, as Descartes said. It is not so gross an error as the newer one of assuming that the minimum categories of physics are the only ones. In spite of the personal unpopularity of Hobbes, his theory became the popular view and it still has many adherents. Berkeley from first to last attacked this, the Mechanical Philosophy or Great Machine Theory of the Universe. For him the physical is not unreal, only subordinate, creating or initiating nothing, and in that sense passive; mind alone is primary and can be fully active. All causation in the full and complete sense of the word was for him mental, of the character of an act of will, and not of mechanical interaction in terms of Newton's laws. As Leibniz puts it, mechanical causes are always considered in terms of external spatial and temporal relations, of *partes extra partes*, and cannot be primary.

In his earlier *Princ.* and *DM*, Berkeley went no further than barely to distinguish between a realm of *noumena*, spirits, minds and wills, and another of *phenomena*, which we humans discover how to construct out of our sense experience with the guidance of God. He was a dualist after the manner of Plato, as he well knew, and avoided the special errors of Monists, like Hobbes, who slur over necessary distinctions and cause confusion, and also those of Triadists, like Descartes, who add unnecessary extras. But he had his own difficulties, which I have already discussed.

When he came to write *Siris* he had made one step further with the philosophy of the Great Chain of Being, but in its traditional and seventeenth-century form, containing too much of the wrong kind of mechanics before Newton. There is no reason to suppose he thought this was the last step and provided him with all he looked for. He was not, apparently, acquainted with the philosophy of Leibniz, nor, by necessity, with that of Kant, but these two could have helped him considerably to take the next steps, if that was the direction in which his mind worked. He would have needed not only the expressed views of these two but also new empirical knowledge and certain twentieth-century philosophical concepts, to go the way I am suggesting or hinting at.

There are two main points to make clear, the first most simply put with the help of questions. Was Berkeley prepared to find links in his Great Chain to bridge the gulf between pure noumenal creative activity and pure phenomenal passivity? Similarly, was Kant prepared to find links to bridge the gulf between noumenal freedom and phenomenal bondage? And are there such links in the *Critique of Judgment*?

Secondly, granted that God's activity is creative in the full sense, so that it is not confined to 'informing' pre-existing but formless 'matter', much less spatial shuffling of pre-existing and fully formed bodies, even though these processes occur in consequence of the primal, perpetual and ordering creative activity; and the last supposedly by human agency. It has to be admitted that all creatures are passive, relatively, but not necessarily entirely. It is absurd for me to claim (consciously and deliberately) that I am purely passive, and equally absurd for you to claim that you are also. It is, if not absurd, at least rash to claim that all animals are entirely passive too. It is unsafe to be too sure even about apparently lifeless things, for we are not of their party. The Great Chain which links all creatures to their Creator should be considered first as a Realm of Ends, but that need not rule out all possibility of considering it also in mechanical terms. For any further development of this concept of a Realm of Ends, we should consult Kant, not Leibniz, for Kant though he puts his case in negative terms, as Berkeley in *Passive Obedience*, has his own contribution on the noumenal side and has also the assistance of Newton on the phenomenal, which deserves to be looked at more closely. Kant's Three Analogies of Experience come of universalizing Newton's Three Laws of Motion. Kant said that they must be worked out through empirical discoveries and these appeared abundantly in the nineteenth century, after his death. In formulating the First Analogy, Kant grossly exaggerated the significance of the first genuine *Principle of Conservation* to be discovered, a pardonable error, for it happened in his lifetime between writing the first edition of the *Critique of Pure Reason* and the second.[1] What he intended to say can now be put more generally and more simply; the First Analogy summarizes all those *relations*, discovered and yet to be discovered in the natural world, which no human effort can alter or control in any way. The best name for them is Postulates of Impotence, and they include all Principles of Conservation (e.g. of Mass and Energy and Specific Properties, as well as the more general one formulated by Einstein as $E = mc^2$) and also at least one other to be mentioned below. The Second Analogy can now be put as the Principle governing all those *relations* that human activity in the natural world can and does alter and therefore controls, subject always to the price paid for control, namely the Law of Dissipation of Energy, another Postulate of Impotence. There is also the Third Analogy which Kant could do little with and which has been too much ignored, but is the reassertion in phenomenal terms of the Great Chain of Being, of the interaction of everything in the natural world under the guidance of God, whereby Berkeley, while seeing all things in God, as did Malebranche, can avoid postulating endless trivial miracles.

These are no more than hints, which could be worked out further with the help of Whitehead's reformulation of the Great Chain Theory, though Whitehead is too Monistic and Naturalistic and needs to be supplemented with Bowman's hitherto neglected reassertion of Dualism.[2]

I have made two suggestions as to the way Berkeley's mind might have worked; that he put forward the Great Chain Theory as being ancient, familiar to the learned, and harmless, even if obsolete, and for those who crave after cosmology better than one that was pernicious as well as obsolete; or that he may have guessed that there was a future for it. There is a third possibility. He may have held that all cosmology is a claim to a kind of omniscience ill-suited to an empiricist or a Christian. He was also

[1] Moreover mass is not a property of an abstract material substance; it is the density of a body, and is that body, as it is measured. Energy unless kinetic and measured as such is potential and abstract.

[2] A. A. Bowman, *A Sacramental Universe*, 1939 (O.U.P.).

N

aware that 'now we see through a glass darkly', and 'persuaded that neither death nor life, nor angels, nor principalities nor powers, nor things present, nor things to come, nor height, nor depth, nor any other creature, shall be able to separate us from the love of God, which is in Jesus Christ our Lord.'

I am not attempting to maintain that Berkeley was always immaculately right, but that he was more far-sighted than his contemporaries and most of his successors. I do also maintain that his genuine Christian faith preserved him from blunders of those whose faith was feeble or absent, and that he was the one eighteenth-century thinker who could have understood a philosophy of *action* in place of *contemplation*.

Take the case of J. S. Mill, who openly professed himself a disciple of Berkeley and skilfully defended his Theory of Vision against the last attacks, delivered in the nineteenth century by Bailey and Abbott. Mill had been from his earliest years 'conditioned' (it is the only word) by his father James Mill in a Benthamite and Hartleian secular faith and against Christianity. In place of futile revolt he had the strength to live through, though almost driven to despair in adolescence. Young Mill recovered sanity and some kind of faith and hope by embracing the Wordsworthian religion, most simply described as a Western kind of Pantheism. Despite lifelong doubts and hesitations he never abandoned it, nor got much further. For most Westerners who in one way or another are excluded from Christian faith and practice or else exclude themselves, Wordsworth provides the most satisfactory refuge. Dabbling in Hinduism or Buddhism is usually the reverse.

Now Berkeley lived in a period when many of his contemporaries lost their traditional faith and practice and he might have been 'conditioned' in the same direction too. Instead he adhered to the concrete, historical, one may almost say, practical doctrines of Incarnation, Crucifixion and Resurrection, the 'stumbling blocks to Jews and foolishness to Greeks'. This 'subjective idealist' sums up his own faith and practice in the words already quoted, 'To feed the hungry and clothe the naked by promoting an honest industry is no improper employment for a clergyman who still thinks himself a member of the Commonwealth.' This was said when he first took up his episcopal duties. Only a few years later he could add, had he wished, 'In time of famine to feed the hungry and clothe the naked directly and to succour the sick and dying in every possible way.'

I am not suggesting that J. S. Mill would have failed in his moral duty as he saw it and in his circumstances, only that his circumstances were never those of a bishop and could not have been, with or without James Mill; but I do want to point out that Mill's philosophy was less coherent than Berkeley's and that the difference is clear. J. S. Mill's view of perception has come to him *via* Hume, Reid, Hartley, James Mill and others, and has not improved on the way. It is too much taken up with 'sensations' as discrete, very nearly atomic units and too little with the given order of experiences only incidentally unitary, if at all. Moreover, the Wordsworthian faith, though it can see the order, and see it as given, does not see it as being created here and now, by 'our Heavenly Father'.

I am not jeering at Wordsworth who has given faith and hope to many souls suffocated by secular creeds, but pointing out that it is pantheistic, not Christian. Berkeley could, when he wished, dabble in a special kind of seventeenth-century pantheism as a not unfruitful speculation, which need not compromise his faith and might supplement it. The writer of the Epistle to the Hebrews says 'God, who at sundry times and in divers manners spake in time past unto the fathers by the prophets, . . .' Had he been writing also to Gentiles he could have included among the prophets, Plato, Aristotle, and Plotinus.

I have done my best to emphasize rather than suppress the metaphysical difficulties in Berkeley's thought. Let me now summarize them:

i. Put first, the objection that a 'natural world', which is said to contain an infinite array of hypothetical experiences, seems extremely 'artificial' and cannot obtain much support from Ockham's Razor. This difficulty I think has only recently been raised and I do not see how he could meet it if he adhered strictly to his original denials.

ii. That space and time can be attributes of God (as More and Newton claimed), and yet not be substantial nor absolute (as Newton claimed). Yet Berkeley has been able to assert that spatial and temporal relations are public, available to all persons and universal so as to form a single system and also as phenomenal as are simple qualities of sense such as those of sounds and smells.

iii. Berkeley has also to make room for a natural science of moving bodies. Within the strict limits of Newtonian theory this seems easy enough, not quite so easy in view of the complications introduced by empirical discoveries of nineteenth-century physics and chemistry. We should, however, be cautious how we criticize Berkeley about this theory of space and time when we remember the classical difficulties of all theories, Newtonian, Leibnizian and Kantian.

iv. The simple Platonic doctrine in *Princ.* of souls or spiritual substances does lead to difficulties about the relation of each mind to its own body. But to help us out of such difficulties there is an Aristotelian doctrine, perhaps there are two, as well as a Leibnizian or a Kantian. Berkeley is in a better position than Descartes or Malebranche, and in a much better one than Hume whose brain could not distinguish between true and false, or genuine and sham, without the assistance of his kind heart; and even that could do nothing against hard hearts of other people. In short, he has less to unsay.

So much for objections to Berkeley, now for a decision about his conclusions. If we were to take the argument of *Siris* as his final word, it might commit him to a kind of Pantheism that is not compatible with views he expressed earlier. He certainly was committed to the kind of view expressed in William Temple's *Nature, Man and God* (1934, pp. 306–7) that unless all human life and experience provides a possible medium for divine revelation no special or particular part can. This means that God is present in all those of his creatures who will and think as well as live, and perhaps in those who merely live also, but the seventeenth-century Platonists found it difficult to exclude even those creatures who appeared to move entirely under mechanical impulses or in well-defined gravitational fields (or electro-magnetic fields). Even the Pan-theist has to draw the line somewhere or he is indistinguishable from the Pan-mechanist, as well as the Pan-zoist. I doubt whether Berkeley would ever have gone beyond Pan-psychism, and whether any Christian could, or indeed any Aristotelian.

Siris is not a success, only a brave experiment, because the time was not ripe for it. Alchemy was only a hindrance, Platonism not much help. Modern medicine with the psychosomatic theory of disease could have helped. But Berkeley did not really need that negative help, for he already had the Christian theory of psycho-somatic health.

Now for my last point. The obstacles to understanding divine revelation, however mediated, are according to Berkeley, our pre-existing habits of idolatry. They are to be seen at work now and on the largest scale. The twentieth-century suburban man, who believes himself civilized, has a plausible excuse for his favourite idols, the Great Machine (Fate) and the very similar Great Lottery (Chance). He repudiates any obligation to act in obedience to any external authority, and he takes all authority as external or con-ventional or arbitrary and never as possibly his own arbitrium. He is like Milton's Satan, always glorifying 'Mein Kampf'. He does not know how moral obligation can be absolute, yet not external, nor magical, nor the subject of a bargain, but autono-mous, one's own, and transcendent, beyond petty appetites, fears and anxieties.

By misinterpreting common metaphors and analogies, he mis-takes God's authority for some kind of human authority. Human authorities are necessarily external; there are a number of them, and some need to be obeyed from time to time, and some can be cheated, deceived or bargained with. Certain of them *ought* to be obeyed as a moral obligation, but only under conditions, for a time and for a special purpose or in terms of a contract, as people used to say. The favourite modern idol differs from those of Berkeley's day, but only slightly. On questions of morals I need do no more than refer to what Berkeley said specifically on political obedience and draw attention to the general likeness of his moral theory to that of the other philosopher-Bishop of his day, Joseph Butler. But I would also draw attention to his last sermon, delivered when he bade farewell to his diocese. The reader must remember that Berkeley belonged to an age and a school of churchmanship which was extremely suspicious of 'enthusiasm' as useless to sober persons and dangerous to others. He shunned poetical utterance in sermons (unlike John Donne), unless in quotations from the Bible.

For those who would end on a more metaphysical note, I would recommend *TVV*, § 38, where Berkeley explains that there are two ways of considering questions of sense perception. There is the synthetic or metaphysical method which he now introduces by stating as a presupposition what he formerly stated as a conclusion, namely that *Vision is the Language of the Author of Nature* and then expounds his theory more fully, in the paragraphs that follow until he comes to the concluding one, where he reverts to the analytical or experimental method and quotes the successful termination of Chesselden's experiment. But Berkeley has already said (*TVV*, § 36):

> In the contrivance of vision, as in other things, the wisdom of Providence seemeth to have consulted the operation, rather than the theory, of man; to the former things are admirably fitted, but, by that very means, the latter is often perplexed. For, as useful as these immediate suggestions and constant connexions are to direct our actions; so is our distinguishing between things confounded, and our separating things connected, and as it were blended together, no less necessary to the speculation and knowledge of truth.

In order to live we usually have to act before we have had time or occasion to think and therefore we trust to an 'animal faith' or 'wisdom of the body' which runs ahead of the slow and difficult process by which we may, through a lengthy process, analyse out how we became possessed of skills we never realized we learnt but supposed to be innate, instinctive, or directly intuited.

Finally let me quote the solitary passage in Locke where he seems to anticipate what is central to Berkeley's relational way of thought:

> This is certain, things, however absolute and entire they seem in themselves, are but retainers to other parts of nature for that which they are most taken notice of by us (Bk IV, Ch. 6, § 11).

[The incompleteness of this book makes itself evident in these last four paragraphs, whose force is obscured by the manner of their presentation. However, Ritchie's main idea is not, I think, in doubt. What he is trying to do is to make the novel and important point that Berkeley, properly understood, *is not a reductive analyst*. A passage from Theodore Jouffroy (the translator of Reid) may, I think, profitably be compared.

> Looking presupposes seeing, in much the same way as reflection presupposes sentiment and free analysis presupposes involuntary synthesis. The property of the initial seeing is breadth combined with vagueness; looking introduces distinctness along with a narrowing of view. So philosophy, if it perceives clearly what it grasps, perceives

only details, whereas common sense, if it has seen nothing clearly, has nevertheless seen things as a whole.

Like Jouffroy, Berkeley, in the TVV extract, is trying to draw attention to an essential point which the one-sided abstracters forget. But at the same time, Berkeley, in contradistinction to the common-sense philosophers, is not anti-analytic. What Berkeley, in Ritchie's interpretation, is after is to replace a reductive analysis based on the principle that the whole is nothing but the sum of the parts by a non-reductive analysis which treats the whole as more than the sum of the parts. From Berkeley's point of view, certain basic distinctions of common sense, (e.g. public and private) are genuinely illumined and up to a point justified by the sort of analysis which regards human knowledge as dependent on the conscious correlation of sight and of touch. At the same time, Berkeley, on Ritchie's view, would, I think, want to add that the illumination analysis thus offered, though genuine, is limited—in the sense that this comparison of sight and of touch is only one of a series of conditions of human knowledge—social, material, etc. —which are, apparently, contingently related to one another and which it is difficult, perhaps in some cases impracticable, to isolate for investigation.]

INDEX